The Belarus Secret

The
Belarus
Secret

by John Loftus
edited by Nathan Miller

Alfred A. Knopf New York 1982

THIS IS A BORZOI BOOK
PUBLISHED BY ALFRED A. KNOPF, INC.
Copyright © 1982 by John J. Loftus
All rights reserved under International and Pan-American
Copyright Conventions. Published in the United States by
Alfred A. Knopf, Inc., New York, and simultaneously in
Canada by Random House of Canada Limited, Toronto.
Distributed by Random House, Inc., New York.
Library of Congress Cataloging in Publication Data
Loftus, John. The Belarus secret.
Includes index.
1. World War, 1939–1945—Atrocities. 2. World
War, 1939–1945—Byelorussian S.S.R. 3. War
criminals—Byelorussian S.S.R. 4. War criminals—
United States. 5. Byelorussians—United States.
6. Byelorussian S.S.R.—History. I. Miller,
Nathan.   II. Title.
D804.B93L63 1982   940.54′05   82-48483
ISBN 0-394-52292-3
Manufactured in the United States of America
FIRST EDITION

015113

13.95

To Solomon, a Jew,
who bore witness to the Holocaust,

and

To Meg, my newborn,
so that she may never have to

Preface

For two and a half years, I was a federal prosecutor in the Office of Special Investigations of the Criminal Division of the Justice Department, which is also known as the Nazi war crimes unit. Our job was to search for and prosecute Nazi war criminals living in the United States. I was coordinator of a highly classified inquiry called the Belarus Project.

This book describes that project, which focused on one particular group of Nazi War Criminals, and on the people who brought them to America. The Department of Justice, the Department of Defense, and the Central Intelligence Agency are in no way responsible for the book's contents.

My conclusions are based primarily upon available public records. To ensure that no sensitive sources or methods were disclosed, I submitted this manuscript to various intelligence agencies for clearance, and agreed to delete a few portions.

Throughout my research, I have been fortunate to have received the support of many good friends, particularly John Cermack, Marc Masurovsky, Toni Chion, Julia Gaythwaite, Ruth Winters, Layne Nothman, Mark Truitt, Margaret Lawrence, Janne Conger, Fred Mauhs, Bernie Dougherty, Jeri Switzer, Dan Harkness, C. Dianne Sloan, and a number of others who must remain nameless but are not forgotten. William Lewis, Robert Wolfe, and Timothy Mulligan were helpful in their official capacity as archivists in the National Archives.

I would also like to acknowledge my many friends and colleagues at OSI and in the intelligence community. Although they are not responsible for the contents of this book, I hope that it will reflect credit upon them, particularly those members of Army Counter Intelligence and the regular staff of the CIA who tried so hard to keep the Nazis out of our country. I hope this book puts the blame where it belongs, with the State Department. I would also like to thank the members of my law firm, Bingham, Dana

& Gould, for their patience and assistance, especially the staff of the word-processing department. I was especially pleased to have the assistance of Nathan Miller, who edited the final draft of the manuscript for publication, and that of Mike Hamilburg and Ashbel Green, whose patient criticisms were invaluable. I am particularly proud of and grateful for the enormous support my family provided during a long and wearing experience. I hope now they understand what I was trying to achieve. My best friend, Susan, was with me through it all.

Most of all, however, I would like to thank a man whom I have never met. His name is Solomon Schiadow, and I hope he is still alive. During the war, he was among 5,000 Jews out of 50,000 in southwestern Byelorussia who survived the first Nazi sweep there. Out of the 5,000, only 200 were kept alive as slaves in the Koldichevo concentration camp. Of the 200, only 80 broke out and fled to the forests. Of the 80, perhaps a dozen survived the war. Of the dozen, only Solomon Schiadow made it to America. After he arrived, he wrote out his history so that the truth would not be forgotten. The Nazis had taken everything from him: his neighbors, his nation, his wife, his children. Ironically, some men who ordered the deaths of his children were living only a few miles away from him in New York and New Jersey. They are living there today; several still work for the U.S. government.

On the door to my office in the Justice Department was a grisly pun on the sign the Nazis put up in their concentration camps: ARBEIT MACHT FREI—"Work Shall Make You Free." My sign read WAHRHEIT MACHT FREI—"Truth Shall Make You Free." If we are to keep our children safe from any future holocaust, we must teach them the lessons of the past. They have to know that there are some crimes that shall never be forgiven, and those who commit them will be hunted for the rest of their lives. There is no statute of limitations for mass murder.

In a way, we Americans are the last victims of the Holocaust, imprisoned by the secrets of the Cold War, locked in a fortress of lies. In a democratic society, there is only one hard way of liberation. *Wahrheit Macht Frei.*

John Loftus
June 1982

The Belarus Secret

Prologue

Rain and darkness blurred the landscape as we turned off the New Jersey Turnpike at Exit 9 one night at the end of October, 1980. As the windshield wipers flicked back and forth, the driver hesitated at the bottom of the exit ramp to examine the road signs. New Brunswick, the home of Rutgers University, lay to the left, but the driver turned right toward South River. Within a few minutes we passed through the outskirts of the town, headlights throwing shadows on the walls of dark warehouses and shopping centers. And then we were in the gritty downtown where the neon beer signs in the tavern windows created little islands of light in the empty night.

While the driver kept his eyes on the road, the three passengers concentrated on a carefully marked map, checking it against a list of names and addresses. I was a federal prosecutor attached to the Office of Special Investigations, the Nazi war crimes unit of the Criminal Division of the Department of Justice; my companions were a State Department security man, a New Jersey state trooper in civilian clothes, and an informant who had put us on the long-hidden trail of the Belarus SS Brigade and the Nazi puppet government of Byelorussia.

For myself, this trip was the culmination of eighteen months of work. Shortly after joining the Justice Department as a member of the Attorney General's honors program, I had seen a notice on an office bulletin board asking for volunteers for the Office of Special Investigations. In May 1979, I applied and was accepted.

My first assignment was to help build cases against several Byelorussians who had been admitted to the United States and allowed to become citizens, despite strong evidence that they were guilty of war crimes. The assignment was not made any easier by my having—as do, I suspect, most Americans—only a passing knowledge of Byelorussia and its tortured history.

I learned that Byelorussia, sometimes called White Russia, is today a Soviet Socialist Republic with a population of some eight million. It borders on Poland in the West, Lithuania and Latvia in the northwest, Russia in the east, and the Ukraine in the south. During World War II, Byelorussia was occupied by the Germans from 1941 to 1944, and was one of the most devastated regions of the Soviet Union. Some of its citizens served the Nazi puppet government and some even served in an SS unit known as the Belarus Brigade which fought against the Americans. It was these ex-Nazis, now thought to be living in the United States, who were the object of our inquiry.

OSI's task was a difficult one, because we were dealing with events that had occurred nearly forty years before in a foreign country. And not only did the Soviet Union refuse to provide witnesses to crimes committed within its borders but American intelligence agencies as well seemed curiously reluctant to cooperate with us. Time after time, I had been told that no one knew where the old files were stored, or even where an index could be located. I spent weeks in underground vaults, learning the intricacies of long-forgotten intelligence operations, and then systematically retrieving the records from their dusty containers. It took years to reassemble all the documents, many of which had never even been translated. But there was one document that I could not forget: the memoir of Solomon Schiadow, who had survived the Byelorussian holocaust. Whenever I felt frustrated by a dead end or an uncooperative agency, I would remember what he had written, and feel renewed determination to keep on sifting through the files for traces of the men who had committed the atrocities he recorded.

Eventually, some of the pieces of the puzzle started to come together in South River. OSI had learned that several Byelorussian Nazi collaborators lived there—little more than a three-hour drive from the nation's capital—but an informant had discovered that their numbers were actually much larger than OSI's estimate. So as not to arouse suspicion, we came on this night to check out the facts of this curious situation.

South River sprawls along the meandering stream for which it is named like a bent and wrinkled arm. Sometimes the damp wind sweeping down from the northeast carries with it the smell of the refineries and petrochemical plants of Carteret and Bayonne that lie just over the horizon. Founded in colonial times, South River has become an enclave of Eastern European immigrants. Russians, Byelorussians, Ukrainians, Hungarians, Poles, Czechs, Slovaks, Slovenes, and European Jews have all found a haven there. As the members of each ethnic group have prospered, they have moved away from the river, up to neat bungalows that line the nearby hills. Perhaps the town's most famous citizen is Joe Theismann, star quarterback of the Washington Redskins.

Shortly after midnight we pulled up in front of St. Euphrosynia's Church on Whitehead Avenue.* Despite the darkness, a tall monument on a mound behind the church was clearly visible. GLORY TO THOSE WHO FOUGHT FOR THE FREEDOM AND INDEPENDENCE OF BYELORUSSIA read the inscription on the base. Atop the stone pillar, flanked by a white-red-white Byelorussian flag and the Stars and Stripes, was a circle of iron enclosing a double-barred cross. This was the same symbol that the Belarus SS unit had worn as it went into battle against American troops toward the end of World War II.

We drove past the onion-domed churches of Russian Alley and up a hill lined by large graveyards. Off to one side, as if holding itself aloof, was another, much smaller cemetery. The iron-barred gate was padlocked, but a plaque to the left identified it as the "White Ruthenian (Byelorussian) Orthodox Cemetery of St. Euphrosynia in South River." A plaque on the right bore a verse from the Twenty-third Psalm: "I will dwell in the house of the Lord forever." I climbed over the low wall while the others kept watch, and in the dim light saw that the plot was only about one-third full. It was too dark to make out the names carved on the tombstones in Cyrillic lettering, so we decided to return when the light was better.

Early the next morning, I went over the wall again. Moving quickly up and down the rows of graves, many of which appeared new, I read the names onto a tape recorder that I had brought with me so we could check them off later against our list of fugitive war

---

*Inside the church is a commemorative plaque listing the members of the building committee. Many of those named were prominent collaborators during the Nazi occupation.

criminals. In the center of the cemetery, occupying the most
prominent place, I found a tall gray stone. It marked the grave of
Radislaw Ostrowsky. The framed photograph affixed to it in accordance with Russian Orthodox custom showed an ascetic, lean-
faced man with a look of righteous intensity. A plaque identified
Ostrowsky as the "President of the Byelorussian Central Council"
during World War II and the founder of the "Byelorussian National Armed Forces." We had found the final resting place of the
highest-ranking war criminal ever to become a United States citizen, as far as is known.

All around him were the graves of his fellow war criminals:
mayors, governors, and other officials—men who had ruled the
Nazi puppet state of Byelorussia; who had guided the SS *Einsatzgruppen*—the mobile killing squads—across a good part of Eastern Europe; who had assisted in the mass murder of thousands of
Jews; whose atrocities had even sickened some of their German
masters.

Suddenly, the gate creaked behind me. I stuffed the tape recorder under my coat and turned to see my companions frantically
signaling me to jump over the wall. A tall man in a leather jacket
was working a key in the lock of the cemetery gates. He had
a narrow face and cold, deep-set eyes that seemed disturbingly
familiar.

It was too late to run, so I decided to act as if I had a right to
be there. I walked over to the stranger and asked if he could help
me find the grave of Emanuel Jasiuk. Obviously surprised, he
asked in strongly accented English for my connection with Jasiuk.

My father had met Jasiuk after World War II, I explained, and
he had requested me to visit his grave if I ever came to New Jersey.

How did your father know Jasiuk? the tall man inquired.

He had been attached to an Air Force Intelligence unit that had
been stationed near Stuttgart in West Germany, I said.

The man nodded and led me to a recent grave near the rear of
the cemetery.

All the other graves had headstones with ornate carvings and
photographs in brass frames, but the plot of Emanuel Jasiuk was
marked by only a bed of flowers and a simple white cross.

Under the approving gaze of the watchman, I stood over the

grave for a few moments with my head bowed. To make a graceful exit, I asked for directions to a florist so I could return with a wreath as a remembrance from my father. With a smile, he furnished directions to a nearby flower shop as he escorted me to the gate, where my companions awaited me.

"You can come by any morning," he said, struggling for the words in English. "I'm sorry it couldn't have been a more joyful occasion."

As soon as our car pulled away, my companions burst out laughing. Somewhat irritated, I demanded to know what was so funny about my narrow escape, and they told me that the watchman I had just talked to was one of the fugitives we were seeking.

And then I remembered the Justice Department file where I had first seen his photograph. He had been a county chief in Byelorussia, and police forces under his command had murdered thousands of his own countrymen, Poles, and Jews. How could such a man be living peacefully as an American citizen in a New Jersey town? I wondered with frustration, incredulity, and outrage. These were feelings I was to experience countless times as I went about tracing the origins of the long-suppressed "Belarus Secret."

Chapter

1

Frank G. Wisner did not look like a spymaster.

Balding and fleshy although he was not yet forty, he appeared to those who greeted him upon his arrival in West Germany in the summer of 1948 like the prosperous Wall Street lawyer he had been. He spoke with a trace of the soft accent of his native Mississippi, and his official title, Director of the Office of Policy Coordination, was innocuous. He had chosen it himself for that reason. Wisner was a veteran practitioner of the black art of covert operations, and the newly organized OPC was in the front line of the secret war against the Soviet Union.

Wisner came to Germany at a time when Europe seemed on the brink of revolutionary upheaval. Berlin was under blockade by the Soviets and depended upon a tenuous airlift for its survival. The Communists were actively trying to overthrow the governments of Greece and Turkey. Italy was on the verge of going communist. A Russian attempt to pinch off a piece of northern Iran had just been repulsed. Half of Europe had disappeared behind the Iron Curtain. To meet the challenge of Soviet expansion, President Harry S Truman had made substantial amounts of military and economic assistance available to nations facing internal and external communist threats. "Our policy [is] to support the cause of freedom wherever it is threatened," he declared.

Energetic, adventurous, and something of a romantic, Wisner seemed an excellent choice to lead OPC. He was a member of a wealthy Southern family and graduated from the University of Virginia Law School in 1934. That same year he joined Carter, Ledyard & Milburn, a prominent Manhattan law firm, and soon became a partner.* At the outbreak of World War II he entered the Navy but, looking for more excitement, joined the Office of

---

*Franklin D. Roosevelt's first job as a young attorney in 1907 had been with Carter, Ledyard & Milburn.

Strategic Services, America's new independent intelligence agency. Wisner spent most of the war in the Balkans, engaged in clandestine activities in Romania and Turkey. After brief service in Germany following the surrender, he returned to Wall Street, but found the world of estates and trusts too tame. During his time with OSS, Wisner had become convinced of the inevitability of a conflict with the Soviet Union—and the Cold War provided him with an opportunity to return to intelligence work.[1]

In 1948, many believed that a Soviet attack on Western Europe was imminent. According to one retired government official, the entire American intelligence community was put on a war footing. Wisner's job was to plan an underground network of commando units to slow down the Communist advance, and then guide allied forces in an invasion. To serve as the nucleus of his guerrilla forces, and to spearhead the invasion, Wisner decided to recruit those Nazi collaborators who had performed similar duties only a few years earlier for the Third Reich. Wisner was ordered to use his underground agents to overthrow the Communist-imposed governments, if possible, without American intervention. To accomplish these goals, Wisner was hired by the State Department as head of the Office of Policy Coordination.

The OPC charter—National Security Council directive 10/2—was sweeping. Wisner's efforts to counter the Soviet threat were limited only by "deniability," the proviso that if any of his operations were blown, the Secretary of State should be able to plausibly disavow any knowledge of his activities. His weapons included propaganda, economic warfare, sabotage, and subversion against hostile states, including assistance to underground resistance groups in Eastern Europe. Wisner was particularly intrigued by this last part of his charter, concerning the recruiting of an anticommunist guerrilla army and turning it loose upon the Soviet Union. He had come to Germany to lay the groundwork for this force.

Before being ordered to leave Bucharest by the victorious Red Army in 1945, Wisner had compiled a list of Romanians opposed to the Soviet Union. Among them were Nazi collaborators and members of the Iron Guard, a fascist organization noted for its hatred of Jews. Now, he was engaged in expanding his lists of anticommunist zealots, and it would soon include men, many of them accused war criminals, from all across Eastern Europe.

Wisner's staff secretly made contact with leaders from four different Nazi ministries who had directed the activities of collaborators in Eastern Europe during the war. First was Gustav Hilger, a diplomat from the Nazi Foreign Office who had served as Hitler's Russian expert. Hilger had helped to plan the invasion of Russia and had worked with SS Intelligence late in the war to build an anticommunist army of collaborators. Wisner also recruited Hilger's counterpart in the SS: Obersturmbannfuehrer Friedrich Buchardt, chief of Emigré Affairs for the SS, who had worked his way up from commander of a mobile killing unit in Byelorussia. He too had used native collaborators to advantage. The third man to supply information to Wisner was Professor Gerhardt von Mende, a deputy in the Nazi Ministry for the Occupied Eastern Territories who had favored using collaborationist politicians to establish a network of Nazi puppet governments as a wall against the Russians. The last man that Wisner needed to consult was hidden behind a different kind of wall.

Before leaving West Germany, Wisner went to Pullach, a pretty little village eight miles from Munich, where he was taken to a heavily guarded compound surrounded by high walls and an electrified fence. A brass plate at the gate bore the name "South German Industries Utilisation Company," but other signs warned, "Beware of fierce dogs."[2]

Pullach was the headquarters of Reinhard Gehlen, Germany's most celebrated spy.* During World War II he had been chief of Fremde Heere Ost (FHO), the eastern military intelligence section of the Armed Forces High Command. After the collapse of Germany, he avoided capture by the Russians, who regarded him as a war criminal, and surrendered himself, his staff, and his exten-

---

*In a recent interview, a senior intelligence official remained adamant that neither Wisner nor any other OPC official met Gehlen face to face in 1948. Historians, however, have described their connections in detail. One thing is certain from the documents of the period: Gehlen's American liaison officer, Captain Erich Waldmann, was recruited by Wisner to conduct secret research on Byelorussian Nazis, and Gehlen's own files conclusively establish that he was providing the OPC with information on Wisner's recruitment targets. Whether Wisner and Gehlen conversed personally or through intermediaries, the fact remains that they carried on a long and profitable relationship under the noses of the other American intelligence agencies.

sive files to the U.S. Army. He was brought to America, interrogated there, and then sent back in July 1946 to Germany, where as head of ORG, Organisation Gehlen, subsidized by the Americans, he directed espionage activities against the Soviet Union and its satellites. Gehlen thus became the only Wehrmacht general to function in the postwar era with his wartime staff almost intact.

Wisner and Gehlen were well acquainted with each other. At the end of the war Wisner had interrogated Gehlen and had been struck by his knowledge of Soviet affairs. Now, Wisner was impressed with the astuteness of Gehlen's reading of Russian intentions in Germany. Gehlen had warned the Americans of Stalin's plan to drive the Western allies out of Berlin, but his reports had not been believed until the Russians blockaded the city. Long before anyone else, he told Wisner that the Soviets were planning to establish the German Democratic Republic in their zone of occupation and that the "People's Police," or VOPO, was being transformed into an East German army, complete with tank divisions and its own air force.[3]

Cementing an alliance with Gehlen, Wisner sought his help in organizing guerrilla units behind the Iron Curtain, to build a clandestine arsenal and to assist and, if necessary, instigate armed rebellion against the Soviets. Believing that it was only a matter of time before the United States became involved in a war with the Soviet Union, Wisner expected the old Nazi intelligence networks to play a major role in undermining the Soviet order. The Gehlen Organization would identify potential recruits for these "special forces."

From his archives, Gehlen produced the names of Eastern Europeans who had served the Nazi puppet governments and would provide the nucleus for Wisner's private army. Among them were the Byelorussians of the Belarus Brigade, hiding out in the refugee camps of Germany from war crimes investigators who knew next to nothing about their history.

Belarus is another name for Byelorussia, as are White Russia and White Ruthenia. Byelorussia is an ancient country, a land of superstition and festering hatreds. The southern half is underwater during the spring when the Pripet marshes are flooded; the northern region is isolated by a maze of rivers and forests. For centuries, Byelorussia's narrow roads and paths were the principal land bridge between Europe and Asia, and in medieval times it boasted of a proud and literate culture. But in addition to being a zone of passage, Byelorussia was also fated to be an area where rival peoples met, merged, and fought for control of the land.[4]

To the east lay the great empire of the tsars, with its Cyrillic alphabet and Orthodox tradition. To the west was Catholic Poland with its Latin script and princely aristocracy. Byelorussia was alternately dominated by either Poland or Russia, and Minsk, the capital, is said to have changed hands more than 150 times. Byelorussian culture was all but obliterated by conquerors who imposed their own language and religion as annexation superseded annexation. The peasants hated the Polish landlords, the tsarist regime, and above all the Jewish shopkeepers and tradesmen who bought their produce. Through an accident of history, Byelorussia had become the center of the Pale of Settlement, the densest concentration of Jews in the world.

After their expulsion from Western Europe in the fourteenth and fifteenth centuries, the Jews had made their way to Poland, the Ukraine, and Lithuania, where they were welcomed. These lands were beginning to stir economically, and there was a need for the enterprise and skills offered by the Jews. Over the next four centuries, Eastern Europe became the center of the Jewish world. At first the Jews prospered, but this prosperity aroused jealousy and anti-Semitism, and eventually restrictions were placed on the types of business and trades in which Jews could participate. When Poland was divided among neighboring Prussia, Austria, and Russia at the end of the eighteenth century, most of the Jews passed under the control of the tsars. A Pale of Settlement was mapped that restricted Jews to parts of Lithuania, Romania, Poland, Byelorussia, and the Ukraine, where they lived in poverty and in fear of periodic pogroms.

For the subject peoples of Eastern Europe, the Russian Revolution was like the breaking of an ice jam in a spring thaw. From Finland to the Ukraine, they joyously threw off the Russian yoke. In Byelorussia, a handful of nationalists gathered in the Minsk opera house on December 17, 1917, to proclaim an independent republic. They were, however, quickly suppressed by the Bolsheviks, who had planted spies among the dissidents—although Lenin had announced a policy of moderation toward Russia's national groups, the Bolsheviks had no intention of presiding over the country's disintegration. The Byelorussian nationalists appealed for help to the German army, which had occupied most of the region since the beginning of World War I. The Germans took over Minsk, and a mixed bag of nationalist politicians, intellectuals, workers, Jews, Poles, eccentrics, and an occasional Soviet informer reassembled to launch the Byelorussian National Republic (BNR) on March 25, 1918.

The new government adopted a flag with three horizontal stripes—white, red, white—ordered postage stamps, and established an administrative framework. Included in the cabinet was Radislaw Ostrowsky, a popular young schoolteacher, who was named Minister of Education.[5] For a few months, a semblance of democracy existed in Byelorussia, but not even the Germans bothered to recognize the nationalist regime. When the Germans withdrew at the end of the war, the BNR quickly collapsed under the onslaught of the Bolsheviks. Some members of the government fled to Vilna (then in Poland) and later to the West, where they established a government-in-exile. Others, Ostrowsky among them, joined the counterrevolutionary White armies that with Anglo-American-French support were trying to overthrow the Bolshevik regime. Wherever they went, however, the Byelorussian dissidents were followed by agents of the foreign section of the Cheka, the newly organized Soviet secret police.

Russia was almost in anarchy as civil war raged along the frontiers and across the steppes. Using the liberation of the Catholic population as a pretext, the Poles took advantage of the confusion to invade Byelorussia. Although the Russians initially suffered heavy defeats, the Poles were thrown back, and by August 1920 the Red Army had advanced to the outskirts of Warsaw. With the vigorous assistance of the French, the Poles drove the Russians back into mid-Byelorussia, where the war bogged down in stalemate. The Treaty of Riga, signed in 1921, drew a line down the middle of Byelorussia, giving the western and Catholic half to Poland, while the eastern and Orthodox part went to Moscow.

Many of the nationalists returned to western Byelorussia, but life under the Poles was oppressive.[6] The old landlords, who claimed hereditary title to the major part of what little arable land was available, were reinstated. The Orthodox religion was persecuted, and the teaching of the Byelorussian language was discouraged. Every attempt was made by the Polish authorities to stamp out Byelorussian nationalism. Only a handful of ethnic Byelorussians were permitted seats in the Polish Senate, or Diet. Among them was Jury Sobolewsky, who would later become Radislaw Ostrowsky's vice-president during the Nazi occupation.[7] Both Sobolewsky and Ostrowsky had clandestinely joined a left-wing organization, the Byelorussian Peasants and Workers Party (known as the Gramada), that included liberals, Socialists, and Communists.

Hoping to discredit its Socialist rivals in the Gramada, the OGPU,* the successor to the Cheka, informed the Polish Secret Service that it was controlled from Moscow. The Poles saw the Gramada as a threat to the economic exploitation of the eastern provinces. By linking the Gramada to the Communists, the Polish government recognized an opportunity to discredit the nationalist movement. On January 14, 1927, more than 3,000 Byelorussian activists were arrested, including Ostrowsky, who was accused of being a Communist agent.[8] Ostrowsky and eighteen other defendants were acquitted following a mass trial, but the rest were sentenced to several years in prison. The Polish government's evidence was so flimsy, however, that the verdict was reversed and a new trial ordered.[9] The outcry from Poles and Byelorussians was so great that the embarrassed government granted a limited amnesty and called off the retrial. Still, a cloud of suspicion hung over the accused, and their civil rights were permanently suspended.

Soviet propagandists used the incident to compare Polish repression to their own treatment of minorities. Byelorussia enjoyed the status (at least on paper) of an autonomous Soviet Socialist Republic—proof that the Communists had no intention of destroying Byelorussian culture and identity. The token concessions

---

*The Cheka became the OGPU in 1923, the NKVD in 1934, the MVD in 1946, and finally the KGB in 1953.

the Soviets had offered their minorities—actually as a means of curbing internal unrest—were presented to the émigrés as illustrating the more enlightened Soviet attitude. The Gramada and BNR leaders were invited to come home to help build the new Byelorussian state.

Most of the Byelorussian leaders formally voted to terminate the BNR as a government-in-exile and move to the Russian half of their divided nation. A voluntary merger with the Communists did not seem a bad political strategy in 1930. The Soviet constitution guaranteed equal rights for minorities and clearly established the right of the individual republics to withdraw from the Soviet Union whenever they chose. It was an enticing illusion for the nationalists. Soon after their return, however, the Gramada leaders were again arrested, this time by the Communists, and were executed as Polish spies.[10]

For many of the nationalists, this was the turning point. Persecuted by the Poles and betrayed by the Russians, they turned toward fascism. Fascism appealed to the Byelorussian émigrés because it provided the best chance for an anti-Soviet crusade. To the embittered exiles, any rule in their homeland—even that of Nazi Germany—was preferable to the continuation of the Communist dictatorship. Besides, it was often argued, the period of foreign domination would be only temporary. And over and beyond its anticommunist aspect, fascism offered much that was attractive to the Byelorussians: discipline, nationalism, adulation of force, promises of social justice, and, last but not least, anti-Semitism. To them, "Jew-Bolshevism" was the cause of the world's problems—a point of view made increasingly popular by the worldwide economic depression and the rise of Adolf Hitler.[11] The White Ruthenian Nazi Party was founded in 1937 with subsidies from Berlin.

The Byelorussians, along with other émigré groups, sought financial support from any source willing to provide it. For example, Stephan Bandera, a Ukrainian with extreme right-wing views, was on the payroll of both the British and German intelligence services prior to World War II. Similarly, Ostrowsky is reported to have worked for several countries simultaneously. The Byelorussians competed with the other nationalities for German money and support—particularly with the NTS, the Alliance of Russian National Solidarists, an organization of right-wing Russian political exiles that was formed in the late 1920's and still exists. The nationalists were aware of the rivalries that were surfacing among the police and intelligence agencies of the Third Reich, which frequently competed with each other.

One of the major agencies was the Abwehr (officially, the Amt/ Ausland Abwehr), the foreign-intelligence and counterintelligence department of the Armed Forces High Command. It was composed of two separate and more or less autonomous compartments: one covering the east, mainly the Soviet Union, the other engaged in operations against the west, primarily France, Britain, and America. The Abwehr was headed by Admiral Wilhelm Canaris until he was arrested as a spy in 1944 and hanged the following year. After Canaris's removal, the Abwehr—many of whose officers were Foreign Office and military academy graduates privately opposed to Nazism—fell into disgrace with Hitler.

Meanwhile, after eliminating Hitler's original supporters, the Brownshirts of the SA (Sturmabteilung), in the Blood Purge of June 1934, the SS (Schutzstaffel—literally, "defense echelon") eventually attained almost absolute power. In 1939 the Reich Central Security Office was set up as the main security department of the Nazi government. Brought under this office were all the existing police forces, including the Gestapo (Geheime Staatspolizei—Secret State Police); the *Kriminalpolizei,* or Criminal Police; and the SD (Sicherheitsdienst—Security Service), the espionage and counterespionage apparatus of the SS.

The Allgemeine-SS (General SS) administered the concentration and extermination camps, as well as portions of the occupied eastern territories, while the Waffen-SS (Armed SS) was primarily a military organization which eventually expanded to thirty-nine divisions and came to rival the Wehrmacht, the traditional German Army. In 1936, Hitler designated Heinrich Himmler as head of the unified police system of the Third Reich, as Reichsfuehrer of the SS and leader of the Gestapo.[12]

In their rush to win the bureaucratic struggle, both the SS and the Abwehr hastily hired scores of foreign recruits, including a number of double agents who had been planted among the émigrés by the Soviets. The outbreak of World War II in September 1939 provided a fresh supply of Slavic recruits for the German espionage apparatus. The Hitler-Stalin pact resulted in a new partition of Poland in which the Soviets regained control of western Byelorussia. Many of the Byelorussian nationalists fled ahead of the advancing Red Army and settled in Warsaw, Prague, Berlin, and Paris, as their predecessors had done after World War I.[13] To return to their homeland would have been suicidal, for their fate would have been the same as that of the unfortunates who had been beguiled into returning in 1930.

These new émigrés to the Third Reich were the cream of the Byelorussian intelligentsia—admittedly a small group after years of Polish oppression, but proud of their cultural and ethnic heritage. The SS had a natural attraction for them. They were impressed by the large number of professionals like themselves who wore the black uniform of the SS. Only racial Germans could become fully accredited members of the SS, but many of the blond, blue-eyed Byelorussians pretended to be of German origin to gain membership. The SD cultivated ties with the new crop of Byelorussian émigrés, using them as sources for recent information about the roads and rail systems of their native land. Even then, Hitler was contemplating the betrayal of his pact with Stalin.

The Nazis funded a network of Byelorussian "self-help" or welfare offices whose purpose was ostensibly charitable; in reality they were covert recruitment agencies.[14] A Byelorussian-language newspaper, *Ranitsa,* was published in Berlin. Each issue carried venomous articles denouncing the "Jewish-Bolshevik world conspiracy" and predicting the early defeat of Britain and France. One of the "self-help" organization's major functions was the screening of prisoners of war captured during the Polish campaign and to recruit imprisoned Byelorussians and Ukrainians who were sympathetic to the German cause. It was rumored that several prison camps were staffed in part by Byelorussian prisoners who had joined the German side.

In their eagerness to expand operations at the expense of their rivals, the various German intelligence organizations recruited émigrés who had once had ties with the Communist Party. For example, Dr. Mikolai Abramtchik, the ambitious leader of the

Byelorussians in Paris, had been active in the Communist youth organization in Byelorussia, and his brother was head of Soviet military intelligence in Minsk. Angry at being superseded in the confidence of the German intelligence services by the newly arrived intellectuals and professionals, the old Byelorussian collaborators, whose links had been with the now defunct SA, denounced the new recruits as Communist infiltrators. But these warnings were ignored in the infighting among the contending agencies. Eager to build up its assets at the expense of rivals, the SS assumed that anyone willing to work against communism could not be a Communist. Such naiveté was visible everywhere as Germany hastily assembled an enormous but inefficient global intelligence network. Faced with similar conditions after the war, American intelligence agencies repeated the same mistake.

Why did the SS, which espoused some of the most extreme racial doctrines in Nazi Germany, become the principal benefactor of the Byelorussians and the other Slavic nationalist movements? The SS was pragmatic. The émigrés could provide a native intelligence network for the invasion of the Soviet Union as well as serve as guides for the invasion spearheads. They could also help in establishing civil administrations in the conquered areas.[15] If so, SS leaders reasoned, it would do no harm to pay temporary lip service to their petty nationalist aspirations. For their part, the émigrés willingly joined the Nazi conspiracy because Germany appeared invincible. Some of the collaborators were willing to accept the slaughter of large numbers of their countrymen if it meant the destruction of Soviet communism. Others hoped that a benign Germany would permit some form of Byelorussian self-government.

The SS established a special test for its Byelorussian collaborators: Only those who assisted the *Einsatzgruppen* (task forces) would be permitted to become part of the civilian administration to be established in the wake of the advancing Wehrmacht and Waffen-SS troops.[16]

The *Einsatzgruppen* were special mobile formations charged with carrying out liquidations of communist officials, partisans, saboteurs, and Jews on the eastern front. They were attached to Amt (Office) IV (Gestapo) of the Reich Central Security Office but were subordinate to Amt VI (SD) for intelligence purposes. Together with other elements of the *Sicherheitspolizei* (security police), they were responsible for the deaths of two million of the estimated six million Jews killed.* Himmler had organized four *Einsatzgruppen;* Einsatzgruppe B would follow Army Group Center along the traditional Warsaw-Minsk-Smolensk-Moscow invasion route through Byelorussia. Since the German Nazis had no manpower to spare, they would welcome any local help in carrying out the special tasks of the *Einsatzgruppen.*

The work of each group was planned with thoroughness. Following the tanks of the Panzer units, an SS forward command *(Vorkommando)* would capture local Communist headquarters and take possession of all documents and records before they could be destroyed. Native guides were essential not only in locating the buildings, but also in translating the documents containing the names of local commissars, informants, and intelligence officers. All Soviet functionaries were to be arrested and shot before they could disappear into the population. Armed with lists taken from the Soviet intelligence archives or drawn up by the collaborators, the *Einsatzgruppen* would then split up into smaller mobile killing units, or *Einsatzkommandos,* to deal with any members of the local population likely to resist Nazi rule. The Byelorussian collaborators would have a key role in singling out particular persons to be executed, but this would be kept secret from the local populace, which would know only that the German liberators had installed fellow Byelorussians to help run the municipal administrations. No one would realize that the mayors and police chiefs were systematically betraying their countrymen to the *Einsatzgruppen* execution squads. If the initial liquidations of Communist officials worked well, the SS planned for the Byelorussian collaborators to help with the much larger task of eliminating the huge Jewish population concentrated in the Pale of Settlement.[17] A week before the invasion, Byelorussians from all over Europe met secretly in Berlin to plan the administration of the soon-to-be-conquered territories.

Sometime in the spring of 1940, Dr. Franz Six, a former profes-

---

*After the invasion, the *Einsatzgruppen* split up into individual command units which centralized all police, intelligence, and execution functions for the SS in the newly conquered areas.

sor of political science and head of the *Vorkommando* for Einsatz-gruppe B, made contact with the local branch of the Byelorussian "self-help" organization in Warsaw and put together a task force of some thirty to forty trusted Byelorussians to serve as guides, administrators, and informers.[18] Among them were Stanislaw Stankievich, who later ran the city of Borissow; Emanuel Jasiuk, who was assigned to the city of Kletsk; and Jury Sobolewsky, who administered Baranovitche, the second-largest city in Byelorussia. Radislaw Ostrowsky, who spoke fluent Russian, was to organize the counties around Minsk and then follow the invasion forces into Russia proper. There were reports that Ostrowsky would be named mayor of Moscow after its capture. In a moment of optimism, the SS had designated Dr. Six's unit "Vorkommando Moskau."[19]

Chapter
2

Operation Barbarossa began at first light on Sunday, June 22, 1941. German troops moved across the Soviet frontier from the Baltic to the Ukraine, and swarms of paratroopers and saboteurs, many of them Byelorussians and Ukrainians, created havoc in the enemy's rear. Although Stalin had been given ample warning by the British of an impending German assault, the Red Army was completely taken by surprise. The Russian air force was wiped out on the ground on the first day of fighting, and entire Russian units surrendered en masse. Minsk fell within a week, and it did not take much longer for the German armies to occupy all the territory incorporated into the Soviet Union since 1939. Hitler appeared to have overestimated when he allocated four months for the subjugation of the Soviet Union.[1]

Einsatzgruppe B followed in the wake of Army Group Center. The Vorkommando and its Byelorussian guides seized the Minsk archives of Soviet intelligence, which had been abandoned by fleeing Communist officials. They had been so panic-stricken that they left behind lists of Soviet informers, and bags of money from the National Bank were found sitting on the ground in the stadium. The people of Minsk greeted the Germans with bread and salt, as they had welcomed conquerors many times before. Most of the population, remembering the freedoms permitted during the German occupation of World War I, were genuinely glad to see the Nazis. Even the Jews, who had fled the city along with the other civilians during the initial bombing, returned after a few nights in the Byelorussian forests. Cut off from the outside world, they had no idea of what the Nazis had planned for them.

Dr. Six nominated teams of two of his Byelorussian collaborators to organize each city and town under military occupation.[2] One was assigned to head the political administration, the other the paramilitary police. General Kraatz, the Wehrmacht counter-

part to the SS in charge of rear area security for Army Group
Center, was impressed by the efficiency of Six's collaborators.
Ostrowsky, for example, had commandeered a German military
staff car and within a week had established a network of pro-Nazi
officials throughout every county in the Minsk district.[3] In Minsk
itself, Ostrowsky formed a municipal government subservient to
the Nazis, while Franz Kushel put together a fledgling police force
to replace the Communist militia.* The SS equipped Kushel's men
with black uniforms and red armbands labeled "Polizei."

Within days of their arrival, the Germans ordered the entire
male population of Minsk to assemble on a field south of the city
known as Drozdy. Drozdy Field was bordered on three sides by
the river which flows through Minsk, making a small peninsula.
At the base of the peninsula, the Germans established a barrier of
barbed wire and machine-gun emplacements. Every man in the
area—Jews, escaped criminals, Soviet prisoners of war, and ordinary townspeople—was present, and Byelorussian collaborators
moved through the mob identifying those willing to work for the
SS. Many of these were funneled to Kushel for his police force,
which eventually totaled 20,000 men. Others were appointed to
positions in the municipal administration being set up by the
collaborators.

The rest were simply left in the open field for several days
without food or water. The Germans divided the plain into areas
for Soviet soldiers and civilians. The civilians began to receive food
from the women of Minsk, who threw it to them over the fence.
At night, Soviet soldiers would crawl over to the civilians and beg
for a little food. For days the Germans debated the matter of

---

*The mayor of Minsk was Dr. Vitold Tumash. Tumash, who now lives in New York City,
acknowledged to Mike Wallace on the CBS program 60 Minutes (May 16, 1982) that he
had been mayor of Minsk for three months but denied having anything to do with the
extermination of the Jews. Captured Nazi documents in the National Archives tell a
different story. They not only identify him as the mayor of Minsk but also reveal that the
municipal authorities supervised the ghetto and issued passports for the elimination of
racial undesirables. (Report of 20 July, 1941, Military Administration Group, Army
Group Center, National Archives Microfilm Section T175, Roll 2533, Frames 292820-
821.) One of Tumash's fellow Byelorussians has written a book in which he states that
Tumash solicited Franz Kushel to organize a Byelorussian police force in Minsk (Konstantine Akula, Combat Trails). There is a copy of this book, published in Toronto in Byelorussian, in the Library of Congress.

rations for the captured soldiers. Although Germany was a signatory to the Geneva convention on the treatment of prisoners of war, Russia was not. The matter of the Soviet POW rations was resolved quite simply: there would be none. In July, all male civilians were permitted to move back to Minsk after a security check, leaving thousands of soldiers behind. As the last of the civilian columns moved back to the city, they could hear the sound of machine guns in the distance.

When the surviving citizens returned from Drozdy, they found that there had been changes in Minsk. All Jews had been ordered to resettle within a ghetto that reached eastward across half the city from the Jewish cemetery to the upper bend of the river and then southward, almost to the old insurance building and the other commercial structures where the German administration and the Byelorussian collaborators had established their offices. In the center of the ghetto was the Ubelanyie marketplace, where the Jews were made to register. Lists were compiled identifying the residents of each house in the ghetto, and Jews were ordered to wear a large yellow Star of David on the front and back of their coats. The system that had worked so efficiently in Germany and Poland had come to Byelorussia.

A few Jews attempted to avoid registration and pass as Christians. To the Germans, all Slavs appeared the same, so that the collaborators' assistance was invaluable in detecting Jews.[4] They knew the accents and physical characteristics that differentiated a Byelorussian Jew from a gentile, and they served the Nazis as enforcers of the racial laws.* When Jews were caught outside the ghetto, the Byelorussian police beat them, if they were lucky; if not, they were shot.[5] Within the ghetto, the Germans established a Jewish police force under the control of a Judenrat, or Jewish council. The Judenrat was responsible for carrying out every Nazi demand, and was subordinate to the municipal council set up by the collaborators. The first demand imposed on the Judenrat was to raise a sizable amount of money to pay for the erection of a barbed-wire fence around the ghetto, which was to be cut off from

*Byelorussian peasants were rewarded with a kilo of sugar for every Jew they caught trying to escape to the countryside.

the rest of the city except for two gates where German or Byelorussian guards were always posted.

Anyone who attempted to approach was shot. On one occasion, the police gunned down Christian Byelorussians who attempted to throw food onto trucks shuttling Soviet POWs to a new concentration camp.

The same scenario was played out in every city and town in Byelorussia. Jews were rounded up by the collaborators and relocated to the ghettos, where, to prevent the possibility of a rebellion, the educated leadership was marked for elimination first.[6] Byelorussian officials ordered the Judenrat to make lists of workers and specialists for the issuance of work passes. Those without permits would receive no food. Believing that educated people might get some special consideration, many falsely listed themselves as teachers or as possessing a college education. The collaborators would turn the lists over to the SS, who would determine which specialists, such as doctors or machinists, were temporarily necessary to the war effort and certify the rest as human surplus. The Judenrat then assembled the persons on the surplus list for a special work detail. When fewer and fewer people returned from these details, the truth began to dawn on the Jews, but the disappearances went on. By August 1941, the ghettos had been effectively purged of their educated leadership.[7]

Radislaw Ostrowsky's men ran everything for the Germans.[8] The streets of Minsk were patrolled by Byelorussian police. Hundreds of people were marked by the collaborators to be sent off to concentration camps. Slave labor projects, utilizing Jews and Soviet POWs, were initiated in factories reopened by the collaborators. Bombed-out buildings were rebuilt to house German troops, and roads were repaired to carry German vehicles. The collaborators opened warehouses to collect goods seized from the Jews. With the help of the Byelorussians,[9] Minsk became an important staging area for the German advance upon Moscow.

Adolf Eichmann, an SS bureaucrat who had made himself an expert on Jewish affairs (he even picked up a smattering of Hebrew), was given the assignment of devising a solution for the Jewish problem. To Eichmann, the only practical way to rid Germany and the rest of Western Europe of their Jewish population was to deport them eastward to the farthest reaches of Poland, Russia, Byelorussia, and the Ukraine. Eichmann planned to resettle them as slave laborers in the ghettos of the Pale, the traditional dumping ground for Europe's unwanted Jews. There they could be worked or starved to death and no one would know—or care.

The ghettos of Minsk and Baranovitche were selected as holding pens for the Jews of Western Europe who were to be shipped in by rail. Eventually all the Jews would be killed. But first the SS and their Byelorussian collaborators would have to make room for them in ghettos that were already crowded with most of the remaining Jews of the region. The *Einsatzgruppen* and local "demonstrations" could kill hundreds of Jews in a day, but the size of the job ahead was mind-boggling. The murder of tens of thousands of Jews was an enormous task even for the *Einsatzgruppen* with their special training, and the cooperation of the collaborators was required.[10] In the fall of 1941 the SS selected the heavily Jewish city of Borissow as a pilot project for the impending slaughter.

Borissow was under the control of Stanislaw Stankievich, another member of the Warsaw group picked by Dr. Six to assist Einsatzgruppe B.[11] Obese and jowly, he held a doctorate in humanities and belonged to an upper-class Byelorussian family active in collaborationist activities. One relative served with the German paratroops that had led the invasion of the Soviet Union; another had been editor of *Ranitsa,* the Byelorussian-language newspaper sponsored by the SS. Immediately following the invasion, Stankievich had worked with Franz Kushel to organize the local security system in Minsk for the Nazis. Moving on to Borissow, a town of some 15,000, more than half of them Jews, he ruled through a police force garbed in black SS-type uniforms with the white-red-white of Byelorussia on their armbands.

Stankievich ordered all Jews to resettle in the poorest part of town. Even as they were complying, his men set fire to a few homes and blamed the incident on Jewish troublemakers trying to deprive the Germans of quarters for their troops. Fearful of provoking more incidents and eager to prove their willingness to cooperate, the remainder of the Jewish population obeyed him promptly. Stalin's censorship had effectively prevented Soviet Jews from learning about Nazi oppression. When Stankievich ordered a wall to be built around the ghetto, they accepted this as an irritating but temporary measure to ensure that there was no communication with Russian partisans operating in the countryside. Anxious to show that they were not Communist sympathizers, the Judenrat leaders insisted that Stankievich's orders be carried out and discouraged attempts to resist.[12]

Following his instructions from the SS, Stankievich imposed taxes on the Jews. Initially, the levies were small, but they soon became extortionate. The Judenrat paid ransom again and again until funds were exhausted. Then came the requisitions for clothing, furniture, medicine, equipment, books, and paper—even part of the food rations now already at the starvation level. The enterprising peasants demanded whatever belongings the Jews had left for every scrap of food sold to the ghetto on the black market.

In mid-October 1941, a Wehrmacht sergeant named Soennecken brought his boots to a Jewish cobbler for repair and found the Jews in a panic. Soennecken, assigned to military intelligence because he could speak Russian, had been detailed to Borissow to inspect defense measures against the partisans—and to observe the SS and its allies. The cobbler told him of the ghetto rumor that the local German military commander had ordered every Jew in the city rounded up the following night and executed. The Judenrat had sent a delegation to Stankievich begging him to intercede, pointing out that Jewish tradesmen and skilled workers were necessary to the war effort. The mayor had assured them that the fears were groundless, and promised that he would remind the military how cooperative the Judenrat had been in the collection of taxes.

Nevertheless, said the cobbler, the Jews were anxious. Borissow had undergone pogroms before, but on those occasions only a few had been killed; now the entire ghetto was threatened. Soennecken tried to reassure the cobbler, but he immediately went to the collaborators' headquarters to speak with David Ehoff, the police chief.[14] Soennecken knew that anti-Jewish measures were usually the responsibility of the SS and the local authorities, not the military. Further, he was convinced that no German general would be stupid enough to order a public slaughter where there was not even a pretext of combat operations to fall back on.

Ehoff told Soennecken that the rumor was quite true. By sunrise on October 20 all the Jews, save for a handful who were temporarily essential, were to be killed. Stankievich had given him orders to murder about 7,000 men, women, and children. Soennecken was horrified, but he suppressed his outrage and merely replied that as a practical matter it seemed impossible to dispatch that many victims in a single night. Ehoff said that he had some experience in these matters. He also pointed out that liquidating the Jewish population was essential to the military security of the area. If the Jews were allowed to live, they would help the partisans attack German supply lines.

Soennecken spoke to some of the gentile citizens and learned that most knew about the planned executions. "It does no good to talk about the dead," they said, as if the ghetto were already destroyed. For them, the impending death of the Jews meant a windfall of free housing. Previously, Stankievich had divided a portion of the seized Jewish property among the Christian citizens to guarantee their continued support. Few, if any, objected to the persecution of the Jews. Centuries of religious prejudice and local superstition had left them with little love for the "Christ-killers" who owned most of the shops and businesses of Borissow.

On the evening of October 19 Soennecken attended a party at which Stankievich and his police and their wives and girlfriends were present. Most of the guests listened with minimum politeness to the mayor's platitudes about the Jewish-Bolshevik menace and the role that the Byelorussian people would play in ridding their country of these vermin. Speeches done, they turned to the refreshments. The younger men quickly became drunk and raucous. Most of the German officers left after a brief, obligatory visit. They planned to be out of town the next day. Stankievich himself did not have the stomach to witness the consequences of his orders. He took a ride out into the country, far away from Borissow.

The roundup of Jews began at 3 A.M. The local police, bolstered by reinforcements from the neighboring town of Zembin, surrounded the ghetto. Entire families were routed out at gunpoint and forced into cars and trucks that took them out the Poletzala

Ulitsa road leading to the airport, where mass graves had already been dug by Soviet prisoners of war. Soennecken watched the columns shuttle back and forth, but he could not bring himself to go to the execution ground, from which he could clearly hear the gunfire. From time to time he stopped some young policemen or German reinforcements and questioned them about what was going on at the pits. He later filed a report that eventually was entered in evidence at the Nuremberg war crimes trials.

> The first contingent, about 20 men, were made to jump into the pits after taking off all but their underwear. They were then shot from above. Of course these dead and half-dead people were lying pell-mell. The next victims had to line them up so as to gain as much space as possible. Then it continued as above. When the bottom row of the mass grave was full, the Jews had to put a layer of sand over the bodies. The most horrible scenes are said to have taken place in these mass graves. . . . The Russian policemen were given a great deal of liquor. . . .[13]

The killing went on throughout the day. Stankievich had underestimated the manpower needed for the operation, and German troops had to be called out to guard the ghetto so more policemen could be sent to deal with the crowds at the execution grounds. Too many trucks arrived at the same time, and there were not enough men to direct the unloading. A few Jews tried to escape, but most were killed before they reached the woods. Others were too frightened to move until prodded toward the graves. Many accepted the futility of resistance and quietly followed the line to the pit to which they were assigned. Some of the guards raped the younger women before forcing them into the pits. Heads were smashed by rifle butts, and bodies were mutilated. Autopsies conducted after the war showed that some babies, out of sheer savagery or to save ammunition, had been thrown into the pits and buried alive.

The SS professed to be shocked by the Borissow massacre—not at the slaughter of the Jews but at the carnival aspects of it. Over the next three years, as the Byelorussian holocaust increased in intensity and dimension, the *Einsatzgruppen* supervised the actual shooting themselves. Then, at least, the moment of execution would be devoid of the demonic games favored by the collaborators. But even after the sport of pulling the trigger at the pits had been taken from them, hundreds of collaborators guarded the roads, chased fugitives, and forced the living down into the graves.[15] Children were thrown into wells and hand grenades dropped down upon them, and Byelorussian policemen swung infants by the heels and smashed their heads against rocks. More Jews perished in Poland and Germany, but the holocaust in Byelorussia was unique. In no other nation under German occupation did the inhabitants so willingly and enthusiastically visit such a degree of inhumanity upon their neighbors.

Borissow was merely the beginning.[16] On November 15, 1941, Franz Kushel's Byelorussian police conducted a roundup of Jews in the Minsk ghetto and trucked them to an execution ground outside the city. The *Einsatzgruppen* did the actual killing. A report prepared by the SS that week contained a map of the German-occupied area of the Soviet Union with coffins representing the number of Jews who had been exterminated. The coffin representing Minsk contained the figure 42,000. Sometimes the desire of the collaborators to kill outstripped their capacity. On one occasion the SS issued orders for the extermination of the Jews of Slutsk, but owing to a major pogrom scheduled for the nearby town of Pinsk, insufficient Byelorussian volunteers were available. Units were brought in from the Baltic, but they were inexperienced. The mass graves were overfilled, and some of the victims, who had only been wounded, dug themselves out.[17]

The ghettos of Minsk and Baranovitche were rapidly emptied of their original inhabitants to make room for the Jews of Western Europe being shipped to Byelorussia. One morning in 1942 some 50,000 Jews in the Minsk ghetto were herded into Ubelanyie Square. Those who fainted in the press of bodies were shot where they lay by black-uniformed Byelorussian police. They crammed dozens of Jews at a time into large, box-shaped vans and closed the doors behind them, pummeling them with their rifle butts until the bolts fitted into the door locks. As each truck drove away, the driver pulled a switch that channeled exhaust fumes into the passenger compartment. Soviet prisoners unloaded the bodies into long graves that had been bulldozed along the highways, and the gas vans returned to the ghetto for a new load of victims. In 1944, victorious Russian troops crossing Byelorussia saw miles and miles of bulldozer scars along the highways and wondered what they were.

When the Jews learned the fate of those taken away in the vans it was impossible to load them except by force. The SS altered procedures and sent the vans to meet transports of Western European Jews at the Minsk railroad station so no one could warn them. Eventually a ring of holding camps was established around the city to handle the overflow of Jews, and a small crematorium was built in the suburb of Malyi Trostynets. During the summer of 1942 the SS ordered the Byelorussian mayors and police officials to liquidate all the smaller ghettos. The Jews were told they were going to be ransomed to America, and they marched out in columns of a hundred at a time to execution grounds where they were shot by the *Einsatzgruppen*. The SS claimed that they were killing ten thousand Jews per week. In all, about two-thirds of the approximately 375,000 Jews who lived in Byelorussia before the Nazi invasion were swallowed up by the Holocaust.

By the beginning of 1943 most pockets of Byelorussian Jewry had been eradicated except for a few thousand technicians and specialists held in special ghettos and concentration camps because they had essential skills. Koldichevo, in southwestern Byelorussia, was one such camp.[18] Built to house thousands of Soviet prisoners, it was administered by a handful of German officers, while most of the staff were Byelorussians. Two hundred Jews remained alive to keep the camp's equipment functioning. They were all that were left of the 50,000 or so Jews who had lived in the district, except for a handful hiding in the swamps.

Solomon Schiadow, one of the few inmates who escaped Koldichevo, later described the conditions there.[19] The Byelorussian guards were so brutal that the prisoners prayed that they would be replaced by Germans. One day a Byelorussian caught a youngster looking at the sky as planes flew overhead and accused the prisoner of attempting to signal enemy aircraft. The guard ordered several other Jews to hold the youth down over a table. He warned them that anyone who let go would replace the man on the table. He took out his knife and began to carve large steaks out of the living flesh of the young man, as if he were a butcher calmly working on a side of beef.

In the early period of the occupation of Byelorussia the peasants got along well with the Germans and the collaborators. The breakup of the agricultural collectives was begun, and taxes were lower than those that had been collected by the Soviets. Opinion polls taken by the SS purported to show that almost 80 percent of the population favored a German victory. The entire nation appeared to have defected to the Nazis.[20]

One of the most powerful weapons in the collaborationist arsenal was the religious fervor of the Byelorussian peasants, despite the years of official atheism under the Communists and the attempt by the Catholic Church to close Orthodox churches during the Polish occupation.[21] The SS "ordained" sympathizers from the Byelorussian seminaries and religious colleges and established an independent, or autocephalous, Byelorussian Orthodox Church free of the patriarch of Moscow, who was actively propagandizing for the Soviet government. (Early in the war Stalin had promised the patriarch religious freedom in return for total support of the Soviet regime.) These priests had considerable influence with the peasantry, and they actively supported the Nazi cause. In every church the *Einsatzgruppen* were depicted as waging a holy war against atheistic-Judeo communism.

This reservoir of goodwill was forfeited by the brutality and arrogance of the erstwhile liberators in their campaign against the partisan bands that lived in the marshes and forests. The Nazis indulged in an orgy of slaughter, murdering the innocent, burning villages, and looting everything of value. The peasantry were also angered by the increasing confiscation of livestock and grain, and by the conscription of their sons and daughters for forced labor. As a result, the partisan ranks were swelled by volunteers from the once-hostile peasantry. "The situation in Russia grows more unstable," noted Joseph Goebbels, the Nazi propaganda minister. "The partisan danger is increasing week by week."[22]

The Soviet secret police, the NKVD, began to infiltrate the collaborationist network in Byelorussia.[23] Soviet "moles" not only engaged in sabotage and spying but tried to provoke even greater atrocities against the local populace in order to inspire hatred of the Germans. Many enlisted in the police and the units organized to hunt for partisans, and some of them rose to become police chiefs and ranking administrators. Others obtained low-level jobs as typists, translators, and even cleaning women in German offices. Nina Litwinczyk, a typist in the Gestapo headquarters in Minsk, had access to lists containing the names of every collaborator on the Nazi payroll. "We would choose the quietest settlement, with a population loyal to the occupants," one Soviet saboteur later recalled. "Then we would kill a German soldier, or we would mine the railroads in the vicinity; the Germans would retaliate upon the whole village and the peasantry learned a cruel lesson."[24]

As the NKVD anticipated, these provocations increased the German determination to rid Byelorussia of its "bandit" underground. Front-line units were diverted to the rear areas to conduct widespread search-and-destroy missions. The Soviets also stepped up their activities. Officers were parachuted in to coordinate the forest warfare, supplies were airdropped, the scattered partisan units were directed by radio from Moscow. The guerrilla war was taking a heavy toll of the Germans. Railroad lines were disrupted, bridges blown up, and supply dumps burned. Generalkommissar Wilhelm Kube, the overseer of Byelorussia, was killed when his mistress planted a bomb under his bed.* Political leaders in the outlying villages were murdered along with their families. Replacements became harder to find as the partisans warned that anyone who collaborated with the Nazis would be killed.

The Germans were alarmed because the Red Army had gone on the offensive, and by the end of 1943 Byelorussia was again close to the front. The need to maintain order was imperative. A year before, General Gehlen had suggested in a memorandum to the High Command that steps be taken to appeal to the Russian

---

*Since most of the SS documents have remained classified, postwar historians have tended to overemphasize the power of Kube's administration without realizing the more powerful and more enduring relationship between the SS and the native political structure.

people to join the Germans in the fight against the partisans.[25] This was a complete break with prevailing German policy, for the invaders, regarding the Russians as racially inferior, had ignored the nationalist ambitions of the collaborators despite their loyalty to the Nazi cause. The Byelorussians had not even been permitted to form their own military organization or national police force. Gehlen called for an end to Nazi racial doctrines, urged self-government for the occupied territories, and suggested recruiting anti-Stalinist Russians into the Wehrmacht.

These suggestions were ignored by Kube, whose faction had displaced SS control over the Byelorussian collaborators for more than a year. During Kube's brief interregnum, Dr. Six's agents were subordinated to a motley collection of German political appointees who envied the SS and looked with disfavor on their Slavic protégés. By the end of 1942, however, even Kube had recognized the importance of the native politicians and allowed them to form a number of nationalist "cultural" organizations which assisted the Nazis with police recruiting and intelligence operations. Kube's chief collaborator was Ivan Ermachenko, called "Herr Jawohl" by those who despised his slavish devotion to the Nazi cause.* Shortly before his assassination in 1943, Kube sensed a change in the political winds and began to boast in letters to Berlin of how he and his collaborators were helping the SS kill thousands of Jews. However, it was the Soviet partisans operating in Kube's domain that gave Hitler pause. After Kube's death, he gave the post of Generalkommissar to the SS chief of anti-partisan operations, General Kurt von Gottberg, a brutal but practical soldier who had little use for Kube's civilian administrators and their counterproductive racial theories.

Taking a gamble, Gottberg decided to adopt Gehlen's suggestions in Byelorussia: he offered the collaborators a limited form of national autonomy if they could mobilize the peasantry against the partisans. Radislaw Ostrowsky was selected by the SS to head the new regime.[26]

---

*The SS arranged for Ermachenko's disgrace by exposing his war profiteering, with the help of a rival faction of Byelorussian collaborators. After the war, Ermachenko settled in Binghamton, New York, where he joined the Byelorussian Government-in-Exile.

Chapter

3

With motorcycle outriders on the alert, a Gestapo staff car drew up in front of SS headquarters in Minsk on December 21, 1943. Ostrowsky was conducted through the barbed-wire barrier and past a heavy guard to meet with General von Gottberg. Security was tight because the Byelorussian capital had become virtually an island in a sea of partisans. The Germans were not even safe within the city itself, for the Soviet underground was active. The nights were filled with explosions and gunfire. Sentries were killed, and their bodies were propped up to be found frozen in a macabre Nazi salute.

Realizing that the Germans needed him if they were to have any hope of recovering their lost support in Byelorussia, Ostrowsky bargained with the SS for an independent Byelorussian state complete with its own army and congress.[1] He was the only person who could unite all the contending factions. He appealed to the Orthodox group in the east because of his role in the abortive Byelorussian government established following the Russian Revolution, and he was acceptable to the Catholic faction in the west because of his association with such old Polish organizations as the Gramada. Ostrowsky also enjoyed the confidence of the Germans. He had played a leading role in establishing German rule in the occupied territories after his return to Byelorussia with the *Einsatzgruppen* in June 1941. Slighted by Kube, Ostrowsky offered his services to the German army. From Smolensk he moved on to Mogilev and then to other cities on the Russian-Byelorussian border, where he mobilized collaborators, trained police, and directed the elimination of Jews. Now he wished to return to Minsk.

Gottberg was unwilling to go so far as permitting Ostrowsky to establish a full-fledged government. At most, the Byelorussians would be permitted to form a temporary national council with restricted authority. As president, Ostrowsky could choose a cabinet subject to SS approval. The puppet regime would be allowed to organize a centralized Byelorussian home defense corps (BKA) from the 20,000 men in the police battalions already in existence, but it was not to be referred to as a national army and would remain under SS control. If operations against the partisans went well, a national convention might be called in six months.

Ostrowsky insisted that he work directly with Gottberg without the interference of German civilian administrators. He was accustomed to collaborating with the "greens"—the dark-green-uniformed officers of the Wehrmacht—and refused to take orders from the remnants of Kube's inept civilians. Gottberg pointed to his own uniform and assured Ostrowsky that he would still be working for the "greens." The general wore the gray-green uniform of the SD, the intelligence arm of the SS. If any German interfered with him or his deputies, Ostrowsky was told, Gottberg would order that person sent to a combat unit.

Despite the limitations imposed by Gottberg, the Byelorussians had accomplished what few other Nazi collaborators had been able to do—convince the SS to allow them to organize their own quisling government. This was possible because Byelorussia was the only occupied nation where the SS gained complete political control. Ostrowsky submitted a list of ministers for a Byelorussian Central Council (BCC) to Gottberg for his approval and organized the collaborators in each of the provinces and districts.[2] However, the BCC was infiltrated by Gestapo informants placed by the SS to ensure that the BCC remained loyal to Hitler, as well as by Soviet agents who permeated every level of the German administration in Eastern Europe.

Ostrowsky had only six months to prove that his government was worthy of continued SS backing. Although he had put together a political organization and a military force, he still lacked national recognition or popular acceptance. Tall, eloquent, and magnetic, Ostrowsky immediately launched a propaganda campaign to drum up support for his regime and the battle against the partisans. He was a compelling orator who not only spoke the polished language of the intellectuals but appealed to the peasants. He called upon them to fight for "order and peace"—not only for the benefit of the Germans but for themselves. A Soviet victory would mean the return of communism, and he blamed past atroci-

ties against the peasantry on the "Jew-Bolsheviks" rather than the
Nazis. "Forward for the struggle and for the liberation of White
Ruthenia with the German people toward victory!" Ostrowsky
told a crowd in Baranovitche. "Long live the German Wehrmacht
and their Führer, Adolf Hitler!"[3]

Warned that one village where he was scheduled to speak was
secretly controlled by the partisans, Ostrowsky brushed off the
pleas of aides that he avoid the place. Immediately upon his
arrival, he went to the village hall and spoke before a crowd that
included many suspected partisan sympathizers. He made an emo-
tional plea for the villagers to come over to his side and to fight
the Communists, who had done nothing for Byelorussia. Over the
next few weeks a significant increase in the number of defections
from the partisans was reported in the area.

Ostrowsky persuaded the Germans to reduce their confiscations
of crops and livestock to conciliate the peasants and to establish
Wehrdorfer, or fortified villages, designed to withstand partisan
raids. He also ordered a general conscription to fill the ranks of
the BKA. All ex-officers of the Soviet and Polish armies were
ordered into service, and draft evasion was punished with death.
Some 60,000 men are said to have been conscripted.[4] But the hard
core of the BKA was Kushel's 20,000-man auxiliary police force,
which had helped the SS murder the Jews, Poles, and partisans.
Recruits wore the Byelorussian white-red-white on their caps and
the SS insignia on their collars. Within a few months Ostrowsky
managed to convince Gottberg that the nationalist strategy had
paid off. The Byelorussian militia was slightly less inclined to
terrorize the peasants than the Germans, and they provided information that led to some local successes against the partisans.[5]
Gehlen was among those impressed with Ostrowsky's organiza-
tional abilities. Ostrowsky had been mayor of Smolensk at the
time Gehlen had his headquarters in the city.

Dimitri Kasmowich, the police chief in the Smolensk region,
was one of Ostrowsky's ablest lieutenants. A strong nationalist,
Kasmowich had fled Byelorussia at the time of the Soviet conquest
of the Polish-dominated region and had gone to live in Yugoslavia.
He returned with the German invaders, and his operations
showed what could happen if the Germans allowed the Russians

to administer the occupied territories. The forests around Smolensk were dominated by a partisan brigade at the time Kasmowich took control of the police force. With Smolensk as the center, Kasmowich established an expanding ring of defended villages and maintained a motorized reserve ready to meet emergencies. Large areas were swept clean of partisans.[6]

As his reward, Ostrowsky received Gottberg's permission to call a convention of collaborators to solidify the power of the Byelorussian Central Council.[7] The sounds of artillery at the front could be heard in the Minsk opera house as the convention was gaveled to order late in June 1944. The 1,039 "delegates" represented all of the feuding Byelorussian factions, including the western group headed by Mikolai Abramtchik. They had been selected by the SS and screened for loyalty by the Gestapo. Nina Litwinczyk, the Soviet agent who had infiltrated Gestapo headquarters in Minsk, made a careful copy of the list of delegates and forwarded it to Moscow. At first the meeting proceeded according to the scenario prepared by the SS. Ostrowsky made an impassioned speech in support of the Third Reich's struggle against communism and pledged undying devotion to Hitler's Germany, which had liberated Byelorussia from the grip of the "Jew-Bolsheviks."

Then Ostrowsky departed from the SS script. He announced that the work of the BCC was ended and that the convention should pick a new president. The collaborators were as stunned as the SS officers monitoring the convention, but they quickly seized the opportunity. Ostrowsky was immediately chosen president by acclamation. It was a great political coup. He could later claim that he was chosen as president by the "elected" delegates of the Minsk Congress, for in Byelorussian the words "elect" and "select" are the same. In actual fact, only the Germans had had any say in the selection of delegates.

An SS officer immediately went to the podium to put the convention back on track. As a show of submissiveness to German rule, he reminded the collaborators that they had failed to send Hitler a telegram of congratulations on his birthday. A pledge of loyalty was drafted and unanimously approved. The remainder of the convention was tame by comparison, and consisted mostly of resolutions blaming the Jew-Bolshevik conspiracy for all the problems of the nation, from crop failure to labor shortages. In the middle of the Congress the delegates received word that the Red Army had ripped a great gap in the German front. And so the second "great congress" in Byelorussian history ended like its post–World War I predecessor—with the delegates frantically trying to flee the country.

The Nazis had originally planned to make Minsk a fortress city, a last-ditch line of defense along with the other urban strong points, but the partisan revolt and the massive Soviet attack rendered this plan impossible. There was barely time to organize the withdrawal of German administrators, their families, and key collaborators. Ostrowsky insisted, however, that the entire congress and their families must also be evacuated.[8] The SS gave in, and a special train carrying 800 collaborators and their families pulled out of the Minsk railroad station early on the morning of June 28, 1944. Ostrowsky remained behind for another two days to direct the evacuation. It is no small measure of the value the Nazis placed upon their Byelorussian allies that they sacrificed an entire train to transport them at a time when some wounded German soldiers could not be sent home. The SS made a list of those to be evacuated—and nearly every person on it ended up in the United States.

These collaborators were more than cooperative politicians. Although few of them had personally murdered anyone, they were directly responsible for the holocaust in Byelorussia. They were the key organizers of the Nazi intelligence network, a principal tool in the four-year subjugation of Byelorussia. Without these few hundred men there could have been no guides for the *Einsatzgruppen,* no volunteers to help with the destruction of the Jews. Only with their help could the Germans have recruited the thousands of volunteers needed for crowd control and other measures during the executions. These men ran the ghettos, built the concentration camps, collected the taxes, established the networks of secret informants, and fought the partisans. They were indispensable to Nazi Germany's control of 10 million Byelorussians.

Before they were evacuated, the collaborators helped the Germans plant explosives beneath every principal factory, office building, warehouse, or granary that had not already been stripped and sent to Germany. When the members of the congress withdrew, they gave the order to scorch the earth behind them. The destruction was appalling. Barely a building was left standing when the Soviet forces recaptured Minsk. The final yardstick of the Nazi occupation was the fact that the civilian population of Byelorussia had decreased 25 percent in three years.

In Berlin, Ostrowsky and his government were warmly received by the Nazis.[9] The ministers were given special ration cards issued only to high-ranking Nazi party members and were assigned to comfortable quarters in the heart of the city. But they must have been shaken by what they saw. Berlin was being bombed around the clock, and the streets were lined with shattered buildings. Bombed-out families lived in the ruins of their homes along with a few rescued possessions. Some of the people were shocked and sullen; others displayed a hysterical merriment often seen in the midst of disaster. Following the raids, a cloud of smoke that reached thousands of feet into the air hung over the burning city, turning day into night.

Kushel's troops marched a thousand miles to their new home. Most of the recruits conscripted into the BKA remained behind —and were given amnesty by the Soviets—but the 20,000 auxiliary policemen who had been absorbed into its ranks were forced to flee. They had earned a special notoriety and knew what their fate would be if they were captured by the Red Army. Along the way these units were absorbed into the 30th Waffen-Grenadier-division der SS-Russiche No. 2.

This infantry division was formed from the remnants of the 29th Waffen-SS Division, which had included Byelorussian and Ukrainian units. Hitler had become suspicious of their loyalty and had ordered them removed from the eastern front, fearing that they would defect to the advancing Red Army. They were transferred to Italy, where in their first encounter with American and Free Polish troops at Cassino a good number of them deserted, as Hitler had predicted. Later, many Byelorussians and Ukrainians were sent to France as members of the 30th Division, where they defected again.

It was not unusual to find Byelorussians serving the Nazis in the

Waffen-SS. The latter was a heterogeneous organization through whose ranks nearly one million men of fifteen nationalities eventually passed. Most were German volunteers, but there were also Frenchmen, Dutchmen, Romanians, Hungarians, Yugoslavs, even Muslims.

The names of some Waffen-SS divisions indicate their diverse national composition: SS-Freiwilligen-Panzerdivision-Nederland (Dutch); Waffen-Grenadierdivision der SS-Charlemagne (French); Waffen-Grenadierdivision der SS-Lettische No. 2 (Latvians). The motives of the foreigners for joining the Waffen-SS were also diverse, ranging from anticommunism to simple opportunism to desire for adventure. But the Byelorussians cannot be singled out as unique for having joined the Nazi cause; what did make them different from most of the other nationalities was their eventual, and curious, fate.

A portion of the division was sent to Warsaw in August 1944 to assist in putting down an uprising by the Polish underground. It was one of the bloodiest episodes of the entire war. The Byelorussian units were accustomed to unrestricted methods of terror against civilians, and murder, rape, and looting were common occurrences. The revolt was crushed, and the Nazis razed the city as an example. While the Poles fought and died in the ruins of their capital, the Soviet army had deliberately stalled outside the gates of Warsaw waiting for the SS to suppress the rebellion. The massacre spared them, at least temporarily, the problem of dealing with Polish nationalism.

The 30th Division was regarded as experienced in anti-partisan tactics, so it was immediately shipped to Alsace-Lorraine to fight the French underground. More important, the division could be quickly sent into combat in the event of an Allied breakthrough in western France. An alarmed Ostrowsky sought a meeting with Himmler in an attempt to persuade the SS chief to change his mind.* He knew that his ill-trained peasant terrorists would never stand up against the Allied armies. Ostrowsky also asked that the Byelorussian brigade of the 30th Division be put under Byelorus-

---

*It is not known whether Ostrowsky had a personal confrontation with Himmler, but he told his associates he would make every effort to meet with him personally.

sian command, not just for nationalistic reasons, but also to make certain that his units did not take part in the fighting against Allied troops. If the Third Reich collapsed, Ostrowsky did not want the Allies to treat the Byelorussians as enemies, for he was already hoping to make a deal with them.[10]

Himmler reluctantly agreed to place the Byelorussian segments of the 30th Division under the control of the puppet government.[11] With the help of the SS, Ostrowsky set up an officers' school and had uniforms and insignia made for the new "Waffen Sturm-brigade Belarus." The symbol chosen was an ancient religious sign, a cross with two bars equal in length and parallel to each other.[12] The Belarus officer cadets had barely time to enroll in the school before they were thrown into battle along with other half-trained units against General George S. Patton's advancing Third Army. They were routed and a sizable number captured, while the survivors retreated back to Germany after burying their dead at Biscenson, near the Swiss border. Orders were issued for the dazed remnants to be absorbed by the Russian Army of Liberation, which had been organized among volunteers from the POW camps by the renegade Soviet general Andrei A. Vlasov, and thrown into battle against the Red Army. But Ostrowsky, deter-mined to keep the Belarus Brigade together, deliberately dragged his feet in carrying out the order.[13]

Ostrowsky also resisted attempts by Gustav Hilger, the Foreign Office liaison to the SS for émigré affairs, to unite all the Russian groups into an anticommunist Committee for the Liberation of the Peoples of Russia. Collaborators were Hilger's specialty.

In the winter of 1944–45 the Third Reich, in the hope of staving off the Russian advance, abandoned its anti-Slavic ideology and enthusiastically embraced its Eastern European allies. Nearly twenty collaborationist "Governments-in-Exile" were formed in Berlin as a belated sop to the nationalist aspirations of the émigrés.* Hilger met frequently with Buchardt of the SS and

---

*Some nationalities had more than one representative body in Berlin. The Byelorussians, for example, had one national committee willing to work with Russian collaborators, and another committee, headed by Ostrowsky, that opposed such a union. Similarly, a faction of the Organization of Ukrainian Nationalists accepted the offer of Nazi political recogni-tion while a rival group continued to haggle over terms.

members of Gehlen's staff to create a political structure to unite the émigrés against the Communists. However, infighting among various Nazi ministries delayed the formation of Hilger's umbrella organization of collaborators. As a strong nationalist, Ostrowsky believed that such an organization would subordinate Byelorussian interests to those of its other members, particularly the White Russian NTS, which opposed all attempts by the various nationalities to break away from a central Russian state.

In the meantime, Himmler had given his blessing to a "special intelligence operations" section within the SS that was to organize resistance behind Soviet lines. SS Colonel Otto Skorzeny, who had led the commandos who rescued Benito Mussolini from captivity in September 1943, was placed in charge. Under Skorzeny's guidance, a paratroop and commando school for Byelorussian Nazis was established at Dahlwitz, near Berlin, where they were trained in radio communication, encoding, sabotage, and assassination. After parachuting into Soviet-held territory they were to make contact with the auxiliaries who had been left behind when the collaborators had fled and to launch a guerrilla war, just as the Russians had done to the Nazis.

Skorzeny began the campaign by airdropping some thirty Byelorussians behind enemy lines. Known as the "Black Cats," the unit was commanded by Michael Vitushka and scored some initial successes. Vitushka capitalized on the disorder in the Soviet rear areas to organize elements of the police force that had been left behind. Other Byelorussian units slipped through the dense Belovezh Forest along the Polish border, and a full-scale guerrilla war erupted. Skorzeny also tried to activate the network of collaborators that had deliberately been left behind during the German evacuation. To ensure cooperation, the agents were told that unless they joined the fight, details of their services to the Nazis would be leaked to the Russians. Such threats would have been effective except for the fact that the NKVD already knew the identity of every secret collaborator.

In evacuating the Byelorussian quislings, the Germans had brought out the Soviet spies among them as well. Soviet intelligence was continually apprised of the latest moves of the collaborators. In fact, several NKVD informants were alleged to have worked their way into the battalion undergoing training at Dahlwitz itself. Even before Ostrowsky reviewed his men at a graduation parade, Soviet intelligence was working on a counter-plan to destroy the guerrilla units before they could do much damage. The entire population along a fifty-mile border strip was removed and transported to Siberia. No more spies could cross from Poland. Armed with reports provided by their agents, the Russians went through each village and town arresting those who had in any way served the Germans. There were many arrests, and many executions. Quickly and efficiently the NKVD rolled up Skorzeny's guerrilla fighters and most of Ostrowsky's informants. Three years of SS effort in organizing the Byelorussian informants network was destroyed in little over three months. Most of the paratroopers escaped and made their way back to Germany, but a few, including Vitushka, never returned. The original Black Cat unit was hunted down, and Vitushka himself was captured and executed.

Ostrowsky realized that it was only a matter of time before his commandos were caught and if he were to make use of them in his bargaining with the western Allies he would have to move swiftly. He had had considerable experience with the thorough-ness of the NKVD in dealing with infiltrators. Earlier, when the SS had tried to place a group of his men behind Soviet lines, the Soviets assigned an entire intelligence division, almost 10,000 men, to comb through each house in the area in search of the spies. Intelligence work is largely the gathering of great quantities of routine information in the hope of discovering an occasional gem. The Soviets guaranteed that they would uncover even the smallest jewel by systematically searching and sifting all relevant sources of information. If it took 10,000 men one week to interrogate a few hundred thousand people, so be it. The spies had been caught and dealt with.

With Germany collapsing about him, Ostrowsky recognized that the only politics that mattered now were the politics of sur-vival. Victorious Allied armies were advancing on all fronts— from the east, south, and west. The cities had been bombed to rubble by thousand-plane raids. The roads were clogged by ref-ugees fleeing the Soviets who spread nightmarish stories of rape and murder. The factories had been either leveled or shut down because of power failure. The machinery of government had been shattered, the telephone exchanges destroyed, and Hitler had disappeared into a bunker deep beneath the Reich Chancellery in Berlin. Nazi Germany was dying in a Wagnerian funeral pyre planned by Hitler, but Ostrowsky was determined to avoid the flames.

Envoys were dispatched to the American, British, and French armies with the Byelorussians' last bargaining chip—the offer of an operating spy network and an "active" guerrilla army to fight Communists. On the surface it looked as if Ostrowsky and his intelligence chief, Mikolai Abramtchik, were the masterminds of a giant espionage network behind Soviet lines. By the time the Allies discovered that Ostrowsky's spies were long since dead or had been "turned" by the Soviets, the Byelorussians would be safely ensconced behind the Allied lines, where they could await the day when the West took up the anti-Bolshevik crusade.

Ostrowsky decided that the best chance for safety lay with the Polish government-in-exile in London and its anticommunist leader, General Wladyslaw Anders. Ostrowsky's son, Wiktor, had managed to escape the Soviet attack on Poland in 1939 and made his way to Egypt, where he joined Anders' army. Franz Kushel, Ostrowsky's minister of war, also had a link to Anders. Kushel and Anders had been cellmates in Moscow's Lubyanka prison after the Russian takeover. They were among a handful of captured Polish officers not slaughtered by the Communists at the Katyn massacre.

With the help of Abramtchik's contacts in Paris and Switzerland a deal was quickly made. General Anders, a bluff professional soldier without political guile, agreed to welcome the Belarus Brigade as part of a Free Polish army to liberate his country from what he feared would become a long Communist occupation. It is one of the ironies of history that the Poles, who had recently suffered so much at the hands of the Byelorussians, were first to give them shelter from the avenging Russians. But there is no evidence that the Polish government-in-exile in London made the connection between the Belarus Brigade and their own intelligence reports on the holocaust in Byelorussia.* To all appearances Ostrowsky was a dedicated nationalist willing to work with any ally who might free his country from Communist occupation. Such views met with much sympathy. There were many officers, especially in the American military, who were ardent in their hatred of communism and openly advocated the immediate conquest of the Soviet Union.

In the spring of 1945, as the Third Reich was collapsing, Ostrowsky ordered Kushel to march the Belarus Brigade toward General Patton's Third Army. Patton was both a friend of Anders and an outspoken anticommunist, so Ostrowsky hoped he would provide temporary shelter for the Byelorussians until they could link up with Anders. The brigade members removed the double cross from their collar tabs, hid their flags and records, and, disguising themselves as escaping POWs, marched toward the sanctuary of the American lines.[14] The Belarus SS settled down as prisoners in an American internment center just outside the city of Regensburg.

*The Polish secret service maintained an active spy network in Byelorussia during 1941–42. Their reports on Byelorussian atrocities under the collaborators were forwarded to the Polish Minister of the Interior in London, and to the OSS. Copies of these reports are in the files of the Sikorski Institute in London and of Yad Vashem in Israel.

Chapter

4

Early on the morning of May 7, 1945, a telephone rang in General George S. Patton's mobile headquarters trailer, which was parked in Regensburg, in southern Germany. General Omar N. Bradley, commander of the Twelfth Army Group, was on the line. "Ike just called me, George," he said. "The Germans have surrendered. It takes effect at midnight, May eighth. We're to hold in place everywhere up and down the line. There's no sense in taking any more casualties now." The truculent Patton had wanted to plunge ahead with his tanks and capture Prague before the Red Army got there.[1] As the Third Army warily settled into place, Dr. Stanislaw Hrynkievich, who had been dispatched by Ostrowsky as the Byelorussian envoy to the Americans, sought a meeting with Patton's intelligence chief.

Hrynkievich's reception by the Third Army was something less than Ostrowsky had hoped. During a routine search, military policemen discovered a food ration card issued only to very high-ranking Nazis, and Hrynkievich was arrested as a fugitive collaborator. Before he was taken away to a POW cage, Hrynkievich did manage to get an interview with an intelligence officer. He proudly announced that he was an ambassador from the Byelorussian Central Council, which was the anticommunist national government established on the formerly Soviet territory. Hrynkievich conveyed the willingness of the BCC to do anything to assist the Americans in defeating communism. As evidence of the good faith of the Byelorussians, Hrynkievich gave the American intelligence officer the name and official position of nearly every senior collaborator—at least a hundred names in all. Hrynkievich's statement constituted a complete table of organization of the Byelorussian-Nazi hierarchy. He described each of the front groups, traced their Nazi affiliation, and even identified those Byelorussians who had been secret Gestapo informants. No mention was made of the empty ghettos or the *Einsatzgruppen,* however. Hrynkievich also withheld the fact that the remnants of the Belarus Brigade, disguised as Polish prisoners of war, had gone to ground in American POW camps in Bavaria, which was under Patton's jurisdiction.

A copy of the Hrynkievich interrogation was sent to the Army Counter-Intelligence Corps. Attached to the Twelfth Army Group, which included the Third Army, was a special CIC section whose primary task was to identify and arrest Nazi war criminals and key officials in every town under occupation. Lists of Nazis wanted for arrest had been compiled from information supplied by the OSS and the British Secret Service, and each of them had been placed in an arrest category. Category One was reserved for high-ranking Nazis, major war criminals, and security threats who were to be automatically arrested. Hrynkievich was a Category One because of his membership in the "self-help" group and the Byelorussian Central Council in Berlin. Every name mentioned in his report was also given a Category One rating and was to be hunted down.

But the denazification program was the responsibility of area military commanders, and Patton was lax in rounding up Nazi collaborators. Instead, he repeatedly urged that several of the best Waffen-SS divisions be incorporated into his Third Army so he could "lead them against the Reds." When General Joseph T. McNarney, the deputy U.S. military governor of Germany, told Patton that the Russians were complaining about the Third Army's lack of diligence in disarming and confining German units in Bavaria, he snapped: "What do you care what those goddam bolshies think? We're going to have to fight them sooner or later. Why not now while our army is intact and we can kick the Red Army back into Russia? We can do it with my Germans . . . they hate those red bastards."[2]

The Belarus Brigade had good reason to be grateful for Patton's reluctance to root out Nazis, especially after they saw what happened to the survivors of Vlasov's Russian Army of Liberation. At the Yalta conference, President Franklin D. Roosevelt and Prime Minister Winston S. Churchill had agreed to Stalin's request that any "fascist traitors" found in their areas of occupation after the war be repatriated to the Soviet Union. As soon as the war ended, Soviet emissaries searched the POW camps for Russian, Ukrainian, and Byelorussian fugitives to be repatriated to either death or exile in Siberia. Stalin had decided that any Soviet soldier captured by the Germans was a traitor—or at least a potential agitator who must be dealt with harshly. Fully realizing that they would be treated as war criminals if they were turned over to the Soviets, the Byelorussians found it even more vital to keep the history of the Belarus Brigade a secret.*

The roundup and mass deportation of some 2 million Russians, known as Operation Keelhaul, is one of the saddest chapters in American and British history. Some of the deportees had fought in Vlasov's army, but the majority were POWs who had cooperated with the Nazis merely to survive. Many were confirmed anti-Stalinists and passionately wanted to remain in the West. But, ignoring every tradition of asylum, the western Allies uniformly treated all the Russians as "traitors" and forcibly loaded them into boxcars for shipment to the Soviet Union. Rather than return, some of the desperate Russians committed suicide by throwing themselves under the trains. Those who escaped execution were shipped to Siberia as slave laborers in the gulags.[3]

Before the Red Army captured Berlin and the abandoned bunker where Hitler had committed suicide, the Byelorussian puppet government fled to the west.[4] Ostrowsky escorted most of the exiled leaders and their families some 300 miles to Hoexter, in the British zone of occupation, and Abramtchik made his way to the French. Unlike the Americans, who did not realize the significance of the Byelorussians and unceremoniously arrested Hrynkievich, the British and French knew whom they were dealing with. The first Nazi code cracked by the ULTRA operation had been the SS communications code, and the British had almost continuously monitored the activities of the Byelorussian *Einsatzgruppen*. They understood what these collaborators had done to gain power, but were willing to employ them nonetheless.

Disillusionment was darkening relations between the Soviet

---

*In his interrogations after the war, General Franz Kushel always referred to his 30th Division as the *29th* Division, thereby hoping to conceal its combat role in France. Twenty years afterward some American intelligence agencies still bought his deception.

Union and its allies. Churchill privately warned President Truman, Roosevelt's successor, that "an iron curtain is [being] drawn down" across Europe by the Russians. At a Big Three meeting in Potsdam in July 1945 Stalin rebuffed every attempt by Churchill and Truman to question Soviet domination of Eastern Europe, and the conference marked the beginning of the Cold War. Having lost Reinhard Gehlen and his organization to the Americans, the British had to pick up intelligence assets where they could find them. Even as planning for the Nuremberg war crimes trials was underway, they began recruiting Eastern European Nazis. One of the chief recruiters was Harold A. R. Philby, head of Section 9, the Soviet intelligence unit of the Secret Intelligence Service. Kim Philby was a Soviet mole who passed on to his employers information about the defectors while warning the Russians when one of their own agents was about to be unmasked.

Abramtchik and the western Byelorussians, maneuvering for independence from Ostrowsky, volunteered their assets to the French secret service. The French had a long history of engagement in Poland and Byelorussia, and many had been involved in the prewar "Prometheus" program—a Franco-Polish effort to instigate an anticommunist revolution in Byelorussia and the Ukraine. Like the British, the French were willing to overlook the wartime collaboration of the Byelorussians. The French approved the establishment of a Polish military mission in Paris, which served as a cover organization for Franco-Polish attempts to recruit the leading members of the Belarus.[5]

The word was soon passed to General Patton, presumably via General Anders, that if the Americans were uncomfortable with the Byelorussians in their zone of occupation the French would be more than willing to accommodate them. The news must have come as a relief to Patton. Although he was sympathetic to the anticommunist cause, he could not go on sheltering large numbers of ex-SS members for much longer. The Western press was attacking him for his laxness in pursuing the denazification program. If it was learned that most of the Belarus Brigade was living in an internment camp under his command, there would be trouble. The pressure was mounting to do something about the Byelorussians before a Soviet repatriation mission arrived.

According to a member of the Belarus Brigade, an American

officer came to the Regensburg DP camp* where most of the unit
was hiding and said they really would have been better off fighting
with the Poles. In such a circumstance, the French government
would be only too glad to give them shelter. The border to the
French zone was only a few kilometers away, and the Belarus
Brigade took the hint. That evening they noticed that every
American guard had been pulled away from the camp perimeter.[6]
By morning they had fled to other DP camps or moved to the
French zone. In early October 1945, Patton was relieved of com-
mand of the Third Army and as Military Governor of Bavaria by
General Eisenhower. He was given command of the Fifteenth
Army, which was largely concerned with historical research and
controlled no divisions or occupation area. Among the reasons for
Patton's removal from Bavaria was his failure to cooperate with
the denazification program. In December, he was fatally injured
in a motor accident.

For many of the Nazi collaborators, the postwar months in the
French zone were an idyllic time. A Byelorussian school was
opened, and an underground community was established. The
men who had presided over the mass murder of the Jews in
Byelorussia were now safely ensconced as employees of the United
Nations Relief and Rehabilitation Agency (UNRRA). Stanislaw
Stankievich was hired as an English-language teacher for the
camps.[7] Dimitri Kasmowich, former police chief of the Smolensk
region and commander of one of Skorzeny's "special" units, was
a refugee rations officer. Throughout the occupied zones, the
French and British intelligence organizations sought jobs for their
new assets with UNRRA in the camps. It was not only good cover
but provided extra funds, since the British and French had no
money to pay a large retinue of ex-Nazi puppets.

These jobs were often a cover for the real work as recruiters for
the Polish Military Mission. The Polish mission itself was an arm
of the British and French secret services, which sought to provide
assistance to the government-in-exile in London. Throughout
1945 and 1946 a task force composed of several of the original

*The "camp leader" at Regensburg was Franz Kushel. He was later placed in charge of
the Michelsdorf DP camp, where the Belarus SS was regrouped.

Einsatzgruppen guides reestablished contact with the now scattered elements of the Belarus Brigade and other Eastern European collaborators hiding in the DP camps. The Byelorussian collaborators had false identity cards showing that they were discharged Polish officers. The cards had probably been printed on one of the high-quality printing presses that the SS had given the Byelorussian Central Council before the collapse.

The chief document-forger for the BCC was Jury Bartishevic. During the war he had run the Nazi warehouses in Minsk that stored arms and food for the German troops. He also collected valuables extorted from the Jews. In 1944, General von Gottberg had appointed him Minister of Administration in Ostrowsky's government. Bartishevic's staff apparently made new identities for each of the leaders of the BCC just before the war ended. Most of the members of the Belarus simply changed their names from the Byelorussian spelling to the Polish, and the confusing conversion from the Cyrillic alphabet to the Latin was enough to conceal their identities. Ostrowsky replaced Astrouski, Jasiuk replaced Yasyuk, Sobolewsky replaced Sabaleuski, Franz Kushel replaced Frantzishak Kusiel.

The forging operation had intelligence implications as well. Large numbers of Byelorussian Nazis had been trapped behind enemy lines, and all through the summer and fall of 1945 survivors came trickling into the western Allied zones of Germany. Travel through the Soviet zone was still possible: Some German units were operating in the chaotic rear areas despite the end of the war. Each arrival often brought news of Soviet military activity and troop movements. The Byelorussians combined these bits of gossip and fact and printed them up to look like captured Soviet documents. Those who had served with Ostrowsky in Vorkommando Moskau had ample experience with real Soviet documents when they pillaged the offices of the Minsk NKVD in 1941. A large number of these authentic but out-of-date documents had been taken to Germany when the Byelorussian collaborators fled in 1944. By mixing real documents with the newly concocted reports, the Byelorussians hoped to convince the Allies that they possessed an active spy network behind the Soviet borders. The sale of the documents from the Byelorussian paper mills brought in a sizable income during the first years after the end of the war. After 1946, however, the last trickle of border-crossers was cut off by the Soviets, and the Byelorussians lost most of their contacts with the homeland.

Realizing that the Allies could not officially embrace a government created by the Nazis, Ostrowsky called the fugitives out of hiding at the end of 1945 to create another front organization.[8] He told a special meeting of the Byelorussian Central Council that it would be in their best interests to dissolve the government in order to avoid being sent back to Byelorussia as war criminals. In fact, following Patton's removal from command, the Third Army had forcibly repatriated 243 Soviet nationals who had fought for Germany during the war. The BCC changed its name to the Byelorussian Central Representation (BCR) and within a month was operating in the British zone under the new name but the same leadership. But whatever unity had prevailed among the exiles was already splintering.[9]

Factionalism is the bane of émigré political organizations. Increasingly remote from the reality of their homelands, the exiles exist in a hothouse atmosphere that breeds a mixture of intrigue and paranoia. Each faction becomes convinced that it alone is the legitimate instrument of struggle for national liberation, and the fights between them take on the bitterness of a family argument. This is exactly what happened among the Byelorussians. The western, Polish faction was growing more and more uncomfortable with Ostrowsky's leadership, complaining that he was too visible a target because he was widely known as the leader of a Nazi puppet government. It split off and formed its own organization under Abramtchik. Unlike Ostrowsky, Abramtchik had worked secretly for the Gestapo and the SS, and his role as a Nazi collaborationist was not widely known.[10] To be sure, he had participated in Ostrowsky's government-in-exile in Berlin as Intelligence Minister, but it would be difficult to connect him with the atrocities committed in Byelorussia. Moreover, Abramtchik had a front organization of his own to offer the Allies, the Byelorussian National Republic, which had been established following the Russian Revolution and had set itself up as a government-in-exile in Paris.

As soon as Abramtchik reestablished the BNR in Paris in 1946 he went to work usurping Ostrowsky's position with the British secret service. By the middle of the year, émigré newspapers were reporting that the BNR was being funded by a combination of anticommunist groups, including the Vatican and the London-based Polish government-in-exile. Far from being a front for funding from the British secret service, as the Soviets have suggested, the London Poles were desperately maneuvering on their own to regain control of a country that was rapidly falling under Communist influence. One of their methods was to finance groups that held themselves out as possible sources of resistance to Communist control. The Vatican supplied support to Abramtchik's group because many members were Catholics from the former Polish provinces of Byelorussia.[11] A special school was established in the Vatican to encourage their postwar nationalism. The curriculum eventually included parachute training, and there is an apocryphal story about a headline in the Vatican newspaper reading "They Fall from the Skies like Angels."

Bitter infighting erupted among the various Byelorussian factions as they struggled against each other for recognition and financial aid from Western intelligence agencies. They were like salesmen competing for a lucrative account. Ostrowsky's Orthodox supporters were opposed to Abramtchik's links to the Vatican; Abramtchik told the British and French that their opponents, loyal to the Moscow patriarchy, were secretly manipulated by the "Communist" Orthodox Church. Abramtchik soon hit upon a more effective technique: Quietly, the word was spread that many of Ostrowsky's followers were war criminals. In order to avoid public scandals, both the British and French cut their links to Ostrowsky and adopted the "moderate" Abramtchik faction as their channel for dealing with the Byelorussians.* Ostrowsky appeared to have been left out in the cold, but it was not long before he found new sponsors—Reinhard Gehlen and the Americans.

Along with the cream of Nazi rocket scientists and engineers, Gehlen was one of the prize catches of American military intelli-

---

*Ironically, the American CIC reports described Ostrowsky's group as the more moderate faction, and Abramtchik's as the organization with the most Nazi collaborators.

gence.[12] As head of FHO, he had amassed a huge amount of information about the Soviet Union.* Even after the Germans were driven from Russia, Gehlen coordinated the processing of intelligence from the Nazi spy network that had remained behind Soviet lines. Realizing at the war's end that he would be sought by the Russians for punishment even though he claimed never to have been a Nazi, he made plans to ensure his survival by placing with the Allies his vast storehouse of information on the Soviet Union. Like many other Germans, he was convinced that it was only a matter of time before the alliance between the Russians and the West would collapse. In anticipation of that day, he microfilmed his entire Soviet intelligence file, stored the microfilm in steel boxes—some fifty in all—and buried them in the Bavarian Alps in the path of the advancing Americans, to whom he and his staff surrendered in May 1945.

Once Gehlen's identity was established, General Edwin L. Sibert, the Twelfth Army Group's chief of intelligence, consulted with Allen Dulles, then OSS station chief in Germany. Unlike many generals who distrusted the civilian intelligence service, Sibert respected Dulles's judgment. Both men agreed that Gehlen would be a prize beyond measure. Through him, American intelligence would obtain an unprecedented opportunity to develop an anticommunist network in Soviet territory. Fearing that the Russians, who were searching for Gehlen to settle old scores, might get wind of the fact that he was in American hands, the military decided to send him to Washington for extended interrogation.

Much to Gehlen's amusement, he was given the uniform of an American general to wear as he was spirited aboard a plane in an attempt to avert the attention of Soviet agents. Upon his arrival

---

*Early in 1945 General Heinz Guderian, the chief of staff on the eastern front, presented Hitler with a survey of the deteriorating military situation and the strength of the Soviet armies prepared by Gehlen. "Completely idiotic!" the Führer shouted, and demanded that Gehlen be committed to an insane asylum. Guderian angrily replied that Gehlen was "one of my best staff officers" and said he would not have shown the report to Hitler if he were not in agreement with it. "If you want General Gehlen sent to a lunatic asylum," he declared, "then you'd better have me certified as well." Hitler relented, but after this both Guderian and Gehlen were on his blacklist (Guderian, *Panzer Leader* [E.P. Dutton, 1952], p. 387).

Not all of Gehlen's forecasts were accurate, however. During the early period of the war in the east he tended to be overly optimistic. See David Kahn, *Hitler's Spies* (Macmillan, 1978), pp. 441–42.

in America on August 22, 1945, he was put in civilian clothes and installed as an honored prisoner in the interrogation center at Fort Hunt, just across the Potomac from Washington, where Nazi VIP's, such as Gustav Hilger, were interviewed. There Gehlen received a steady stream of visitors from the faction-ridden American intelligence community, each of whom had his own ideas how this windfall should best be used. From their conversations and from the Washington newspapers he was permitted to read, Gehlen discovered that his interrogation coincided with an intense struggle among U.S. intelligence agencies for control of future operations. Rather than being a supplicant, he now found himself the center of a bureaucratic tug-of-war.

The American intelligence system was almost as complex as the Nazi apparatus, and the infighting among its members was equally Byzantine. Until World War II, the United States had no centralized intelligence agency. There were the Army's G-2, the Navy's ONI, the State Department's small "research bureau," and the Federal Bureau of Investigation's activities in domestic counterespionage. The devastating Japanese attack on Pearl Harbor spotlighted the lack of cooperation among these agencies and the vital need for coordination. President Roosevelt authorized the creation of the Office of Strategic Services to meet this need and appointed Colonel William J. Donovan, a World War I hero and an old classmate from Columbia Law School, as its head.[13]

"Wild Bill" Donovan shaped the OSS in his own image. Flamboyant and daring, he recruited agents from among Wall Street law firms, Ivy League schools, and big corporations. The old-line military intelligence agencies, contemptuous of the new organization, claimed its initials stood for "Oh So Social." Nevertheless, after a shaky start, the OSS achieved a credible record in the secret war against the Nazis and the Japanese. Impressed with the success of the OSS, Roosevelt planned, as the war neared its end, to create a permanent, centralized intelligence organization with Donovan's agency as its nucleus. But he had failed to reckon with J. Edgar Hoover, the longtime chief of the FBI.* Hoover believed

*The rivalry between the FBI and OSS was intense. When Hoover learned that the OSS had penetrated the Spanish embassy in Washington and was secretly photographing code books and other documents belonging to the Franco regime, he decided to put an end to it. One night after the OSS had broken into the embassy, two FBI cars pulled up in front

that he, rather than Donovan, should head such an intelligence apparatus. A plan prepared by Donovan for the President's consideration was leaked to the rabidly anti-Roosevelt Chicago *Tribune,* which warned that FDR was trying to create an "American Gestapo." Following Roosevelt's death, the generals and admirals who had also resented Donovan's power persuaded President Truman to disband the OSS as of October 1, 1945.[14]

The surviving intelligence agencies began competing for the remains of Donovan's organization. The War Department took over the OSS counterintelligence section, where it became the Strategic Services Unit after its entire staff threatened to resign if they were forced to work for Hoover.[15] As a result, the task of detecting Soviet spies became split between the FBI and the Army, a division that would later have tragic consequences. The State Department obtained the political intelligence section of OSS, including all its files.*

Reinhard Gehlen benefited from this struggle. Each of the American agencies coveted his services, and he dictated a high price for them. Gehlen entered into a pact with the U.S. government and returned to Germany in July 1946, where he was permitted to establish his own intelligence empire. He was under contract to the Americans with the understanding that once a German government was established he would be transferred to its authority. (On April 1, 1956, Gehlen became chief of the Bundesnachtrichtendienst, the official intelligence service of the Federal Republic; he retired in 1968.)

The Army and Navy, State, and the FBI were each to receive the intelligence Gehlen produced, but access to his original sources would be strictly limited. Gehlen had good reason to be cautious. He needed to keep the Americans from learning how

---

of the building and turned on their sirens. The entire neighborhood was awakened, and the shaken interlopers fled. Donovan protested to the White House, but instead of reprimanding Hoover, the President ordered the infiltration project turned over to the FBI (R. Harris Smith, *OSS: The Secret History of America's First Central Intelligence Agency* [University of California Press, 1972], p. 20).

*The State Department's intelligence operation was unable to rival the military's growing dominance of the field because it was hampered by congressional charges that some of the transferees from the OSS had "strong Soviet leanings" (William R. Corson, *The Armies of Ignorance,* Dial Press, 1977, p. 272).

badly his organization had been penetrated by the Soviets during the war. He possessed a pipeline to the Soviet Union all right, but it would be years before the Allies learned that the pipeline flowed in both directions.

Upon his return to Germany, Gehlen began to reassemble his staff of intelligence analysts at his headquarters at Oberursel, near Frankfurt. Former members of the FHO staff in American prisoner-of-war cages were surreptitiously released in Gehlen's custody. American military law prohibited him from employing war criminals and ex-members of the SS or the Gestapo, which had been indicted as criminal organizations at the Nuremberg Trials, but Gehlen reasoned that what the Americans did not know would not hurt them. Blacklisted men were hired and given aliases and false personal documents so he could claim he knew nothing about their past associations. Only one problem remained: Where would Gehlen obtain sufficient amounts of raw intelligence for his machine to digest and process? The Americans were pressing for immediate results to justify the substantial amount of money, not to mention the risk involved, in setting up the Gehlen organization.

Gehlen had a solution. During much of the war, the headquarters of FHO had been in Smolensk, part of the territory that was intended by the Nazis for absorption into Byelorussia. The leader of the collaborators in Smolensk was an energetic Byelorussian nationalist named Radislaw Ostrowsky, who had impressed Gehlen and commanded a network of secret informers who could provide a great deal of intelligence. Gehlen learned that Ostrowsky was hiding in the British zone and proposed a plan for collaboration. In return for information collected by Ostrowsky's network in the displaced persons camps, Gehlen offered the prospect of protection from prosecution for war crimes from his American sponsors.

Chapter

5

Gehlen and Ostrowsky had much in common. Both had the knack of survival, and both were professional conspirators who would serve any master to achieve their goals. And they both had an inordinate amount of luck. Their secret alliance was cemented at a time when their American benefactors were deciding to get into the intelligence business in a massive way. By early 1946 President Truman realized he had made an error in dismantling the OSS and launched a more than year-long process which eventually led to creation of the Central Intelligence Agency. "Conflicting intelligence reports flowing across my desk from the various departments left me confused and irritable, and monumentally uninformed," he complained.[1]

The first step was the organization of a Central Intelligence Group to regulate the information that flowed into the White House from the State Department, the military services, the FBI, and a myriad of other sources.[2] The President wanted an intelligence service that would tell him what the Russians were up to. But Truman's choice as Director of Central Intelligence was less than inspired. Although Truman was an admirable man in many ways, the President's idea of good government was to give a friend a job. Rear Admiral Sidney W. Souers was one of Truman's poker cronies who had owned the Piggly Wiggly stores in Memphis and then operated an insurance office in St. Louis before offering his wartime services to the Navy. Two days after Souers was sworn in there was a party at the White House in which Truman jokingly presented him with a black hat, a cloak, and a wooden dagger. Souers was out of his depth and was replaced within six months by Lieutenant General Hoyt S. Vandenberg, who had commanded the Ninth Air Force in Africa and Europe. He was no stranger to Soviet affairs, having served as chief of the U.S. Air Mission to Russia from 1943 to 1944.

Vandenberg viewed the CIG as a stepping-stone to a fourth star and the post of Chief of Staff of the Air Force as soon as it was created, but in the year he was DCI he built an intelligence empire. He was not hampered by the fact that he was the nephew of Arthur H. Vandenberg, Republican chairman of the Senate Foreign Relations Committee. When aides presented the general with a proposal for a research department with a staff of eighty, he sent it back with an order to come up with a plan for eight hundred employees. Vandenberg's most important acquisition was the OSS intelligence operation, which had been transferred to the War Department at the time of the dismantling of Donovan's agency. It was renamed the Office of Special Operations (OSO) and brought with it a staff of a thousand people. The CIG also obtained a share, along with the Army's G-2 Military Intelligence Service, in the supervision of the Gehlen organization and the fruits of its efforts.*

Gehlen was delighted, and foresaw a significant increase in his funding and mission. Omitting their Nazi backgrounds, he informed his new employers that there was a network of Byelorussians operating in the DP camps which would like to assist the Allies. In return for recognition of their anticommunist nationalist movement, the Byelorussians would secretly target Communist spies working in the émigré community. The proposal attracted interest, because for some time Soviet espionage had been dramatically increasing among the exiles. Gehlen originated Operation Tobacco, a plan to use Byelorussian informants to help the Army's Counter-Intelligence Corps to smoke out Soviet agents. He hoped not only to ingratiate himself with the CIG, but also to neutralize the mounting opposition from the Nazi hunters of the CIC.

Gehlen flooded the Americans with "authentic" documents provided by the Byelorussians. Because the information pertained to Soviet activity in areas where verification was impossible, the Americans had no choice but to view Gehlen's information as genuine. In reality, most of the secret intelligence that Gehlen furnished came from recently arrived émigrés, Soviet newspapers,

*According to a recent interview with a senior CIA official, the Gehlen organization was not completely relinquished by the Pentagon until 1949.

and mail from Byelorussia and the Ukraine, which was permitted
to continue with only varying degrees of censorship until 1948.
Much of Gehlen's information concerned the DP camps themselves. Hundreds of thousands of displaced persons and survivors
of Nazi brutality lived in these camps, where the International
Refugee Organization was making heroic attempts to feed and
clothe them until a permanent solution could be found. With the
German economy in ruins, cigarettes and chocolate were the main
items of exchange, and there was a thriving black market.* For
a few years after the war, black-marketing and espionage were
among the chief means of livelihood. Communists were infiltrat-
ing these large, disorganized communities of refugees and establishing intelligence collection networks. Operation Tobacco was
only the first of many sweeps in which the CIC investigators
picked up Soviet agents who had been identified by Gehlen's
organization.

The CIC was unhappy with Gehlen's prowess, however. Not
only did he make their own efforts seem ineffective, but, to their
credit, CIC officers deduced that much of Gehlen's information
could have been planted by the MVD, the latest version of the
Soviet state security apparatus. These suspicions were heightened
when the CIC stumbled across some of Gehlen's agents in its
denazification sweeps. Time after time, CIC agents arrested Nazis
hiding in the DP camps, only to have the suspect produce a special
card with a phone number to Gehlen's military liaison.[3] Invariably, higher headquarters would order the CIC to release the
Nazis. It did no good for the CIC to protest that Gehlen's men
were ex-Nazis who were suspected of selling the same information
to the Soviets. By now Washington had become addicted to
Gehlen's reports, and he could claim his successes.

For example, Gehlen's interrogations of German soldiers strag-
gling home from Russian prison camps occasionally produced

---

*Although the American military government tried to crack down on the black market,
military intelligence subsidized it by paying its informants in cigarettes and other hard-to-
get goods. Gehlen augmented his cash subsidies from the Americans by taking payment
for his own network of informants in cigarettes and cocoa, which he sold on the black
market. There was a rumor that the Americans had given him the Lucky Strike cigarette
concession as a permanent subsidy for his organization, but it does not appear true.

significant intelligence. Some had worked in Soviet factories and mines, others on rebuilding dams and highways. By piecing together bits of information obtained from these interrogations, Gehlen was able to deduce a significant portion of Soviet plans for reconstructing its military and economic machinery. One of the POWs brought back with him an ordinary-looking piece of ore which turned out to be fragments of radioactive uranium pitchblende, which was thought to be unknown in the Soviet Union. Another provided a soup bowl made out of a piece of special aircraft metal, which enabled Gehlen to come up with a precise estimate of the level of development of Soviet metallurgical processes.

Within two years after Germany's surrender the Byelorussian Nazis had, with Gehlen's assistance, virtually seized control of the DP camps in which they lived.[4] Most of the Belarus Brigade had been reassembled at Regensburg and Michelsdorf, where Franz Kushel acted as camp coordinator. Kushel organized military training units in the camps; to evade regulations forbidding such organizations, the units were disguised as Boy Scout troops and veterans' social clubs.[5] Stanislaw Stankievich ran the Osterhofen camp. Those who resisted his authority were cut off from food rations. Osterhofen contained a large number of refugees unconnected to the Belarus underground, and, when they protested to the American authorities about the brutality of Stankievich's regime, their complaints were ignored. Some of the protesters were beaten by Stankievich's thugs. Stankievich had never been elected camp leader, as required by the IRO rules, but those who demanded a free election were told by the U.S. military representative that there would be no changes. Eventually the dissidents were transferred to other camps.

A dual camp system was being established—one for legitimate refugees, who barely survived, and another for privileged refugees like the members of the Belarus Brigade. Under the guise of realigning the DP locations along ethnic lines to facilitate administration, the Byelorussian and Ukrainian collaborators were given their own private camps. The Backnang, Michelsdorf, Osterhofen, and Aschaffenburg camps all came under the control of one or another of the Byelorussian factions. Ex-Nazi collaborators who were now employed by the Gehlen organization were placed in charge of these camps, and they obtained jobs as schoolteachers, rations distributors, translators, and clerks. The sale of secrets was a cottage industry, and some of them worked not only for Gehlen but for other intelligence services as well.

One of the most embarrassing examples of multiple loyalties surfaced when the Americans conceived the idea of "repatriating" their own agents into the Soviet zone to collect intelligence. Gehlen provided the Americans with the services of Jury Bartishevic, the man who ran the Byelorussian forgery operation. Bartishevic was asked to prepare sufficient documents to enable Russian-speaking agents to move freely through the Soviet zone. The enterprising Bartishevic printed several duplicates of each forged document, which he promptly resold to a number of willing purchasers, including the Soviets. When Bartishevic's duplicity was uncovered he was dismissed, and a scathing comment was placed in his file at the CIC central registry to the effect that Bartishevic's loyalty would follow whoever paid him.* This was apparently a dig at the all-too-visible lack of coordination among the many organizations which sought to develop an intelligence presence among the refugee populations in Germany.

Fighting Russians with Russians was a concept that had long intrigued American Army intelligence. The Army hoped to build an underground force to disrupt the Soviet empire in advance of the inevitable conflict between East and West. In preparation for this mission, the European Command Intelligence School (EUCOM G-2) had been assembling Eastern European experts, particularly Ukrainians, as the nucleus for such a force. But the paramilitary units that could actually conduct this secret war were lacking. Even Gehlen was no help, because his charter limited him to gathering and analyzing information rather than engaging in covert activities. During the first years of his operation he had successfully concealed the fact—despite CIC probing—that most of the refugee sources he had recruited were members of the Nazi underground community. But early in 1947 the Americans accidentally discovered the key to the Belarus network.

*Bartishevic emigrated to the United States shortly thereafter.

The disclosure came about when Dr. Friedrich Buchardt, who was wanted as a major war criminal, emerged from hiding with an offer designed to save himself from execution.[6] Buchardt had been one of Dr. Franz Six's assistants in Einsatzgruppe B, and had later commanded a detachment of the mobile killing units in the Minsk and Smolensk areas. Toward the end of the war, Buchardt became chief of "émigré affairs" of the SS. In this post he acquired an encyclopedic knowledge of the role of the various Eastern European and Russian collaborators. Most of the other *Einsatzgruppen* commanders had already been captured and were awaiting trial before the Nuremberg War Crimes Tribunal on charges of having systematically liquidated millions of Jews and other Eastern Europeans.

Buchardt offered to trade a secret history of SS operations in Russia, with particular emphasis on the work of the native collaborators, in exchange for help from Army intelligence in avoiding punishment for his crimes. Omitting no details, Buchardt described how his colleague Dr. Six had recruited the Byelorussian collaborators in Warsaw and had imported about thirty of them along with the first wave of the invasion. He named several —including Ostrowsky, Kushel, and Stankievich—and described in detail the functioning of Ostrowsky's government. The manuscript was also a manual on the art of psychological warfare and the winning over of an occupied population through the effective use of collaborators. All the mistakes made by the Nazis during the occupation of Russia were enumerated, and methods were discussed to avoid repeating them during a future occupation.

Buchardt arranged for a copy of his manuscript to be passed on to Army intelligence, and it was rapidly handed up the chain of command until it reached the office of the Army Chief of Staff for Intelligence in the Pentagon where it was immediately classified Top Secret and placed in a special safe for sensitive documents. Buchardt was taken under the wing of Army intelligence—and the U.S. government thus recruited a major war criminal. With few exceptions, the other *Einsatzgruppen* commanders were sentenced to death at Nuremberg. Army intelligence protected Buchardt so effectively that no further trace of him has been found.

The Army soon linked the names in Buchardt's manuscript to

the Byelorussians living in the DP camps. Within a month after the manuscript was received in the Pentagon a courier from the Polish Military Mission in France was caught passing sensitive information to the Polish Communists. The courier claimed to be a double agent for Free Polish Intelligence, jointly supported by the French and the British, and was trying to penetrate the Communist intelligence service. He said he had been requested by the Polish Communists to establish the whereabouts of the former leaders of the Byelorussian Central Council, and to ascertain whether or not they were working with any Western intelligence agency.

The courier had contacted Kushel, Stankievich, and other leading members of the western Byelorussian faction, and had obtained a list showing the residences of several cabinet-level collaborators. This list matched the names in Buchardt's manuscript. Kushel and the others had willingly furnished it to the courier to establish his bona fides as a spy. The Byelorussians realized Soviet agents were monitoring their activities and would have secured the information anyway.[7] Up until this time the Americans had no knowledge of the importance of the Byelorussians to Soviet intelligence. The Russians had made no request for their arrest, and their names had never been published on any list of wanted war criminals. The Soviets seemed content to track their every move but not to disclose an interest.

Primed by these fragments of information, Army intelligence launched a crash program to learn everything it could about the Byelorussians, who seemed made to order for a guerrilla campaign against the Soviet Union. But the Americans faced serious problems in enlisting the Byelorussians for a secret war. The various factions showed no inclination to cease their internecine feuding, while officially the United States was committed to the policy of repatriation for all Russian war criminals, including Byelorussians. With the trials of the *Einsatzgruppen* commanders soon to begin at Nuremberg, this was hardly the time for the Pentagon to make it known that it had recruited any of their colleagues. And the Soviets chose this moment to break their silence regarding the Byelorussian Nazis.

On October 31, 1947, the delegate to the United Nations from the Byelorussian Soviet Socialist Republic unleashed an attack that revealed just how closely the MVD had monitored the activities of the Belarus in the DP camps.[8] Almost every one of the men denounced by the Soviets as war criminals was associated with one or another Western intelligence agency. Few of the UN delegates realized, however, that the denunciation was a skirmish in the rapidly heating Cold War between the Soviet Union and the West.

The Government of the Byelorussian Soviet Socialist Republic has available a substantial list of German fascist criminals and their accomplices who committed crimes on the temporarily occupied territory of Byelorussia [the Byelorussian delegate declared]. Some of the criminals are still hiding in camps for displaced persons, while others are living on in the western zones of Germany and Austria, where they are forming all kinds of organizations hostile to Soviet Byelorussia and engaging in subversive activity against the United Nations.

Thus, according to our information, there [exists] in Munich, in the United States zone of occupation, a so-called "Byelorussian National Committee" which is composed of war criminals and is a centre of subversive activity directed against Soviet Byelorussia. . . .

A "Byelorussian Committee" . . . also operates at Regensburg (in the United States zone of occupation). This "Committee" has a considerable number of members who committed crimes against the Byelorussian people [among them] . . . Lieutenant-Colonel Franz Kushel, who lives in Amberg (United States zone of occupation), and who, during the German occupation of Byelorussia, was a member of the so-called "Byelorussian Central Council" set up by the fascists. Kushel was one of the most active workers of the "Byelorussian Territorial Defence Organization," which took part in the fighting against the Soviet Army and the Byelorussian partisans. With Franz Kushel lives his wife Arsenieva, one of the chief contributors to the fascist newspaper *Ranitsa,* which was published in Berlin by the German authorities and called for bloody reprisals against the unyielding Byelorussian people. . . .

The following members of the "Byelorussian Central Council" which existed during the German occupation of Byelorussia are also at Amberg: Evgeni Kolubovich (or Geny Golubovich), who worked as head of the Department of Culture and Propaganda of the "Byelorussian Central Council"; Stanislaw Stankievich, who was chief of the Borissow district at the time of the German occupation, directed the massacre of the innocent inhabitants of this district, and afterwards became editor of the fascist newspaper *Ranitsa;* Yosif Dashkevich, who served as an SS captain and conducted punitive operations against the population of the Slonim district of the region of Baranovichi; and many others whose hands are stained with the blood of the Byelorussian people.

In the town of Hoexter in the United Kingdom zone of occupation of Germany lives the butcher of the Byelorussian people, the President of the so-called "Byelorussian Central Council" set up by the Germans when they were temporarily in occupation of Byelorussia. He is Radislaw Ostrowsky, whose misdeeds the Byelorussian people will never forgive, wherever he may hide and whoever may hide him. . . .

When Washington made inquiries, in an attempt to meet Soviet demands for repatriation of the collaborators, the charges were brushed off, and so were similar accusations against Stankievich and the Ukrainian Stephan Bandera.[9] Bandera was advised by military intelligence to go underground while the CIC searched for him. Stankievich constituted a more difficult problem. The CIC picked him up in 1948 for "aggressive interrogation," and upon being shown a copy of *Ranitsa* with his name on the masthead, he broke down and sobbed out a partial confession.[10] While Stankievich acknowledged having held numerous posts in the occupation regime, he did not mention the atrocities committed while he held those positions. The staff of General Lucius D. Clay, the military governor of the American Zone in Germany, persuaded the CIC not to prosecute, pointing out that Stankievich was now working for British intelligence. The CIC agreed, and Clay's intelligence staff notified Washington that Stankievich was merely an anticommunist politician whom the Soviets wished to discredit. "All other indicated files . . . disclosed no derogatory information," the letter said.*

Meanwhile, the American intelligence establishment was undergoing another shake-up. In September 1947 the Central Intelli-

*This letter was recently discovered in Stankievich's "blue"—or sensitive—file at Fort Meade, along with his confession and other incriminating documents. It is listed under "Stanislav Stankievic, date of birth, 23 February 07, File No. AE5296:75."

gence Group became the Central Intelligence Agency, with a greatly enlarged field of operations.[11] Rear Admiral Roscoe H. Hillenkoetter, Vandenberg's successor at the CIG, was named its head. Unlike his predecessors, the admiral had considerable intelligence experience, which he had garnered in the Pacific during the war, and he was fluent in German.

Army intelligence, which lost its share of the supervision of the Gehlen organization to the CIG, was determined to prevent further erosion of its privileged position in the intelligence community. Military intelligence was particularly alarmed about the influence of old OSS hands in the civilian-oriented CIA, for the Army had always regarded the OSS as too liberal in its political coloration. Many of the G-2 staff were convinced that the OSS had been effectively penetrated by the Communists during the war, and the FBI claimed that Allen Dulles had hired "a bunch of Bolsheviks" to work with him.[12] In point of fact, while the OSS made use of Communists in its work in occupied Europe, its prevailing political ideology was for the most part a vague sort of Eastern Establishment liberalism. By comparison, the Army intelligence staff was largely conservative in its political and social outlook.

The CIA and G-2 also clashed over the proper function of an American intelligence agency. Military intelligence favored infiltration of "liberation groups" such as the Byelorussians into the Soviet Union, while Hillenkoetter disdained "unconventional warfare." He did not believe the high risk of exposure justified actively engaging in sabotage and subversive activities or recruiting paramilitary cadres even on a standby basis. He regarded the CIA as a consumer of intelligence rather than a producer, and was content to receive Gehlen's reports and pass on analyses to the President.

Many of the OSS veterans in the CIA argued that 90 percent of all American intelligence needs could be met by a careful examination of open source material, such as newspapers, or by questioning returning visitors to foreign countries, while the rest could be supplemented by a few well-placed agents. The OSS faction convinced Hillenkoetter that espionage was an industry for craftsmen, requiring a great deal of skill, enormous concentration, and large amounts of money and patience. To support their arguments the OSS veterans maintained that every American intelligence failure in the postwar era could have been prevented by making better use of information already in the files. More emphasis should be placed in gathering information about foreign industry, mineral resources, and political patterns to supplement the heavy doses of purely military intelligence. Hillenkoetter was determined that analysis and collection would be the foundations of the CIA's success, and that the agency should not become involved in schemes to prepare liberation groups for a war that might never come.

The military had important allies, however. Many ranking Republicans regarded the Truman administration's efforts to contain the Soviet Union as ineffectual. Containment of communism was not enough; America should roll back the frontiers of the Soviet empire and liberate the captive nations of Eastern Europe. The "liberationists" included Thomas E. Dewey, the front-runner for the Republican presidential nomination in 1948; John Foster Dulles, Dewey's top foreign policy adviser; Allen Dulles, his brother and an old OSS hand; and Nelson A. Rockefeller, who had headed the U.S. propaganda-espionage effort in Latin America during the war.* Within the government, their allies were James V. Forrestal, the first Secretary of Defense, who possessed a fanatical hatred of communism; George F. Kennan, chief of the State Department's Policy and Planning Staff; and Robert P. Joyce, Kennan's assistant for Eastern Europe.

Alarmed at the prospect of a Communist victory in the Italian parliamentary elections scheduled for April 1948, Forrestal pressed Truman to use the CIA as an active weapon.[13] Following considerable debate, the National Security Council ordered Hil-

---

*During the war, Rockefeller foreshadowed the anticommunist policies of the Cold War by cozying up to dictatorial regimes in Latin America. Niccolò Tucci, head of the State Department's Bureau of Latin American Research, resigned and asked Secretary of State Cordell Hull to abolish his bureau. "My bureau was supposed to undo the Nazi and fascist propaganda in South America and Rockefeller was inviting the worst fascists and Nazis to Washington." Tucci took his objections to Rockefeller and was told: " 'Everybody is useful and we're going to convert these people to friendliness to the United States.' And then, Rockefeller's lawyer Larry Levy said to me, 'Don't worry, we'll buy those people' " (Peter Collier and David Horowitz, The Rockefellers: An American Dynasty. Holt, Rinehart & Winston, 1976, p. 236).

search of potential sources for resistance movements behind Soviet lines. His staff came up with a copy of Stanislaw Hrynkievich's statement to Third Army intelligence, with its detailed description of the Nazi puppet government of Byelorussia.

The Byelorussians appeared ideal for Wisner's purposes. They had run a complex system of secret informants, most of whom had remained behind Soviet lines and were now vulnerable to blackmail by threats to expose their wartime collaboration with the Nazis. They had also proven their willingness in Operation Tobacco to collaborate with the Americans by informing on Communist penetration of the DP camps. The counterintelligence angle would also provide good cover for Wisner's guerrilla warfare operations, which he wanted to keep hidden from the rest of the American intelligence community. Wisner was going to make General Patton's dream a reality—continuing the fight against communism by recruiting guerrilla bands of former SS men.*

Although there was some resistance to a suggestion by Allen Dulles that Wisner be named to head OPC—William R. Corson states that military intelligence regarded him as "another Donovan who'll run away with the ball"—he had strong backing.[16] Forrestal supported him, and so did General Edwin L. Sibert, Gehlen's original sponsor, who was a deputy director of Central Intelligence, as well as General Clay and the Dulles brothers. Each of these men was sympathetic to Wisner's desire to create a "standby" force to carry out guerrilla warfare in case of a war with the Soviet Union. In fact, the State Department had drawn up a plan to overthrow the governments of several Eastern European countries.[17]

---

*Recently, Marc Truitt, a graduate student working on his doctoral dissertation in Albanian history, came across references to State's Top Secret plans for the overthrow of the Communist regime in that country. The documents that he discovered at the National Archives plainly establish the role of the Policy and Planning Staff in recruiting a network of Albanian anticommunists, principally from among those who had previously been denied visas as Nazi collaborators and war criminals. In 1948, Robert Joyce arranged for one such person to be brought to the United States "outside of the regular visa division" channels. In arranging this patently illegal transaction, Joyce laconically explained that "our friends" had determined that the person was of interest to the national security. From subsequent documents, the identity of the Nazi's friends became clear. He and his fellow collaborators were later placed in charge of an OPC front group in New York, and began recruiting agents for OPC's abortive invasion of Albania.

In the early days of OPC, Wisner projected an air of affability and optimism. A man of independent means—he could afford to leave his uncashed salary checks in his office desk for a year—he lived well and entertained lavishly. He and his wife, Polly, knew everyone in Washington who counted, and at their parties one might meet James Reston and Arthur Krock of the *New York Times;* George Kennan and Charles Bohlen, the State Department's Soviet experts; the journalists Joseph and Stewart Alsop; Randolph Churchill; and British editor (and former intelligence agent) Malcolm Muggeridge.[18] Although Wisner drank regularly and heavily, no one ever saw him drunk. And despite his active social life he was a hard worker, sparing neither himself nor his staff. Wisner was obsessed by an anticommunism that he had developed in his encounters with the Soviets in the Balkans and postwar Germany, and it was the driving force behind the OPC. He threw off ideas for rolling back the Soviet empire—some good, others wildly impractical—like a human pinwheel.

Wisner established OPC in the temporary buildings near the Lincoln Memorial* and the Reflecting Pool and recruited a staff of what Stewart Alsop called "Bold Easterners" and less-admiring observers described as "Ivy League dilettantes."[19] They included Kermit Roosevelt, Tracy Barnes, Desmond FitzGerald, Richard Bissell, and Cord Meyer, Jr. The OPC, wrote William Colby, who later became Director of Central Intelligence, operated "in the atmosphere of an order of Knights Templar, to save Western freedom from Communist darkness—and from war."[20]

By the summer of 1948, when Wisner flew to Germany, circumstances had combined to permit him to lay the groundwork for a unique intelligence operation. The presidential election was approaching, and Wisner, a dedicated Republican, was looking forward to a Dewey victory over Truman. This would mean that his program for funding underground guerrilla movements would soon be implemented. It also meant that he would no longer have to conceal his plans from the rest of the American intelligence community, which floundered about in various stages of disarray. As far as Wisner was concerned, the CIA under Hillenkoetter was

*At the top of the Washington Monument is a picture of the old OPC headquarters on the site now occupied by the Bicentennial Gardens.

"a bunch of old washerwomen exchanging gossip while they rinse through the dirty linen."[21]

Wisner explained his plan to re-create the SS underground networks in Eastern Europe, Byelorussia and the Ukraine to General Clay in several lengthy meetings.[22] Once these networks were revived, they could be used to cache supplies of arms and equipment for his "special forces." Soon, Wisner believed, the Soviet Union would begin to disintegrate from internal rebellions, rebellions which he intended to assist and, if necessary, instigate. It was only a matter of time before the Western powers became involved in war, and then Wisner's underground armies would play a major role in helping to overthrow the Soviet empire.

Of course, Wisner added, it would take several years for the plans to come to fruition—probably not until the 1950s—but it was necessary to begin preparation immediately. He knew that many of the people he wished to recruit were still being hunted because of their pro-Nazi activities and they had to be protected. The CIC, at the direction of Congress, was about to launch a major campaign to prevent Nazi war criminals from emigrating to the United States. It was important that the CIC not obstruct Wisner's training program, which for reasons of secrecy would have to take place mostly in America.

With the leading collaborators in New York, safe from the prying eyes of other intelligence agencies (not to mention Soviet war crimes investigators), Wisner would be free not only to have his Nazi politicians recruit commando units to guide western forces in any future invasion of Russia, but he could also establish entire "governments-in-exile" to assist with the occupation. Although President Truman had never sanctioned this extension of OPC's charter, Wisner and General Clay were confident that Dewey's election would guarantee their freedom of operation. After all, the Dulles brothers were key figures in the Republican election campaign and they were the most ardent supporters of OPC's political action program.* But until the defeat of Truman, it was essential that the Byelorussian Nazis and the other

---

*One retired CIA official recently said that the Dulles brothers were "fanatical" adherents of covert liberation programs. Another, who visited with John Foster Dulles during the Dewey campaign, described the OPC Cold War mentality as almost "surrealistic," and inexplicable outside of the context of the times.

collaborators hiding in Clay's refugee camps remain protected.

New EEI's (Expected Elements of Information) were drawn up by Clay's intelligence staff and forwarded to the field. The EEI's for Byelorussia and the Ukraine were so sensitive that they were not published even in the Top Secret CIC *Consolidated Orientation and Guidance Manual,* but were issued to the commanders in a special memorandum. The effect was immediate. A special team of CIC agents had been working in West Germany to confirm Hitler's death by interviewing his bodyguards and chauffeurs, many of whom had gone underground in the displaced persons camps. When the CIC team went into the Byelorussian camps, they were quickly ordered to withdraw and were told that the persons they were seeking would not be found there. Instead, the CIC was ordered quietly to collect all intelligence on the political activities of the Byelorussian refugees and their links with other intelligence agencies. No mention was made of prosecuting the ex-Nazi politicians, only of observing them.

Apparently the CIC's analysts were disgruntled by this hands-off treatment given the Byelorussians. In their Top Secret *Consolidated Orientation and Guidance Manual* for 1948, they devoted a special chapter to the Byelorussian Nazi underground that was encyclopedic in its thoroughness. More than a hundred Byelorussian leaders were identified by their wartime services to the Nazis, present status in the DP camps, and relationship to the various Byelorussian factions. Virtually the entire puppet government was identified, and the CIC made it clear that every one of the factions had collaborated with the Nazis. Their claims to be leaders of a legitimate nationalist political movement were plainly without foundation, for, as the *Manual* pointed out:

To ease occupational problems and to take advantage of native nationalist feeling, the Germans created the puppet state of White Russia during their invasion. . . . When the Red Army threatened to reoccupy the country in 1944, the puppet government moved to Berlin and continued its activity as a government in exile. The Germans, in the meantime, put their agents into the Central Rada [Council].

With an extra twist of the knife, the CIC listed the Byelorussian collaborators by atrocity as well as by the other classifications.

Massacre after massacre was linked to the residents of the Byelorussian DP camps, who, despite their war crimes, now seemed to lead a charmed existence.[23]

Nevertheless, Wisner's plans for a "standby" guerrilla movement were proceeding smoothly. General Clay, the most powerful American in Europe, was on his side, and he had neutralized the troublesome CIC by making it a part of the program. Now he began recruitment of his force. The old SSU had already established intelligence operations in Poland, Czechoslovakia, and the Ukraine, and had even made brief contact with the Byelorussians. Wisner's program was more comprehensive, and less susceptible to exposure by the CIA, which was at that time actively assisting with the prosecution of war criminals at Nuremberg. Wisner's staff contacted each of the German intelligence chiefs who had worked with the émigrés during the war. It was not hard to find them: Hilger had given his State Department friends a great deal of information, and most of the key Nazis were already working for the Americans at Gehlen's secret base in Pullach, where Wisner now went to visit him. This elaborate new headquarters, built in 1938 as a large housing development for SS officers and their families, had been converted into a sort of fortress at a cost to the United States of $3 million. The Gehlen Organization left Oberursel near Frankfurt and moved into Pullach in the second week of December 1947, prepared to continue its espionage activities against the Soviet Union, now backed by substantial American financial aid.*

---

*According to a recent interview with a senior intelligence official, only Gehlen and five of his top associates were transferred from Army control in 1947, while the final integration of the Gehlen Organization into the CIA did not take place until 1949.

Chapter
6

Gehlen must have envied Wisner. The Office of Policy Coordination had access to unlimited funds, and the entire world was its area of operations.* Sensing that OPC was the wave of the future, he became Wisner's firm ally. Wisner offered financial support, which Gehlen repaid with information—particularly about the Byelorussian DPs, who so much interested the American. They conferred together on several occasions during the Cold War. The two men presented a striking contrast: Wisner, bulky and given to orotund utterance; Gehlen, short, slight, and precise as he provided a briefing that filled the gaps in Wisner's knowledge about the intended recruits for his secret army.

For example, the CIC, despite its extensive digging into the background of the Byelorussians, realized only that Franz Kushel, who had taken over control of the Michelsdorf DP camp, was a Nazi police commander who had served with the Waffen-SS. They did not know that Kushel's camp was the home of the Belarus Brigade, which had fought on the western front. Gehlen was aware of the facts because his organization employed many of the SS and SD men who had supervised the Byelorussians during the war. The leaders of the SS intelligence network in Byelorussia were now "research analysts" in Pullach, and over the next four years Gehlen recruited most of the original staff of the Byelorussian *Einsatzgruppen*.

Gehlen believed that the émigrés who had most recently collaborated with the Germans were the ones in closest touch with the thinking of the populations behind the Iron Curtain.† For this

---

*As early as 1949 the OPC had 302 agents in five stations and a budget of $4.7 million. By 1952, the number of employees had jumped to about 4,000 in forty-seven stations and the budget had reached $82 million. This did not include funds spent by other American intelligence agencies on behalf of OPC, nor did it represent the expenses of OPC proprietary operations such as Radio Liberty.

†Tragically, those refugees who opposed both the Nazis and the Communists were ignored.

reason he had immediately recruited Ostrowsky and his followers after they had been dropped by the British in favor of Abramtchik's group. He urged Wisner to put his political backing and financial support behind Ostrowsky, and suggested that they try to bring about a merger of various factions. Ostrowsky had taken such a step early in May 1948 by convening a mass meeting of Byelorussian refugees at the Ellwangen DP camp. Abramtchik did his best to disrupt planning for the session, and his people were ordered to boycott it.

When he learned that Ostrowsky had petitioned General Clay to be accredited as head of a legitimate government-in-exile,[1] Abramtchik launched a fresh campaign to discredit the Ostrowsky group as war criminals—even though Stankievich and Kushel were leading figures in his own organization. The charges and countercharges of Communist infiltration and Nazi collaboration were so strident that they reached the Byelorussian-language press. Fortunately for both factions, few outsiders were able to read the camp newspapers. The infighting gradually subsided, but not before Abramtchik's divisive tactics caused lingering resentment in both groups.[2]

To eliminate the endless feuding, Wisner and Gehlen planned to establish an umbrella group—known as the KTsAB for its Russian acronym—to lead the various nationalities in the struggle to liberate the homelands. The Byelorussians were to be used as a link to the other British groups, especially the more numerous Ukrainians. The Americans planned eventually to supplant the British and take control of all émigré anticommunist activities.

Kennan's Policy and Planning Staff had already convinced the State Department to fund a series of innocuous-sounding cover organizations in New York. With the help of the old OSS political intelligence files, Joyce arranged to have these organizations staffed with the "émigré leaders" that Wisner would select. In turn, they could fund each of the KTsAB's émigré committees headquartered in Paris, Munich, London, and Rome.* Under the

---

*During a series of recent interviews with former CIA officials, they conceded that nearly every American intelligence organization, including OPC, had utilized ex-Nazi émigrés for intelligence purposes in Europe during the Cold War. To do otherwise, they insisted, would have been negligent, since there were so few sources of information available with any

guise of carrying on anticommunist propaganda, the émigré committees would also identify potential recruits for the paramilitary section of OPC.

Wisner's immediate strategy was to locate enough Nazi intelligence officers to train the nucleus of the private armies that were to fight in the expected guerrilla war behind the Iron Curtain. Gehlen was to identify those to be recruited, and General Clay would provide cover for the training activities at the European Command Intelligence School near Oberammergau in Bavaria, or at OPC's "Air Force" units near Wiesbaden. Money for the project would be drawn from untraceable government accounts, such as those of the CIA, and laundered through American corporations whose leaders had expressed a willingness to work with Wisner and OPC.

Gehlen suggested that Wisner hire Dr. Franz Six to head the recruitment and training of the special forces. Six knew most of the leading Byelorussians, he explained, having recruited them for Operation Barbarossa, the invasion of Russia. Six, however, was at that moment on trial for his crimes at Nuremberg. Wisner asked General Clay to intercede with the Nuremberg prosecutor and judges. Whether Clay took such action is unknown, but Six received only a twenty-year prison term, while the rest of the *Einsatzgruppen* commanders were sentenced to death. In 1950, Clay's successor, High Commissioner John J. McCloy, commuted the sentence to time served, and Six went to work for Gehlen on the special forces project.

Wisner and Gehlen found the DP camps fertile ground for recruits. Hundreds of thousands of young refugees—Byelorussians, Poles, Balts, Ukrainians, and anti-Stalinist Russians—lacked work or prospects of emigration. The only jobs they could find were as ill-paid farm workers or as laborers clearing bomb rubble. The "secret army" provided good pay and living conditions, and within a few months recruits were assembled at various camps. American and former Wehrmacht and Waffen-SS instruc-

expertise on Eastern Europe. All of them disavowed any knowledge that the Nazi émigrés were later assisted in entering the United States. Several conceded that in view of the bitter rivalry between CIA and OPC in the late forties, it would have been most unlikely that Wisner would have apprised them of his plans.

tors provided training in hand-to-hand combat, wireless operation, parachuting, small arms, demolition, signals, and all the other "trade craft" of the spy.

In the early 1950s, several of these agents were parachuted into various regions of the Soviet Union from planes supplied by Wisner. They had excellently forged documents and carried miniature radio transmitters, as well as a few thousand rubles and small bags of gold coins with which to buy favors from peasants whom they might have to ask for food and shelter. Some of these agents were to attempt to make contact with the agents Gehlen had left behind in Russia after the German retreat; others were to take jobs in Soviet industry and report back on what they found. A few were successful and provided information for a brief time, but most were quickly captured and executed. Some were "turned" by the Soviets and transmitted false information to Gehlen until the Russians decided to make a show of them at well-publicized press conferences.[3]

Many of the recruits from the Byelorussian SS were put on the government payroll as members of "Polish" labor service battalions and detailed as armed guards at American PXs and commissaries.[4] The Byelorussian units kept the same command structure used under the Nazis and simply changed uniforms as they went on the American payroll. Some had "Polish army" papers signed by Joseph Danikevich, who had been an officer in one of the Byelorussian police units absorbed into the Belarus Brigade. One of the benefits of joining a labor service unit was the fact that character references were provided. For example, a document in Stankievich's file from the commanding officer of the U.S. Army's 59th Supervision Company stated that "in the opinion of the undersigned, Stankievich, Stanislaw, is a good prospect for providing the United States with a loyal, useful citizen of excellent integrity."

The other intelligence agencies were not oblivious to the preparations taking place in Germany, although Wisner did his best to keep the CIC and the CIA away from his operations.[5] His cover was that he was planning to train psychological-warfare operators and secret agents who would help downed American fliers escape from behind the Iron Curtain in case of war. Most of the American agencies were content to believe that was all Wisner intended with his rather small operations in West Germany. The MVD was not fooled, however.

Soviet intelligence had penetrated every corner of the Byelorussian network and had even entered into active competition with Gehlen and Wisner for recruits in the DP camps. Anticipating that the western Allies would sooner or later try to establish an anti-Soviet underground movement, the Russians engaged in a preemptive strike. The Byelorussian BCC, Ukrainian OUN, and Russian NTS were all riddled with Soviet agents. From almost the beginning, as we have seen, Ostrowsky had repeatedly charged that many of Abramtchik's associates were former Communists and his group had been honeycombed with Soviet informers. Wisner went to the best source for comment on these charges—Kim Philby, who had been head of anti-Soviet operations for the British secret service at the time the British recruited Abramtchik and his followers. Philby, then in Washington as liaison between the British and the CIA and FBI, assured Wisner that Ostrowsky's warnings were merely the sour grapes of a disaffected politician.

In later years, however, Ostrowsky's warning of Communist penetration of the Abramtchik faction received independent corroboration. CIC records show that several Soviet moles were unearthed who furnished derogatory information about the group. Other intelligence agencies learned that one of Abramtchik's deputies had been trained as an intelligence officer by the Soviets. (He is now living in the United States.) Military intelligence identified several Byelorussians as part of a network that passed sensitive information to east-bloc intelligence services. (Another of these alleged Communist agents is currently working in America.)

Stanislaw Stankievich was pressured by Soviet intelligence to work for them, but he reported the recruiter to the CIC. She was Nina Litwinczyk, the typist at Gestapo headquarters in Minsk during the German occupation who had supplied the Soviets with the names of Nazi collaborators. Since 1945 she had been blackmailing these fugitives in an effort to turn them into Russian agents.[6] Years later, the FBI received three separate reports concerning a Communist agent living in the United States. Each informant said he had been part of a group of collaborationists who had been captured by Russian partisans during the war. To their surprise, one of the prisoners revealed himself to the captors to be a Communist agent. The others managed to escape and, following the war, eventually made their way to the United States, only to find that the spy had preceded them.[7] The FBI filed the reports without acting upon them.*

Time after time, American intelligence officials ignored their own informants or were persuaded by Kim Philby that the charges about Communist agents among the Byelorussians were merely mud-slinging by the out-of-favor Ostrowsky faction. Philby's biggest coup was to unload the Communist-infiltrated Abramtchik organization upon the all-too-eager Wisner.[8] Pleading a lack of funding from Britain's impecunious postwar government, he allowed Wisner to take over the group, emphasizing the extensive espionage network that Abramtchik was supposedly developing in Poland. Philby also threw in the entire NTS network to serve as the foundation for a Pan-Slavic anticommunist bloc in exchange for access to the intelligence produced. Delighted by Philby's willingness to cooperate with the OPC, Wisner accepted the offer.

As chief of the Soviet section of British intelligence, Philby could claim his successes—in which he was assisted by his Soviet masters—and was considered a preeminent authority on anti-Soviet espionage. Wisner apparently believed that Philby's endorsement provided the "special forces" concept with a cachet that might have taken him years to acquire on his own. The sardonic Philby must have smiled to himself as he turned over the hollow shells of his Eastern European intelligence operations to Wisner. In his memoirs, published after he escaped to the Soviet Union, Philby dismissed Wisner as "a young man for so responsible a job, balding and running self-importantly to fat."[9]

Wisner wanted to train his Nazi protégés in the United States out of sight of both Soviet spies and other Allied intelligence agencies. Plans were made to bring recruits to Fort Bragg, North Carolina, for parachute instruction, and a secret base was estab-

*The FBI terminated several internal security investigations when the suspect identified himself as working for an OPC front group.

lished near Williamsburg, Virginia, where they could be trained in guerrilla warfare without even knowing they were in the United States. In order for this to happen, however, Wisner had to evade a ban imposed by President Truman on admitting ex-Nazis to this country without alerting the Immigration Service.

Precedent existed for such sleight of hand. Following the end of the war, the Pentagon had become alarmed at the extent of the Soviet roundup of German rocket and atomic scientists. To make such recruitment easier, the Russians had classified virtually every significant German physicist as a "war criminal" subject to immediate arrest. The Pentagon asked Truman for permission to "deny" these scientists to the Russians by smuggling them into the country. The White House was concerned that the United States might be accused of breaching international agreements against sheltering war criminals, and issued an order forbidding admission into the country of any scientist who had voluntarily aided the Nazis. The scientists brought over in Operation Paperclip, therefore, were to be classified as prisoners of war so as not to violate immigration laws. Top Secret White House documents recently discovered among State Department archives conclusively establish that Truman was under the impression that no American agency had ever brought any Nazi "quislings, traitors, or war criminals" into the country.*

Assistance in earmarking which German scientists to recruit was offered by Donald Maclean, the First Secretary of the British embassy in Washington and liaison for atomic secrets.[10] Maclean was also a Soviet mole. Among the Top Secret documents in the Operation Paperclip files is a letter from him advising the Pentagon that certain German scientists were too unimportant for recruitment. Later it was determined that several of these men were physicists of international reputation. And the Pentagon soon began to notice that with unsettling regularity many of the scientists whom it wanted to bring to the United States were disappearing, apparently kidnapped by the Russians.

The Pentagon had other worries. The CIC, which had been

---

*Clark Clifford, special counsel to President Truman, recently confirmed that the White House had not been informed of any illegal smuggling program.

assigned to scrutinize the candidates for entry into the United States to ferret out Nazis, was coming dangerously close to discovering that several Paperclip candidates were war criminals who had participated in experiments on human beings or had employed slave labor under inhuman conditions. The Pentagon had apparently decided, without informing the President, that the interests of national security in using these scientists far outweighed any notion of prosecuting them for war crimes. The names of several scientists were deleted from the Army's war crimes suspects list, and the CIC was directed to accelerate background clearances for them. The war crimes investigations were closed, and a "no derogatory information" report was issued. The scientists were simply listed as cargo on an aircraft weigh bill and flown to the United States. Several years later they would be paraded across the Mexican border and back again so as to create a "legal" entry to present to the Justice Department.[11] It was almost an article of faith that any deception was permissible to protect valuable scientists such as Wernher von Braun from Soviet apprehension.*

There were, however, several incidents that graphically illustrated the haphazard nature of postwar security checks for German scientists. According to one CIA agent, Klaus Fuchs was given clearance to work on the atomic bomb project despite the fact that the agency possessed a classified SS report identifying him as a Communist spy. The document was discovered only after Fuchs had sent much important information off to Moscow. (I have since found this document in the National Archives.)

---

*Not all the scientists, of course, were von Brauns. Not until many years later, when one of the Paperclip scientists turned down a job requiring a Top Secret clearance, did the Army first begin to suspect that it may have been too hasty in expediting the earlier background checks. The "scientist" confessed that he had simply made up a host of academic credentials in the hope that the Americans would grant him sanctuary. Upon arrival in the United States he had sought out managerial positions where his fictitious degrees would not be challenged. The "scientist" feared that if he accepted the better-paying job offer and underwent a Top Secret clearance investigation his fraud might be discovered. To the consternation of the Army investigator conducting the interview, the man also confessed that before his departure to the United States he had been solicited to become an informant for Soviet intelligence. For years the "scientist" had lived in dread that one day the Soviet agents would blackmail him. After an investigation the Army decided that he was telling the truth and had not been in contact with the Soviets since coming to America.

With the Paperclip example before him, Frank Wisner designed a program to smuggle his "freedom fighters" into the United States, where he could prepare them for the coming war of liberation. He instructed OPC to concentrate on refugees who had been high-level political collaborators. They were to be brought to the United States to set up "national committees for liberation" for each country behind the Iron Curtain, with money funneled through the OPC's secret accounts. Clay's contacts ensured that the CIC would not conduct war crimes investigations involving them, while Wisner used his influence within the State Department to make certain that the Nazis' visa applications were expedited.[12] Incriminating information was removed from the files and false identities were created as necessary. And so, while other government agencies were actively engaged in pursuing Nazi war criminals, the State Department was importing their leaders to the safety of the United States.

It was not a large operation at first. A few dozen obscure politicians from countries under Soviet occupation were brought to New York and put to work in "private" organizations dedicated to opposing communism.* Outside of a handful of State Department officials, few even knew of their Nazi collaboration, fewer still realized their connection to Nazi intelligence operations. Between 1948 and 1950, while the CIA was still being organized, the State Department systematically imported the leaders of nearly all the puppet regimes established by the Third Reich from the Baltic to the Black Sea. Hilger's dream was coming true.

The OPC insiders were hardly ignorant of the fact that these men were responsible for war crimes involving thousands of innocent civilians. Joyce himself had fought the Nazi collaborators in Yugoslavia. Wisner had been stationed with the OSS in Istanbul during the war when refugees escaping from Eastern Europe described the role of these political leaders in the Holocaust. Kennan, the State Department's Russian expert, must have had access

---

*George Kennan, who designed the administrative structure of OPC for the State Department, was also instrumental in forming the National Committee for a Free Europe. However, there is no conclusive evidence that he knew that Joyce and Wisner were staffing these committees with former Nazi collaborators.

to the reports of atrocities in Byelorussia and the Ukraine from the OSS, the Polish Secret Service, and the U.S. Military Attaché in Moscow. The Department even maintained a Political Biographic Section which cross-filed all the reports on the émigré leaders. In the Library of Congress is a 1948 publication by the government of Albania, identifying its major collaborators and war criminals. Across the top is the signature of the State Department official who donated the copy. A few months later, many of the war criminals listed were placed in charge of the "National Committee for a Free Albania" by the State Department. A review of State cable traffic in the National Archives, Diplomatic Branch, Decimal Files Section, shows that they possessed similar information on the backgrounds of the collaborators in each country prior to OPC's recruiting drive in 1948–50.

Kennan's friend in the German Foreign Office, Gustav Hilger, can hardly deny that he knew of the atrocities. Foreign Office records in the National Archives show that weekly reports from the *Einsatzgruppen* were forwarded to Hilger's Russian desk. Hilger's records were cited in a CIA report (now declassified) listing "S.S. officers wanted for atrocities and mass murders." Ironically, the report lists Friedrich Buchardt, Hilger's counterpart in the SS, for his war crimes in Byelorussia. Several of the persons named in the report, including various Ukrainian collaborators, were recruited by OPC. In a secret report, an Army intelligence officer noted with amusement that one wing of the CIA (apparently OSO) was hunting Ukrainian Nazis, while another wing (OPC) was recruiting them. All of the intelligence officers with whom I spoke placed full responsibility for the initial recruitment of collaborators on the State Department.

Chapter
7

Paradoxically, at the same time that Wisner was trying to smuggle Byelorussian and Ukrainian Nazis into the United States, these very same people were being denounced in Congress as examples of those who should not be allowed entry. In the summer of 1948, Congress approved the Displaced Persons Act, which permitted some 400,000 refugees to come to America, but only after extensive debate because of widespread concern that war criminals might slip through the screening process. The strict standards established by the International Refugee Organization to bar war criminals, Nazi officials, and collaborators from emigrating were tightened by Congress. Even membership in any "movement hostile" to the United States was made sufficient cause for denial of an immigration visa.

On August 7, 1948, during the debate on the DP bill, Congressman Arthur G. Klein of New York cited Stanislaw Stankievich as an example of the war criminals hiding in the refugee camps who should never be permitted to enter the United States. Klein inserted into the *Congressional Record Appendix* an article prepared by an OSS officer who was then assisting the Nuremberg prosecution, giving a detailed account of the Borissow massacre and other atrocities in Byelorussia and the Ukraine. The documentation included Sergeant Soennecken's report on the events of October 19–20, 1941, which had been entered as evidence at Nuremberg.[1]

For the first time Congress learned of the holocaust in Byelorussia, as Klein read Soennecken's account of the slaughter of the 7,000 Jews of Borissow. He also noted the OSS agent's belief that among the refugees in the European camps were many Eastern European Nazis, including Stankievich, who were trying to emigrate to America.

No doubt every one of them now bears a new name, passes [himself] off as a martyr of Soviet oppression, and answers to all the specifications of a "political refugee."

The story of Borissow was enacted in every one of the hundreds of towns of [Byelorussia and] the Ukraine, and when the Jews were no more, the same present-day martyrs were used to hound partisans, recruit forced laborers, confiscate property, supervise labor gangs, operate the crematoria.

A different kind of quisling received their awards in terms of jobs and property. They, too, were recruited among the Lithuanians, Ukrainians, and White Russians. [Nuremberg] Document E.C. 326, a memorandum [dated] November 26, 1942, on the treatment of Poles, instructed the Nazi administrators in Poland to take care that "in particular, mayors, district and region chiefs of Polish nationality or pro-Polish leaders of large industrial plants and estates will be dismissed and replaced by members of other nationalities (Lithuanians, White Russians, Ukrainians). . . . The Polish language . . . must neither be put on the same level nor be preferred to the use of Lithuanian, White Ruthenian, or Ukrainian."

To buttress his contention that large numbers of SS men who persecuted the Poles and Jews were also hiding in the DP camps, Klein produced additional comments from the OSS expert. He described how the Nuremberg documents clearly showed that many non-German collaborators had served the SS in Byelorussia, the Ukraine, and the Baltic states:

The Baltic and Ukrainian collaborationists proved so loyal to their Nazi masters that the latter incorporated them in the elite corps, in the SS. For a non-German to qualify for membership in the SS, he would need to have proved his total loyalty to Himmler, in short, to be a superkiller. As an isolated report (1137-PS, October 19, 1944) indicates, the Nazis were few, widely distributed, stationed almost entirely in the towns and lost in the maze of villages. To carry out the confiscations, requisitions, recruitment for forced labor, the Nazis used a large force of collaborationists, made up of local residents, without whom these tasks could not have been carried out.

Alerted by such testimony, Congress intended to make certain that Stankievich and others responsible for equally horrifying atrocities would never be permitted to enter the United States. Even persons who had merely been members of collaborationist movements were to be barred. A three-tier system of review was established. First, the IRO had to certify that a visa applicant was eligible under its standard as a victim of Nazi oppression. Then the CIC would investigate to determine whether he had ever been a member of a "movement hostile" to the United States. After CIC clearance, a U.S. Displaced Persons Commission created by the law would require an American organization to sponsor and certify that the applicant was of good moral character and had a job waiting for him in the United States.[2] Only then could the State Department issue an immigration visa.

As soon as the Displaced Persons Act became law, American religious and charitable organizations went to the DP camps of occupied Germany to sponsor refugees for immigration. Among the camp leaders who played a key role in selecting "worthy" candidates for emigration were Franz Kushel of the Belarus Brigade and Stanislaw Stankievich of Borissow.

The CIC was proud of its role in helping to assure that Nazis were barred from entering the United States. As early as 1945 the agency had assigned a special denazification section to each major district in the American zone in Germany to apprehend Nazi war criminals and prosecute them before special tribunals that supplemented the Nuremberg trials. The CIC's record of prosecutions was an admirable one, and, on the whole, it carried out the will of Congress with integrity and efficiency. To be sure, the CIC recruited its share of Nazis to help track down other Nazis, but for the most part these informants were rewarded only with cigarettes or scarce rations. Only a handful of extremely valuable agents were helped to emigrate—and they were sent to the United Kingdom rather than the United States. Unfortunately, a few zealots in the CIC knowingly permitted Nazi informants to process through for immigration to the United States. Such instances were rare, however, and must be considered in the context of the hundreds of thousands of German denazification and refugee investigation cases that the CIC conducted.

This is not to say that the Pentagon was precluded from employing Nazis as intelligence agents, especially in Germany, or that the U.S. government never assisted their escape to other countries. In fact, the opposite seems to have been true. A Pentagon official acknowledged recently that Military Intelligence (not CIC) sent so many Nazis to South America that one government "passed the word that they would not take any more." Another official admitted putting his own fingerprints on documents belonging to a former SS officer who was spying for the military in East Germany. Equipped with a new set of documents and a safe set of prints, the SS man was free to emigrate wherever he chose. Although it was a violation of the Treaty of Montevideo to assist Nazis to find shelter in the Western Hemisphere, the Pentagon, at least where its own interests were concerned, was willing to ignore any Nazi migration to South America. The Soviets got wind of the exodus, and *Pravda* charged that thousands of Soviet nationals in the American and British zones of occupation were being sent to South America by way of Trieste.

It was quite clear that anyone wishing to bring Nazis into the United States would have to do so over the express prohibitions of Congress, in violation of several criminal laws, and against the direct orders of the Commander-in-Chief. Congress and the President were not blind to the needs of national security, however, and exceptions were made. In 1949 a special law was enacted to permit the CIA to bring in not more than a hundred persons a year who were "ineligible" for visas to the United States. For the most part the CIA acted in an exemplary fashion under the "Hundred Persons Act."* The Pentagon had a similar mechanism for special entry where intelligence considerations were involved.

The State Department had no legal authority to waive immigration provisions for OPC recruits. The power to suspend entry requirements temporarily did not even exist until 1951, and even then Congress insisted, as it had in the "Hundred Persons Act," that entry would be permitted only for a brief visit for reasons of national security.[3] Even then, some congressmen argued that the waiver law and the "Hundred Persons Act" would provide a mechanism for Nazis and fascists to enter the United States. Wisner's plans to build an anticommunist liberation movement required that large numbers of "freedom fighters" be brought to America, but it was too substantial an operation to escape CIC scrutiny. Inasmuch as Attorney General Tom C. Clark was helping prepare the Nuremberg war crimes prosecutions, Wisner did

---

*With several notorious exceptions, most of which appear to have been instigated by OPC.

not even bother to ask him for special treatment. As the Deputy Assistant Secretary of State for Occupied Countries, Wisner had already placed his own agents in key State Department visa offices, and his knowledge of Operation Paperclip helped him circumvent the CIC's screening process.*

There was a weak point in the CIC's system. All of its information on Nazi war criminals was stored in one consolidated file in West Germany. During the period in which the DPs came to the United States it was located first at Frankfurt and then Stuttgart, before being moved to its current home at the United States Army Investigative Records Repository (USAIRR) at Fort Meade, Maryland. The CIC gathered information from every conceivable source: agents in the DP camps, Nazi personnel records, and from other intelligence services, most of whom maintained liaison officers at the Stuttgart central files.

Not all the information in the CIC's files was released to CIC agents, however. Each of the American intelligence agencies devoted a great deal of effort to spying on the others, and jealously guarded the Nazis in its employ. If a CIC field agent in Frankfurt conducted a visa check on a Nazi who was secretly working for Military Intelligence in Munich, the MIS liaison to the CIC Central Records Repository would simply "red-flag" his agent's records so that any queries would come to him. Consequently, no information would be released. CIC Stuttgart would then report to the field agent that the central files contained "no derogatory information" and the MIS agent would be allowed to emigrate, in spite of his Nazi background. Under General Clay's direction, the MIS had used this system to sanitize incriminating information in the CIC files about the German scientists brought to the United States by Operation Paperclip.

Wisner approached Clay and received similar access for his "special forces" staff. This file-laundering system worked well,

*In recruiting the German scientists, the Pentagon's Joint Intelligence Objectives Agency reported to the State-Navy-War Coordinating Committee, a predecessor of the National Security Council. In the State Department's 1947 telephone directory, the room assigned to the SNWCC liaison at State was also the office of Frank Wisner, Deputy Assistant Secretary of State for Occupied Countries. According to State Department Security officials, this office had almost unlimited access to the visa channels of persons wishing to emigrate to America from occupied Germany.

and derogatory information was withheld from the CIC field investigators checking on visa applicants. For example, the CIC had a thick dossier on Stanislaw Hrynkievich which listed the fact that he had been arrested in 1945 as a security suspect, had confessed during imprisonment to being a Nazi collaborator, and had also admitted being vice-president of the White Ruthenian "self-help" committee in Berlin, which was enough by itself to place him in the CIC's "automatic arrest" category. Moreover, he had been a ranking member of the central committee of the Byelorussian government, which made him both a "quisling" and a member of a "movement hostile." Placed on top of all these incriminating documents is a letter from the Central Repository to the CIC visa investigator stating that its records showed that Hrynkievich was a medical-school student in Berlin who was staunchly anticommunist. This was the only information furnished to the DP Commission,* and Hrynkievich was permitted to go to the United States despite his having been imprisoned by the Americans for his Nazi activities, and his denial of this fact on his visa form.[4]

After the CIC check was evaded, the rest was easy. Few immigration officials had even heard of Byelorussia. Since the Soviets did not furnish information to the IRO, it was barely mentioned in the agency manual. Most of the émigrés did not even bother to change their names, since usually all that was necessary to defeat the CIC filing system was a minor variation in spelling. For example, the highest-ranking collaborator under the administration of General Wilhelm Kube, Dr. Ivan Ermachenko, emigrated to the U.S. as Dr. John Jermaczenko, a permissible phonetic transliteration from the Cyrillic alphabet of Byelorussia into the Latin alphabet of Poland. Most Belarus émigrés had already listed their birthplace as Polish Byelorussia to avoid the earlier repatriation efforts, and so use of the Polish form of their surname was consistent with their previous cover stories. The name translation ploy was so successful that it enabled the majority of Byelorussians to escape detection from the even more antiquated filing systems of

*For reasons of national security, the author has been requested to delete certain details of the file-laundering process and to state only that "various intelligence agencies had access to the central files at the Stuttgart CIC."

the FBI. The Immigration and Naturalization Service of the Department of Justice did not even pretend to maintain an efficient filing system.

Some Byelorussians were picked up in a post-emigration check by the CIA's more efficient cross-language indexing system and were referred to the FBI, but Wisner had arranged for prominent religious leaders in various ethnic groups to vouch for the émigrés as anticommunists who were being victimized by accusers of dubious backgrounds. These religious leaders, many of whom were themselves described in SS documents as key collaborators, played an important role in defeating the CIC screening system. Since few legitimate refugees, especially concentration camp survivors, had retained their birth certificates, the IRO permitted priests to issue substitute baptismal or marriage certificates.

Father Mikalaj Lapitski, an Orthodox priest mentioned favorably in *Einsatzgruppen* reports and a delegate to the Minsk congress in 1944, was a prolific producer of instant documentation for the Belarus network. The papers almost invariably listed a Polish birthplace, were translated to show a Polish variant of the Byelorussian surname, and, at least for the younger collaborators, included a slight change in the date of birth so as to show that they had not been old enough for military service during the war. Lapitski's forgeries appear in numerous immigration records, and his monument in the Belarus cemetery at South River, New Jersey, is equal in prominence to that of Ostrowsky.[5]

Some of the Byelorussian Nazis, however, had become so notorious that merely withholding information from the CIC would not be enough. Kushel, for example, had already been described in the 1948 CIC *Consolidated Orientation and Guidance Manual* as the Byelorussian Minister of War, a member of the puppet government, and the leader of the Regensburg DP camp. It was one thing for the CIC to ignore General Clay's favored Nazis while they were living in Germany; it would be another to defy Congress and clear them for visas.

Apparently acting on instructions, Kushel moved to another part of Germany, where he was less well known, and there applied for a visa to the United States. The local CIC investigator reported to the DP Commission that "Franzischak Kushel" was a high school teacher from 1936 to 1939 in Poland, worked on his parents' farm at Dorey, in Poland, from 1939 to 1943, was employed by the AEG Company in Berlin from 1943 to 1944 (presumably as a slave laborer), and until the end of the war was a farm worker in Geissling, Germany.[6] Not only had the spelling of Kushel's name been changed, but his entire background had been forged.

In fact, central CIC files in Stuttgart contained several indexes for Kushel under various spellings, but which clearly established that he "controls the White Ruthenian Veterans League and was also the leading figure for the German SD" (USAIRR file No. XE198433-I18I045) and was the same Kushel who "was in the 29th SS Grenadier Division, Russische No. 2" (which later became the Belarus Brigade of the 30th SS Division). Other CIC files connect Kushel's "Veterans League" with reports of an anticommunist guerrilla force being recruited in the DP camps and list Kushel as a former cabinet official in the Nazi puppet government of Byelorussia. Not only was this information withheld from immigration officials, but a cover story had been fabricated in its place. Kushel was issued a visa (No. 5291/73) at Munich on May 18, 1950. In New York, he established an OPC front group.

Stankievich's route to the United States was less direct. Having emerged unscathed from his denunciation by the Soviets in 1948, he had been put to work running an OPC-funded newspaper for Byelorussian émigrés in the American-zone DP camps. Soon after the CIC rejected his first visa application, Stankievich moved to another region of Germany and applied again. And again, the CIC blocked the application. Stankievich filed an appeal to the U.S. Displaced Persons Commission, but before Clay's staff could intervene, the CIC submitted a series of scathing reports to the DP Commission to the effect that:

Information on file at this headquarters reveals that Subject [Stankievich] made false statements on practically all major points in his Personal Data Form in an effort to hide his past history. The Personal Data Form of Ziniaide Stankievich, wife of Subject, has also been falsified.

The CIC report then went on to list chronologically every Nazi position held by Stankievich, including mayor of Borissow, national deputy of the Byelorussian Central Council, and, finally, editor-in-chief of *Ranitsa* in Berlin just before the collapse of Nazi Germany.[7] To make sure the DP Commission did not miss the point, the CIC noted that *Ranitsa* was "a pro-Nazi, anti-Allied paper printed in the White Ruthenian language under full control of the German authorities. Subject assigned many positions of trust in the German administration throughout the war."

As a result of the Stankievich report and other documentation, the U.S. Displaced Persons Commission simply stopped considering visas from Byelorussian collaborators in 1950; anyone found to have been a member of the Ostrowsky government in any position from the lowest municipal official to national deputies was automatically rejected as a member of a "movement hostile" to the United States. As if to chide Wisner for the dubious backgrounds of the people he was recruiting, the CIC mentioned a secret file to the DP Commission which showed that Stankievich was a possible Soviet double agent:

Briefly, Subject worked first with the Soviets, then with the Nazis, then again for the Soviets. He appears to be an opportunist who will work for anyone who will pay him. . . . Subject is considered a security risk. . . . This should be sufficient to preclude [Stankievich's] appeal beyond Amberg. However, we have additional information in our Secret files still more damning, which can be forwarded. . . .

Even this did not keep Stankievich from trying to emigrate again. His "blue file" at Fort Meade contains four separate visa applications over the next ten years, all of which were rejected before he finally got to the United States in 1959. By that time CIA officials abroad were circumventing the Parole Powers Act by issuing their own visas to foreigners recruited for intelligence purposes. The State Department urged the CIA to make these visas look "as normal as possible."[8]

The American consulate in Stuttgart was the center of Wisner's visa mill. As soon as news of the Displaced Persons Act reached the camps, the handful of American officials were besieged by refugees who wished to emigrate to the United States. Some of them were in a state of panic, fearing that there would not be enough visas for everyone. The wife of one consular official said that her husband was approached by a woman who offered to trade a handkerchief of diamonds for visas.

Procedures established by the Displaced Persons Act that governed the issuance of visas were complex, and consular officials depended upon inquiries made by other agencies in determining eligibility. The system required American charities to obtain blank sponsorship forms for a certain number of refugees and then to receive lists of eligible applicants from the IRO. The IRO forwarded each individual refugee application and sponsorship form to the U.S. Displaced Persons Commission, along with a detailed questionnaire to make certain that the applicant met the IRO's qualifications as a victim of Nazi oppression. The commission sent the paperwork to the CIC for a further background investigation. Making false statements on the form was a criminal offense, but many refugees altered their backgrounds to avoid repatriation to their Communist-occupied homelands. Neither the Army nor the Displaced Persons Commission could do much to detect such falsifications, for the Soviet Union refused to cooperate with the IRO by providing background information on the refugees.

Strong efforts were made to identify war criminals and Nazis attempting to flee to the United States and other Western countries, but the harassed officials had almost no investigative staff and were faced with a mountain of paperwork. With applications for visas piling up in Stuttgart, attempts were made to decentralize operations. Consular sub-offices were opened up in the larger DP camps, such as Regensburg, which was controlled by the Belarus Brigade, and the OPC used its agents to help subvert the system.[9]

Having short-circuited the CIC background checks, the Byelorussian Nazis had little trouble with the rest of the visa process. Most of the applicants sailed with their families to the United States from Bremerhaven on converted troopships. Passenger manifests show that many of the collaborators traveled in groups, an indication that their visas had been processed simultaneously. The voyage to America was supposed to give the CIA and the FBI sufficient time to run final background checks, since in the rush to help the starving refugees neither agency had been given enough advance warning to investigate before the visas were issued.*

As a result, the CIA frequently identified Byelorussian Nazis to the FBI only after they had arrived in America. Unlike the regular "quota" émigrés, the displaced persons were not subjected to long delays at Hackensack, Ellis Island, or the other immigration ports. They were expedited with the help of American charities, such as the World Church Service, which had provided initial sponsorship. Once the Nazis were in America, tracing them became difficult. They only had to register once a year, and the Immigration Service's record-keeping was abysmal.

By the time the CIA's objections reached the FBI, the Byelorussian Nazis were already settled in South River, Cleveland, Chicago, New York, or in numerous smaller communities in America. There they became part of the well-funded émigré apparatus. The Byelorussians had lawyers to defend them, politicians to endorse them, and, most important, trusted FBI informants to vouch for them as good anticommunists. The CIC's denunciations had little effect, other than to help the FBI identify potential recruits for its network of informers. By the end of 1949, most of the leading Byelorussian collaborators, with the active assistance of Wisner and the OPC, had either evaded the restrictions designed to keep them out of the United States or were on their way. Once the leaders had arrived, they arranged sponsors for their followers, and the pyramid of Nazi emigration was begun.

Wisner's scheme was not without its problems, however.† Arendt Wagenaar, his man in the Stuttgart consulate, lacked a

---

*At least one Byelorussian Nazi entered the United States illegally from Canada and came back and forth several times. Immigration and Naturalization Service files indicate he was never issued a visa, and no visas are on record for several other émigrés.
†In one case, in 1951, a State Department official named Vedeler stumbled across evidence of Wisner's recruiting efforts. Believing that the operation was being conducted by CIA/OSO, he was delighted to blow the whistle on a rival agency and sent a lengthy memorandum to the State Department. It was immediately given to Wisner. Vedeler's memorandum and a cover letter are one of the few extant documents discussing OPC activities during this period. One of the interesting features of the Vedeler memorandum is the notation that the agent in charge of setting up one of the Baltic "governments-in-exile" was the same person previously employed by the Displaced Persons Commission to

passion for anonymity, the hallmark of a good covert agent, and his erratic behavior focused an unwelcome spotlight on the OPC plan. A Dutchman who had worked for the OSS during the war, Wagenaar had been hired by the State Department as the chief visa investigator in the consulate. His true position became apparent after some of the consular officers complained to the consul general that he did no work. They were bluntly told to stay out of Wagenaar's business, making it obvious to the entire staff that he was an intelligence agent. Wagenaar also attracted the attention of the CIC because his mistress had been secretary to the local Gestapo chief, and he appeared to be selling visas to refugees.

The CIC missed the mark by only a slight margin. Wagenaar *was* selling visas, but not for money. He exchanged them for information from Emanuel Jasiuk, one of the most important Byelorussian collaborators.

Jasiuk had a remarkable history. He was a native of Nezvish, Byelorussia, and attended the University of Liège in Belgium. Following graduation, he and his wife attempted to make their living as schoolteachers during the harsh Polish occupation of Byelorussia. When the Soviet Union annexed his homeland in 1939, Jasiuk fled along with many other anticommunist intellectuals to German-held Warsaw. There he worked with other disgruntled teachers who formed the hard core of pro-Nazi nationalist agitators. He was among the first to join Byelorussian "self-help" committees sponsored by the SS in 1940–41.

When Dr. Six came to Warsaw to recruit guides for his *Einsatzgruppen*, Jasiuk was an early volunteer. He returned to Byelorussia soon after the invasion of the Soviet Union and was installed by the SS as mayor of Kletsk. With broad Slavic features almost always wreathed in smiles, Jasiuk was regarded as an amiable fellow. One of his main tasks was to draw up lists of Polish intellectuals and Communist sympathizers for the Germans. The

---

advise it on which Baltic collaborators should be granted or denied visas. The agent had previously worked for Military Intelligence, and, according to his Army dossier, was something of an expert on the role of Baltic collaborators in the SS auxiliary police. Recently, the same agent, now retired, candidly admitted working on covert operations in the Baltics, but he denied the very information which I had obtained from his own reports to the Army.

Einsatzgruppen swept through Kletsk, rounded up hundreds of suspects at Jasiuk's direction, and murdered them. In 1942, Jasiuk, now county chief, or "Kreisleiter," was energetic in preparing the "final solution" of the Jews of Kletsk. Jasiuk's police herded all the Jews in the area—thousands of men, women, and children—into a barbed-wire compound in the middle of the city. The usual pattern of extortions, threats, and increasing acts of violence followed, until Jasiuk arranged for the massacre of the entire ghetto.

Soviet eyewitnesses, Jewish survivors, and some of Jasiuk's colleagues who later informed on him reported that his police did not repeat the mistakes of Borissow. They dug large trenches behind the Arinskaya Church in Kletsk, out of sight but within walking distance of the ghetto. The Byelorussian police lined the roads and escorted the Jews in columns of a hundred, men first, according to the familiar pattern, then women and children. A small detachment of Germans and specially selected Byelorussians accomplished the actual execution. Guards were left atop the graves until the ground stopped trembling and the muffled cries were still. There was no chance for anyone to crawl out. In one day Jasiuk murdered the entire Jewish population of the county, conservatively estimated at more than 5,000 people.

The Nazis took notice of Jasiuk's efforts and promoted him to county chief of Stolpce, a much larger area. Contemporary newspapers related that Jasiuk proved adept at giving pro-Nazi speeches, but he apparently lacked the flair for anti-partisan operations that caused many of his contemporaries to advance under the SS to key positions in the national puppet government. Jasiuk was a valuable utility man, working tirelessly with religious collaborators and others to increase the SS stranglehold on the civilian population, and Ostrowsky selected him as one of the featured speakers at the collaborators' convention in Minsk in 1944. Jasiuk was one of the first to be evacuated to Germany when Byelorussia fell to the Red Army in the summer of 1944. In Berlin he worked to organize other exiled collaborators into the Belarus Brigade. Just as the Reich was about to collapse, he was given forged identity papers listing him as a prisoner of war who had joined the Free Polish forces led by General Anders. Like many of the Belarus Brigade, Jasiuk fled to the French zone, where he lived for a time under the name of Max Jasinki, until the American attitude on repatriation became known.

Jasiuk crossed back into the American zone and became a courier for the Belarus network sponsored by OPC. Learning that Wagenaar was seeking intelligence information, Jasiuk brought him some maps of the Soviet airfields in the Urals that the Byelorussian collaborators had taken from the SS files and captured Soviet archives in Minsk. Much of the information furnished by Jasiuk was later discovered to be worthless. Nevertheless, he provided Wagenaar with an introduction to the Nazi underground that the agent exploited vigorously. Wagenaar and Jasiuk, who was hired as his translator,* traveled all over occupied Germany establishing liaison with the scattered battalions of the Belarus Brigade. As official State Department employees, the two were permitted unrestricted travel. Usually a vice consul from Stuttgart, more or less oblivious to Wagenaar's true role, accompanied them on their rounds to provide cover.

When Wisner directed that an attempt be made to reconcile the various Byelorussian factions, Jasiuk accompanied an Ostrowsky delegation to France to try to reach an agreement with the Abramtchik group. During this journey cover was provided by the Polish Central Commission at the request of General Anders. Wisner decided to bring Jasiuk to America, where he could continue his recruiting activities among the Byelorussians already there. The CIC was asked by the consulate to convene a special hearing to expedite Jasiuk's visa. Wagenaar and two State Department officials appeared on Jasiuk's behalf and testified that he had performed invaluable services "of a highly confidential nature" for an unnamed American intelligence agency. The State Department officials then corroborated Jasiuk's fictitious biography, which put him in a monastery and then on a farm in Bavaria as a slave laborer during World War II.[10]

The CIC was not taken in, and subsequently launched a burglary of Wagenaar's office in order to inspect the documents on Jasiuk.[11] They recognized most of Jasiuk's paperwork as recently

---

*Jasiuk spoke Byelorussian, Russian, Ukrainian, Polish, German, French, and English.

produced forgeries and notified the State Department that they were preparing to arrest Jasiuk and Wagenaar. Wagenaar had friends in the French Sûreté who were called in to provide cover, and a high official in the French intelligence service protested that the CIC was meddling with one of its most valuable operations. After being reprimanded by the State Department, the CIC dropped its investigation of the allegation that Wagenaar was selling visas.[12]

Within a few months after Jasiuk had emigrated, the CIC received a tip from an informant linking him to Dimitri Kasmowich, the former Smolensk police chief, who had applied for a visa. The CIC learned that Kasmowich had been previously rejected for emigration and was taken into custody for falsifying a visa application. Under questioning, Kasmowich ran through a variety of cover stories and false identities before acknowledging that he was being recruited by the Americans for a secret intelligence mission. The OPC tried to persuade the CIC to drop the charges against him, but the CIC sensed there was something suspicious about the connection between Kasmowich and Jasiuk.*

The CIC had obtained a copy of a letter from Jasiuk to his old friend "Captain Wagner" (the copy is in Wagenaar's CIC file). The letter introduced Kasmowich as a former police chief in Byelorussia under the Nazis who Jasiuk said "would be perfect for the purposes of your organization." Wagenaar told the CIC that a "Mr. J." had obtained valuable intelligence information from Kasmowich. The CIC, however, was not fooled.

CIC investigators now realized that Jasiuk was the central figure in a Nazi underground railroad that assisted war criminals to come to the United States, and they blamed the Air Force, which they believed was Jasiuk's controller, for allowing it to

---

*The agency pressed ahead with the case against Kasmowich until State Department officials requested that he be released. In return, State promised to make certain that he would never receive a visa to come to the United States. Instead, Kasmowich was smuggled to England, where he lived under the name of Zarechny.[13] The incident was not yet closed, however. Suspicions aroused, the CIC located several informants who identified Jasiuk and Kasmowich as Nazi collaborators. In fact, Kasmowich was a cousin of Michael Vitushka, who had led the Black Cat guerrilla band behind Soviet lines at the end of the war. Kasmowich himself had undergone parachute and commando training at the SS school at Dahlwitz, but had fled to Switzerland at the end of the war.

operate. The Air Force was mystified; Jasiuk had been only a routine source who had turned over some minor documents on airfield runways and had assisted in putting together an information handbook on Byelorussia. In fact, Jasiuk had been working for an OPC mission wearing Air Force uniforms. Still oblivious to the OPC connection, CIC officials were even more angered at the realization that Jasiuk had orchestrated the escape of at least eight major war criminals by means of the visas he had secured from Wagenaar when he was only a minor informant for the Air Force. To prevent the cancellation of any more of its prosecutions, the CIC submitted a formal complaint on the handling of Jasiuk up the chain of command.

The protest finally reached General John Weckerling, chief of Military Intelligence at the Pentagon, who agreed that the Nazi smuggling operation was deplorable.[14] The FBI had jurisdiction over fugitives wanted for trial on war crimes charges who had entered the United States, so he personally apprised J. Edgar Hoover of the affair. Weckerling told Hoover on January 2, 1951, that the Air Force had apparently used a Nazi war criminal as an informant and the State Department had permitted him to enter the United States. Hoover expressed an interest in the case, for it seemed likely to fit in with his plans to expand the FBI's domestic intelligence capabilities. When FBI agents went to visit Jasiuk, it was not to arrest him but to recruit him.

Following his difficulties with the Byelorussians, Wisner attempted to circumvent similar immigration problems with Ukrainian Nazis. But the repeated denunciations by the Soviets of the alleged links between Stephan Bandera and other Ukrainian war criminals and American and British intelligence agencies kept the spotlight focused upon them. The Ukrainian delegate to the United Nations charged that Bandera and other Ukrainian Nazis, such as Andrei Melnik, were running special schools to train cadres in sabotage and intelligence work against the Soviet Union and listed numerous atrocities committed by them.

The IRO as well as the U.S. DP Commission had long regarded the Ukrainian Nazis as ineligible for visas and had placed their organizations on the "inimical list"; but that did not deter Wisner.

In the spring of 1951, he learned that one of Bandera's intelligence agents had been detained at Ellis Island, charged with possession of false documents as well as being a member of the torture squad (SB) of the Nazi-sponsored Organization of Ukrainian Nationalists, the OUN/Bandera. Wisner decided to meet the challenge head-on, and had the following letter sent to the headquarters of the Immigration and Naturalization Service:

1. . . . It was definitely established that [the agent] is a member of OUN/Bandera, although he at first denied any connection with the organization and even went so far as to perjure himself in writing . . . with the explanation that he was under an oath of secrecy which he could not break.

2. There are at least twenty former or active members of the SB of OUN/Bandera in the United States at the present time. Although the SB is known to have used extra-legal methods while investigating or interrogating suspected Soviet agents, there have been few cases to date where it was possible to pin a specific criminal activity on any individual belonging to the SB and take court action. Since the SB kept elaborate files and conducted investigations on Ukrainians and suspected Soviet agents of other nationalities, no serious attempt has ever been made by American officials in Germany to disband the SB. In the past five years the SB has been chronically unable to cooperate wholeheartedly with American intelligence representatives in Germany, primarily because the price set by Stephan Bandera for complete cooperation involved types of political recognition and commitments to his group which no American in Germany was in a position to make.* Operating independently, the SB has upon occasion been more of a headache to American intelligence than a boon. Nevertheless in war time a highly nationalistic Ukrainian political group with its own security service could conceivably be a great asset. . . . Alienating such a group could, on the other hand, have no particular advantage to the United States either now or in war time.

. . .

At the end of the last war many members of the OUN came to Western Europe to avoid capture by the advancing Soviets. The OUN re-formed in Western Europe with its headquarters in Munich. It first

---

*Thus, U.S. intelligence had actually been in touch with the Ukrainian Nazis since 1946, despite denials of this to Washington and the UN.

came to the attention of American authorities when the Russians demanded extradition of Bandera and many other anti-Soviet Ukrainian nationalists as war criminals. *Luckily the attempt to locate these anti-Soviet Ukrainians was sabotaged by a few far-sighted Americans who warned the persons concerned to go into hiding.* [Emphasis added.] From 1945 to 1948 members of OUN and of UPA arrived from the Soviet Ukraine to Western Germany on foot. The messages they and returning German prisoners of war brought conclusively confirmed that the OUN and the UPA were continuing the fight against the Soviets, with the weapons and ammunition which the retreating German armies had left behind. Over 35,000 members of the Russian secret police (MVD-MKGB) have been killed by OUN-UPA since the end of the last war. In other words, the main activities of the OUN in the Ukraine cannot be considered detrimental to the United States.[15]

Wisner's letter must have caused a commotion at the INS. It was as close as he dared come to disclosing that he was using CIA money and CIA cover to provide "left-behind" arms and ammunition to underground assassination teams inside Eastern Europe. But that was not all. The letter conclusively established that Wisner lied to the INS.* It fraudulently claimed that the OUN was not a Nazi-sponsored organization and that its members had never collaborated with the Germans. At the end of several paragraphs of fictional history, Wisner stated:

In simple terms, the Germans wanted from the Ukrainians only food and supplies for their armies and forced labor for their factories. The Germans used all means necessary to force the cooperation which the Ukrainians were unwilling to give. Thus, by summer 1941 a battle raged on Ukrainian soil between two ruthless exploiters and persecutors of the Ukrainian people, the Third Reich and Soviet Russia. The OUN and the partisan army it created in late 1942, UPA, fought bitterly against both the Germans and the Soviet Russians.

*The letter also enclosed two visa applications—one admitting service in the OUN/SB, and the other concealing that fact. Apparently, the State Department knew all along that the agent had lied to get into America. It was not the last occasion on which State suddenly produced a second visa application to prevent deportation of an OPC agent who had misrepresented his SS connection on one form and concealed it on another.

This was a complete fabrication. The CIC had an agent who photographed eleven volumes of the secret internal files of OUN/ Bandera. These files clearly show how most of its members worked for the Gestapo or SS as policemen, executioners, partisan hunters, and municipal officials. The OUN contribution to the German war effort was significant, including the raising of volunteers for several SS divisions. It was precisely because of its work with the Nazis that Wisner wanted to hire the OUN for his special forces. The Ukrainian letter succeeded in fooling the immigration officials, however, and OUN/Bandera was subsequently taken off the inimical list.

By the time the DP Act expired in 1952, 400,000 immigrants had come to the United States. Among them were important Nazi collaborators from Byelorussia, the Ukraine, the Baltic states, and the Balkans, including the nucleus of Wisner's "special forces." During the same four-year period, Wisner's OPC enjoyed virtually unlimited freedom of action and had grown to the point that it was consuming more than half the CIA's annual budget. Wisner's private army had launched an undeclared war against the Soviet Union. He had defied the congressional ban on smuggling Nazis; he had misappropriated government funds to buy arms for ex-Nazi terrorists; and he had obstructed justice by sheltering fugitive war criminals who had been denounced by the Nuremberg Tribunal, the United Nations, and the Congress of the United States. He had, moreover, inflicted a crucial defeat on his arch-rivals in the CIC and CIA. The State Department had won the first round.

Chapter

8

On June 25–26, 1949, the remaining members of the Belarus network in Europe held their last conference in Germany at the Backnang DP camp near Stuttgart. A motion was made and approved to "transfer the entire organization to the United States, inasmuch as all the officers were there." This was not an understatement: with the exception of Radislaw Ostrowsky, who had gone to Argentina because his record was too well known for him to obtain a visa, virtually every cabinet-level Byelorussian Nazi had been smuggled into America. Franz Kushel, Jury Sobolewsky, Emanuel Jasiuk—the leadership of a movement branded "hostile to the United States"—had been issued visas in violation of federal law, and were now on the road to becoming American citizens.

One needed only to compare the *Consolidated Orientation and Guidance Manual* for Byelorussia prepared by the CIC in 1948 with the immigration rolls to realize how effective Wisner's smuggling operations had been. More than 300 Byelorussian Nazis arrived in the United States, most of whom would become American citizens. (An even larger number of Ukrainian Nazis are suspected to have been smuggled in.)

Wisner's own star had risen too. The announcement of the Soviet atom bomb in 1949 and the outbreak of war in Korea the following year led to sweeping changes in America's intelligence community. Dissatisfied with Admiral Hillenkoetter's performance, President Truman replaced him as Director of Central Intelligence with General Walter Bedell Smith.[1] Brilliant and acerbic, Smith had been General Dwight D. Eisenhower's chief of staff during World War II and was credited with being the driving force behind the American victory in Europe. A postwar tour as envoy to Moscow had left him with a hatred of the Soviet Union. Smith was determined to increase the effectiveness of the CIA by bringing the OPC under his control.

Although the OPC was formally a part of the CIA, Wisner had acted independently, and there was considerable bureaucratic infighting between his shop and the CIA's Office of Special Operations. They had squabbled over local jurisdictions, stealing each other's agents, and, occasionally, blowing each other's operations. Such intra-agency raiding was not uncommon. A retired military intelligence agent revealed recently that OPC had offered him a high-paying job with the stipulation that he steal the list of agents working for the Army in that part of Germany and turn it over to his prospective employers. He refused, but others did not. OPC was envied, feared, and resented by the other agencies because of its power, influence, and limitless financial support.

Between 1950 and 1952, Smith took several steps to encourage cooperation between OPC and OSO. Allen Dulles, Wisner's old friend and chief, was brought in as Deputy Director of Plans to supervise Wisner's operations. Not long afterward, Dulles was named Deputy Director of Central Intelligence, and when Eisenhower was elected President in 1952 he became DCI. Among Smith's last acts was to merge OSO and OPC into the Directorate of Plans with Wisner in charge. All CIA covert actions were now controlled by the men who had planned the "special forces" program. The use of Eastern European émigrés to fight a clandestine guerrilla war against the Soviet Union had not received official sanction from the White House, but in 1953 its two most ardent advocates, Dulles and Wisner, were in a position to continue the secret war on their own.[2]

With unlimited funds and support available, Wisner stepped up his activities among the Byelorussians in the United States. Soon after his arrival in this country, Franz Kushel, now the leader of the old Abramtchik faction, was able to establish the White Ruthenian Institute of Arts and Sciences at 8 Alabama Avenue in Brooklyn, New York. Abramtchik himself remained in Paris. The institute churned out intelligence reports supposedly generated by Kushel's network of spies in Eastern Europe. In reality, most of these agents had long since been captured by the Soviets. Kushel fabricated his reports from newspapers, old books, radio broadcasts, and gossip among the émigrés. Nevertheless, Wisner was so pleased by the results that he expanded the number of émigré institutes, and established a headquarters in Munich where access to the "informants" would be greater. The secretary and later chairman of the board of the Institute of Russian Research in Munich was Stanislaw Stankievich.[3] Funding for these "research institutes," which were little more than front groups for ex-Nazi intelligence officers, came from the American Committee for Liberation from Bolshevism, now known as Radio Liberty.*

The committee was actually a front for OPC. AMCOMLIB was originally a subsidiary organization of the National Committee for a Free Europe (NCFE), which was set up by George Kennan in the State Department long before the CIA became involved.[4] Money for the NCFE and AMCOMLIB was raised through the "private" fund-raising efforts of the "Crusade for Freedom." General Clay, who had retired from his post as military governor of the American Zone of Germany in 1949, was chairman of the Crusade. Dwight Eisenhower and Ronald Reagan were among those who solicited public contributions. (The newsreel collection of the National Archives has a film clip of Reagan urging the American public to send their contributions to General Clay's "Crusade for Freedom.") Over 90 percent of its income came from the unvouchered accounts of the CIA rather than public donations, however. The State Department laundered the money through private charities, such as the Rockefeller Fund, the Carnegie Fund, and the Ford Foundation's Russian Research Committee, which in turn claimed credit in public for their generous donations. Some of the funds went through corporate conduits, such as the Radio Corporation of America, which in turn "donated" equipment to Wisner's front groups.[5]

Only a few of the more favored Byelorussian Nazis found employment with AMCOMLIB. While the intelligentsia, who held advanced degrees, obtained jobs at local hospitals, academic

*The State Department organized "national committees for liberation" for each Eastern European ethnic group, recruiting officials from the exile governments that Gustav Hilger had worked with in Berlin and bringing them to the United States (e.g., Top Secret State Department Decimal File for Albania, Declassified Diplomatic Branch of the National Archives). Money for these committees came from the "Governments-in-Exile" sections of Radio Liberty and Radio Free Europe.

institutions, and architectural firms, the rest took positions as laborers and factory workers. Almost without exception, the Byelorussians filed applications to become American citizens. Now that they were safely in the United States they needed only to wait out the five-year residency requirement. While the Abramtchik faction was centered upon Kushel's base in Brooklyn, Ostrowsky's followers, led by Jury Sobolewsky, were expanding their foothold in South River, New Jersey, the headquarters of a growing Belarus network.

Between 1948 and 1950 over 200 Byelorussian Nazis, together with their families, arrived in South River. It was a quiet little town on the fringe of New Jersey's industrial belt where large numbers of Ukrainian and Byelorussian refugees had settled after World War I. The new arrivals kept to themselves and, unlike other émigrés, did not encourage publication of their social activities in the local newspapers. They built their own parish church, established a meeting hall and business offices, and began organizing charities and religious groups to sponsor still more émigrés. Relatives brought in relatives and arranged jobs for them in the factories of Passaic and Newark. In time, a local lawyer was hired to assist with the immigration process.

Later on, as the number of immigrants increased, new parishes were established near the old Byelorussian communities in Chicago, Cleveland, and Toronto.[6] Belarus activity in America was directed by Sobolewsky, vice-president of the Byelorussian Central Council. As time went on, it became necessary to expand into the New York area. Formal charters were obtained for various front organizations, but most of the leaders of the local groups had one thing in common: They had all been Nazi intelligence officers who had helped the *Einsatzgruppen* direct the subjugation of Byelorussia.[7]

With Ostrowsky still in hiding in Argentina, where he had gone with the assistance of the British, Sobolewsky decided to try to gain public recognition for his organization.[8] He sent Emanuel Jasiuk, now head of the South River chapter, to speak at a Ukrainian convention in Washington, D.C.[9] Vice-President Alben Barkley unwittingly shared the same platform with men who had fought against America and helped obliterate the Jewish population of their countries. To establish his credentials, Jasiuk carried a commission which read:

> Mr. Emanuel Jasiuk is appointed by the Byelorussian Central Council as Chairman of the delegation to represent the Byelorussian people and the government of the Byelorussian Democratic Republic in the United States of America.

The commission was signed by Radislaw Ostrowsky as President of the Byelorussian Central Council and bore the seal of his wartime administration. Ostrowsky was once again trying to rehabilitate his government by dropping the cover name of the "Byelorussian Central Representation," which he had used since 1945.

In February 1951 the first Belarus convention in America was held at South River. It was decided to link up with similar exile organizations from the Ukrainian, Latvian, and Estonian communities. The Belarus network hoped to persuade American public officials that the "White Ruthenian" émigrés in America were willing to do anything to defeat the Communists. Letters were sent to both President Truman and General Eisenhower, promising to supply armed troops for the struggle against communism. American politicians were sought out to endorse Byelorussian nationalism, press releases were issued, and a series of local newspapers were established to link the scattered collaborators.[10] Everything was in readiness for the day when Americans would realize that it was Ostrowsky's Nazis, not Abramtchik's, who offered the best chance of penetrating the Soviet Union. They did not have long to wait.

By the spring of 1951 the Abramtchik faction had begun to collapse. The few parachutists that had been sent to Byelorussia had been captured or killed. Several turned up at press conferences in Moscow to exhibit the American and British equipment with which they had been supplied and to proclaim themselves as having been Soviet agents all along. The "special forces" training school in Germany was later discovered to be riddled with Soviet moles, one of whom had even earned a place on the faculty. Kim

Philby, who was kept informed of Wisner's secret operations, is usually blamed for the defeat of the first waves of special forces. An attempt to parachute in Ukrainians with the hope of linking up with partisans left behind failed, prompting a macabre epitaph from Philby: "I do not know what happened to the parties concerned. But I can make an informed guess."[11] In another, much-publicized incident in 1950, Wisner had recruited a force of some 500 Albanians, armed and trained them in Greece, and sent them over the Albanian frontier to depose the Communist dictatorship of Enver Hoxha. They were met by waiting Communist forces and slaughtered.

After Philby's connection with the Soviets was discovered, he was charged with betraying to Moscow the plans for the invasion. But it appears that much of the damaging information came to the Soviets not by means of high-level agents such as Philby but through the low-ranking Communist informants who had permeated the émigré community at every level. Since Wisner's plans centered on the émigrés, it was not surprising that Soviet moles were among his very first volunteers.[12] Walter Bedell Smith told a class at the Army War College that the "covert agents" that the intelligence agencies were trying to slip into the Soviet Union had an enormous fatality rate.

Philby's exposure in 1951 as a Communist agent led both the FBI and Wisner to drop the British-sponsored Abramtchik faction and take a new look at Ostrowsky's group.* The anticommu-

---

*The Americans had begun to suspect Philby before the British, when it was noticed that projects with which he was associated had a tendency to blow up. Believing that the CIA was on Donald Maclean's trail rather than his own, Philby tipped him off, and Maclean and Guy Burgess, another mole, fled to the Soviet Union. After questioning, Philby was dismissed from the SIS, but conclusive evidence that he was a Soviet spy did not turn up until 1963. Philby got wind of it and defected to the Soviet Union. Another version of the story is that wiretaps on the British embassy strongly implicated Philby, but before conclusive evidence had been gathered, the CIA demanded in 1951 that the SIS recall him. Philby bluffed his British superiors with the admission that of course he had been giving information to the Soviets, he had been posing as a double agent for several years, with the full knowledge of the SIS. The British were convinced that their bumbling American cousins had made a mistake, and continued to employ Philby as an SIS agent in Turkey until, to their chagrin, he showed up at a 1963 press conference in Moscow. Philby probably did more damage to British-American intelligence relations after he came under suspicion than he ever achieved while his cover was still secure. Interview with Military Intelligence official, 1980.

nist chorus from South River began to sound better and better. The large numbers of Ostrowsky's people with Nazi backgrounds had once been a source of embarrassment for American intelligence, who could not expose them without risk of disclosing that Abramtchik's group was working for Wisner. Now the Ostrowsky faction appeared to be an alternative source of recruitment.

Meanwhile, the FBI decided to do some recruiting of its own. On March 28 two agents went to South River to question Emanuel Jasiuk. The agents knew about Jasiuk's Nazi background from the CIC complaint to J. Edgar Hoover; what they wanted was information on the Byelorussians in America. Jasiuk agreed to provide it. He described how the Germans had allowed the Byelorussians to form an independent state during the war, but characterized the government as democratically elected, with a president and a congress. No mention was made of atrocities, and most of the postwar history was concealed. Jasiuk was not sure how much the FBI knew about the special forces network behind the Iron Curtain, so he simply denied that his organization had any contacts with Communist countries.

The FBI agents departed, but after reviewing the CIC allegations that Jasiuk had worked for the SS and had submitted lists of anti-Nazi Poles to be executed by the Germans, they returned three days later for a more thorough interrogation. This time, Jasiuk confessed that he had obtained his immigration visa through fraud. He admitted lying to the CIC screening officers when he concealed his background as mayor of Kletsk under the Nazis, because it would have caused him to be deported to the Soviet Union, where he would have been executed as a war criminal. Jasiuk defended the collaboration of himself and others with the Nazis on the ground that resistance would have been useless.

The FBI now had all it needed to arrest Jasiuk for fraud and illegal entry, not to mention deporting him as a quisling and a member of a "movement hostile." Instead, he was left alone. In return, Jasiuk provided a great deal of information to the bureau about the Byelorussians in America.

In the fall of 1951 the FBI had enough information to confront Jury Sobolewsky, the head of the Ostrowsky network in America.

Sobolewsky admitted that the Byelorussian Central Administration was the same as the Byelorussian Central Council, which had collaborated with the Germans during World War II. He told the FBI the SS had permitted the government to be formed and said he had served as vice-president under Ostrowsky. He admitted that the government had raised sixty-five battalions for a national militia, but he neglected to mention that the battalions were later formed into the Belarus SS Brigade and had fought against the Americans. He described the worldwide network under Ostrowsky, with branches in England, Canada, Argentina, Australia, Brazil, and Germany, and emphasized that his organization was dedicated to fighting communism.

Again, no attempt was made to arrest Sobolewsky for his Nazi background. Instead one of the FBI agents suggested that he register with the Department of Justice to avoid any entanglements with the Foreign Agents Registration Act.

Sobolewsky took the hint and ordered one of his lieutenants to write to the Attorney General, displaying his anticommunist sentiments and downgrading the wartime collaboration with the Nazis.[13] On April 13, 1952, one of Sobolewsky's aides appeared at FBI headquarters in New York. Confident that he had nothing to fear, the aide provided a complete rundown of the postwar emigration from the DP camps, and even admitted that the BCC had changed its name to the BCR "so that the members could avoid being called war criminals during the time of crisis in Germany." The FBI not only overlooked this remark but helped him prepare the information that he would need for the Foreign Agents Registration Act. It was the beginning of a most cooperative relationship: the Byelorussians in South River assisted the FBI in untangling the charges of Soviet penetration permeating the émigré community, while the bureau protected the Byelorussians from being prosecuted as war criminals.

Hoover's decision not to bring the collaborators to court provided him with agents who turned in information on what his rivals in American intelligence were doing. In 1952 the OPC finally dumped the Abramtchik group and began shifting AMCOMLIB's funding and programs to the Ostrowsky faction. Ostrowsky had moved to London with the approval of the British secret service, where he was working with OPC and the British in a new attempt to penetrate the Iron Curtain. Hoover's informants started to provide information on AMCOMLIB's change of strategy. They even discovered that Zarechny (Jasiuk's old friend Dimitri Kasmowich, the Smolensk police chief) was heading up the military operations in London.

Sobolewsky's aide petitioned the Justice Department for clearance under the Foreign Agent section of the Internal Security Act of 1950. Joseph M. McInerney, the Assistant Attorney General for the Criminal Division, forwarded the request to the FBI to help determine whether the Byelorussians should register as agents of a foreign power. The FBI responded with a sanitized summary of some of its early interviews, showing that the Byelorussians were a truly anticommunist organization with no international connections. Sobolewsky was advised that a problem had arisen, and he subsequently mailed the Justice Department a lengthy report on the Byelorussian struggle for "liberation." As a result of these letters, McInerney and Charles B. Murray of the Criminal Division of the Justice Department concluded that the Byelorussian group was not in violation of the Foreign Agents Registration Act because it did not communicate with foreign principals and all major officers were resident in the United States.[14] In a sense it was true: those Byelorussian Nazis who mattered, with the exception of Ostrowsky, were now living in America.

Like Frank Wisner, Ostrowsky was never at a loss for ideas. With his organization revived by the transfusion of American funds, he assigned Kasmowich to the task of recruiting volunteers in the United States, Germany, and Britain for a Byelorussian Liberation Movement to cause trouble for the Soviets. Ostrowsky also had a more subtle plan in mind. As a result of their membership in the Gramada in post–World War I Poland, both he and Sobolewsky were acquainted with some of the Communist officials who now ruled the country. In fact, the Byelorussians had hidden a few of their Polish Communist friends during the Nazi occupation. Ostrowsky informed Wisner that some of these men were now high officials in Polish security. Although they were Communists, they were also opposed to Russian imperialism and were willing to cooperate with the West.

Such "black" operations appealed to Wisner. Not long before, he had masterminded a scheme in which scores of Communist Party officials had been discredited in Poland and the Soviet Union itself. Stalin was apparently convinced that a mass defection was taking place within the Communist Party and ordered a sweeping purge. If the reports are correct, Wisner's disinformation campaign resulted in the liquidation of several thousand Party members who were falsely denounced for collaborating with Western intelligence.

Wisner saw in Ostrowsky's proposal a chance to penetrate deep into Communist territory by organizing a string of double agents who would feed false information to the Communists while alerting the OPC to Stalin's moves. Millions of dollars in gold, bank notes, arms, and equipment were smuggled into Poland. Wisner believed it was important to establish the bona fides of his double agents by giving them valuable secret information. Once these agents were accepted by the Communists the pipeline could be reversed. Within a few months dozens and then hundreds of Polish agents were reporting back to Wisner.

The Polish "double agent" operation was in fact a scheme concocted by the KGB, the latest incarnation of the Soviet security apparatus. Wisner's double agents were actually Communist triple agents. They had been using Ostrowsky's men to identify the real traitors among them.[15] The lists of anticommunists were sent to Moscow almost as soon as they were transmitted to Washington and London. Several of the leading agents were "turned around," and more and more money and supplies were demanded for spy networks that were only a fiction created by the KGB. Wisner fell for it. Millions of dollars and an untold number of agents were dispatched before the Communists decided to roll up the operation. Ostrowsky's friends in Polish security helped direct the roundup of American- and British-funded agents in Poland. When the arrests were completed in 1952, nearly every important anticommunist contact with the West had been seized. For the first time, Wisner realized that his émigré agents had been thoroughly penetrated by the Soviets.

Angry at the loss of AMCOMLIB funding, the Abramtchik faction chose this moment to strike back. In 1953 an article was published in a Byelorussian-language newspaper in Germany attacking Kasmowich, Ostrowsky's military coordinator. Kasmowich was described as a former Communist official, a major Nazi collaborator, and now an employee of the British secret service. His cover blown, Kasmowich fell into a depression and began drinking heavily. One night he returned drunk to the apartment he and Ostrowsky shared, and was ordered not only from the premises but out of the Byelorussian Liberation Movement as well. Kasmowich refused to be dropped, and started proselytizing for public support. The few surviving operations in Poland and Byelorussia were threatened by the continuing factional rivalry.

Wisner's rivals in CIA/OSO and military intelligence were quick to criticize his failure. By 1954 he had spent, conservatively, tens of millions of dollars in an utterly fruitless effort to destroy the Communists from within. In fact, his reckless activities may have destroyed any hope of ever building an effective anticommunist intelligence network in Eastern Europe. One after another his "underground armies" had been eliminated, along with the innocent citizens who had helped them.

Recently, Wisner's deputy for certain Eastern European operations candidly admitted that OPC, like the other intelligence services, had recruited a number of ex-Nazi intelligence agents, and had engaged in a series of "political action" programs against regimes behind the Iron Curtain. Faced with a series of defeats, Wisner's deputy had in 1952 presented Allen Dulles with a lengthy memorandum criticizing these programs as reckless. He visited Dulles at his home in Georgetown and explained that, as each program grew in size, the risk of Communist penetration had increased proportionately, leading inevitably to the disasters which had occurred, and which would occur in the future unless the programs were scaled down. Dulles and he debated throughout the day, with the result that Dulles persuaded him to water down his appraisal. Soon afterwards, he resigned from OPC.

Other CIA and OPC officials confirmed that both Wisner and Dulles had been repeatedly warned that these grandiose programs were doomed to failure, but the advice was ignored. One official, who knew Wisner well, suggested that Wisner, Dulles, and the other OSS veterans were captives of a "guerrilla war" mentality —it was difficult for them to see that what had worked so well in France during World War II might not be applicable in Eastern Europe. Another official suggested that one effect of the McCarthy purges was to pressure the intelligence community to "do something, anything" about the Communist takeovers while at the same time making it politically unsafe to use any but the most right-wing groups to fight the Communists. The example was given of a senior OPC official in Germany who was hounded out of the government for alleged left-wing sympathies.

The most cogent explanation came from a woman who had participated in covert operations in Germany during this period. In her opinion, it mattered little whether the émigré groups were penetrated or not. If they produced good propaganda or intelligence, so much the better; if not, the group would be dropped after it was blown, and another recruited in its place. OPC simply wrote blank checks and waited to see if any of its investments paid off. It is easy to see how Wisner could have believed that, sooner or later, his apparently inexhaustible supply of money was bound to produce something more than a paper army of anticommunists.

Sensing a congressional investigation of the Wisner debacle in the offing, President Eisenhower appointed a special committee to conduct its own inquiry, headed by General James Doolittle, who had led the first bomber raid on Tokyo during the war. Wisner had nothing to fear, however, because Doolittle was an old friend, and another member, Morris Hadley, knew Allen Dulles well. Even the policy guidelines for the committee were drafted by the OPC clique within the CIA. To no one's surprise the Doolittle committee, far from condemning Wisner, issued a report in September 1954 suggesting that his operations be expanded:

It is now clear that we are facing an implacable enemy whose avowed objective is world domination by whatever means and at whatever cost. There are no rules in such a game. Hitherto acceptable norms of human conduct do not apply. If the United States is to survive, long-standing American concepts of "fair play" must be reconsidered. We must develop effective espionage and counterespionage services and must learn to subvert, sabotage and destroy our enemies by more clever, more sophisticated, and more effective methods than those used against us. It may become necessary that the American people be made acquainted with, understand and support this fundamentally repugnant philosophy.[16]

For the first time since he became Deputy Assistant Secretary of State for Occupied Countries in 1947, Frank Wisner had received a form of official endorsement for his covert action program. The Belarus was a direct beneficiary of Doolittle's "Anti-Communist Manifesto." Funding for the Byelorussian community in America was increased, and large numbers of them were hired as researchers for various government projects. Many of OPC's research requests were farmed out to public and private groups in order to provide cover, and more jobs for informants.

The Operations Research Office of the Pentagon was one such agency. ORO was doing historical research into the use of native collaborators by the Nazis in the hope of obtaining information of value in the event of an American invasion of Russia. Operation Pow-wow was the code name given the project. The voluminous material produced by ORO included a series of classified manuals analyzing the Nazi documents concerning Byelorussia. One entire manual was devoted to the Nazi use of native police in the area around Borissow. Only cursory mention was made of the atrocities that had been committed there.

Still another paper discussed the political organizations established by the Nazis to control the population. Ostrowsky's government was mentioned in detail, as was Sobolewsky's earlier work under General Kube. Some of the reports on operations in Baltic countries indicated that they were written by persons who had been high-ranking Nazi collaborators themselves. Obviously, the "researchers" employed by ORO were either Nazis or individuals with a great deal of familiarity with their history.*

Harvard University was also linked to Wisner's research pro-

*An ex-Army sergeant named Henry A. Kissinger was one of the ORO consultants. Kissinger had served with the 970th CIC unit in Germany, where his specialty was identifying Gestapo and SS officers hiding out among the civilian population. Another ORO consultant was Erich Waldmann, formerly Gehlen's liaison to the Army.

grams. The Harvard Institute for Russian Research was funded by OPC, using the Air Force Human Resources Research Institute as a conduit.[17] Wisner commissioned a team of historians to interview Eastern European émigrés in the DP camps. The first series of interviews was legitimate; the refugees provided historical, medical, sociological, and ethnological data on the Soviet Union. But any émigrés who displayed knowledge of Nazi collaborators or intelligence networks were subsequently referred to a second set of interrogators.

The B-6 series of interviews, for example, covered such nonacademic topics as the best method for dropping paratroopers, the utility of Nazi anti-partisan operations, the popularity of Nazi-sponsored political organizations, the successful uses of anticommunist propaganda, and the kind of reception certain Nazi leaders such as Ostrowsky had received from the local population. Several of those interviewed candidly acknowledged that they had held positions in Nazi police or intelligence organizations. One even admitted that he was hiding out because he was wanted as a major war criminal. Apparently they were more than willing to confess participation in criminal activities because they suspected that the person conducting the interview was more than just another Harvard researcher. One even demanded that he be provided with a visa to the United States through special channels so that he would not have to go through the usual screening.

But Wisner's OPC did more than finance research. Large numbers of Byelorussians and other Eastern European Nazis were hired to work in propaganda agencies. The two most important were Radio Free Europe and Radio Liberty, both of which were funded by the Crusade for Freedom. After 1953 these agencies turned sharply conservative in their staffing and in their funding of émigré groups in the United States. Instead of a representative mix of moderate nationalists and right-wingers, the various "national committees of liberation" became dominated by those who had been outright Nazi collaborators—at least no one would ever accuse *them* of being soft on communism.

Radio Liberty was a haven for the Byelorussian Nazis. The operation had a White Ruthenian desk, and several members of the Belarus network who had served as Nazi propagandists were

Radislaw Ostrowsky when he was president of
the Byelorussian Central Council in 1944.

Dr. Mikalai Minkevich (left), who married Ostrowsky's daughter, Melina (right).

The leadership council of the Byelorussian Self-Help Committee in Minsk, 1942. Seated at far left: Ivan Kosiak, later a provincial governor; seated fourth from left: Dr. Ivan Ermachenko; at far right: Vadlay Ivanousky, later mayor of Minsk; standing, second from right: Anton Adamovitch.

Joachim Kipel, president of the Second All-Byelorussian Congress.

Jury Sobolewsky, vice-president of the
Byelorussian Central Council.

Left: Major Michael Vitushka, who was sent by Otto Skorzeny behind Soviet lines in the winter of 1944–45. He was purported to be the leader of a large underground army at a time when he was probably already dead. Right: Major Dimitri Kasmowich, the collaborationist police chief of the Smolensk region during World War II. Forces under his command burned entire cities and towns suspected of aiding the Soviets.

Emanuel Jasiuk, who as mayor of Kletsk directed the killing of 5,000 Jews in a single day, and was later minister of immigration in the Ostrowsky government-in-exile.

Father Mikalaj Lapitski, who forged baptismal certificates for Byelorussians in German DP camps after World War II. He is buried under a large monument in South River, N.J.

B. Д а д а т к і

КІРАЎНІЦТВА БЕЛАРУСКАЙ ЦЭНТРАЛЬНАЙ РАДЫ ПАДЧАС 2-ГА УСЕБЕЛАРУСКАГА КАНГРЭСУ

1. Прэзыдэнт БЦР — праф. Р. Астроўскі,
2. 1-шы Віцэ-Прэзыдэнт БЦР, справы прэсы і прапаганды — мгр. М. Шкелёнак,
3. 2-гі Віцэ-Прэзыдэнт БЦР, справы сацыяльнай апекі, самапомачы і кантролю — Ю. Сабалеўскі,
4. Фінансы — Сымон Кандыбовіч,
5. Справы культуры — А. Калубовіч,
6. Школьныя справы — др. А. Скурат,
7. Вайсковыя справы — Франьцішак Кушэль,
8. Юрыдычныя і рэлігійныя справы — Павал Сьвірыд,
9. Лясная гаспадарка — інж. С. Калядка,
10. Прафэсійныя справы — інж. С. Стаськевіч,
11. Саюз Беларускай Моладзі (Аддзел Хлапцоў) — М. Ганько,
12. Саюз Беларускай Моладзі (Аддзел Дзяўчат) — др. Надзея Абрамава,
13. Аддзел Сельскае Гаспадаркі — інж. Пётра Орса.

АБСАДА НАМЕСЬНІЦТВАУ БЕЛАРУСКАЙ ЦЭТРАЛЬНАЙ РАДЫ ПАДЧАС 2-ГА УСЕБЕЛАРУСКАГА КАНГРЭСУ

1. Баранавіцкая Акруга — др. Станіслаў Станкевіч,
2. Берасьцейская Акруга — Міхал Васілеўскі,
3. Вялейская Акруга — др. Язэп Малецкі,
4. Ганцавіцкая Акруга — кап. Сокал-Кутылоўскі,
5. Глыбоцкая Аруга — інж. І. Касяк,
6. Лідзкая Акруга — інж. А. Клімовіч,
7. Менск-Горад — А. Комар,
8. Менская Акруга — інж. Жук,
9. Наваградзкая Акруга — Барыс Рагуля,
10. Слонімская Акруга — Александар Аўдзей,
11. Слуцкая Акруга — Іван Хіхлуша.

The official roster of the leadership of the Byelorussian Central Council at the time of the Minsk convention in 1944. The top listing includes R. Astrouski (Radislaw Ostrowsky) (1) as president of the Council, Yu. Sabaleuski (Jury Sobolewsky) (3) as second vice-president and social affairs minister, and Frantzishak (Franz) Kushel (7) as war minister. The first name on the bottom list is that of Stanislaw Stankievich, as representative of Baranovitche county.

Monument to Byelorussian war veterans in the White Ruthenian (Byelorussian) Orthodox Cemetery of St. Euphrosynia in South River, N.J. Inside the cross at the top is the emblem of the Belarus SS division. (Washington *Post* photograph by Bill Snead)

Headquarters of the Byelorussian Central Council in Minsk in 1943.

Unmarked South River grave of Emanuel Jasiuk. (Washington *Post* photograph by Bill Snead)

Photograph and biography of Radislaw Ostrowsky on his gravestone in South River, N.J. (Washington *Post* photograph by Bill Snead)

PROF. RADASLAŬ ASTROŬSKI
(RADOSLAW OSTROWSKI)

BORN IN SLUCK-BYELORUSSIA, OCTOBER 25, 1887.
GRADUATED UNIVERSITY OF DORPAT-ESTONIA (1913)
EDUCATOR, PROFESSOR OF PHYSICS AND
MATHEMATICS, JOURNALIST.-SINCE EARLY SCHOOL
YEARS FIGHTER FOR FREEDOM AND INDEPENDANCE
OF BYELORUSSIA.-POLITICAL LEADER IN
BYELORUSSIAN NATIONAL MOVEMENT, DELEGATE
TO FIRST AND SECOND ALL-BYELORUSSIAN
CONGRESSES IN MINSK (1917-1944) SECRETARY OF
EDUCATION IN THE GOVERNMENT OF THE
BYELORUSSIAN DEMOCRATIC REPUBLIC
(1918).-PRESIDENT OF BYELORUSSIAN CENTRAL
COUNCIL OF THE BYELORUSSIAN DEMOCRATIC
REPUBLIC AND FOUNDER OF BYELORUSSIAN ARMED
FORCES (1944).-DIED IN BENTON HARBOR, MICHIGAN,
OCTOBER 17, 1976.

employed, among them Anton Adamovitch, who acknowledged in a television interview that he had been a Nazi collaborator and worked for U.S. Army intelligence. He said he had told the FBI about his background at the time he was admitted to the United States and no objections were raised.*

Stankievich became chairman of the Learned Council of the Institute of Russian Research in Munich, which had been placed under Radio Liberty. After Stankievich was overheard bragging about the mass execution at Borissow, one of the other émigrés asked an OPC liaison man whether it was wise to place a notorious war criminal in such a prominent position. The discussion was cut short. Stankievich was credited with being an important source of information. Moreover, he had exposed the Soviet agent who attempted to recruit him. Moreover, he was a major politician in the Abramtchik faction, having risen to become its vice-president. Many of his followers were employed at Radio Liberty and its research staffs. Their academic credentials served them in good stead. When the famous Berlin wiretap tunnel was dug in 1953, the Byelorussians were hired to translate the voluminous Soviet conversations. Many took jobs with government research institutes or served as translators for the State Department and other government agencies. A few, including Kushel, were hired as consultants by military and academic organizations.

For the most part, the Byelorussian émigrés in the United States possessed modest jobs. They lived in old but well-maintained neighborhoods and kept to themselves. In South River, for instance, they concentrated in a triangle between Whitehead Avenue, Main Street, and Hillside Avenue, although several of the more prominent collaborators were located on the southwestern side of town, near Route 527. They kept their lawns trimmed, their houses painted, and they never got in trouble with the police.

---

*Adamovitch was not an ordinary journalist who merely kept his job on a newspaper when the Nazis overran his homeland. Eventually he rose to become a member of the presidium, the ruling body of the Byelorussian government-in-exile in Berlin in 1944–45. This is the group that authorized the organization of the Belarus SS Brigade (Ivan Kosiak, *For the National Independence of Byelorussia* (Byelorussian language publication), Ukrainian Press, London, copy in the National Archives).

Most of their neighbors knew little about them. No one who was not part of the Belarus, or a relative of a collaborator, was allowed to join their social groups.* No one who was not a member of the parish could be buried in St. Euphrosynia's cemetery. The Belarus even had its own youth group, the Byelorussian-American Youth Organization, or BAYO. Now a social organization, BAYO was an outgrowth of the paramilitary "Boy Scout" units organized by Kushel in the DP camps.

The BAYO monthly magazine was a valuable tool for learning the names of the Belarus members living in America, as nearly every issue contained a picture of some of the parents. The magazine also published a grossly distorted history of World War II, apparently in recognition that the children had learned some of the truth. The BAYO article admitted, for instance, that an SS brigade known as the Belarus Legion had been formed, but it denied that the unit had gone into battle. The Ostrowsky government was portrayed as the culmination of centuries of Byelorussian striving for nationhood and independence.

The BAYO article went to great lengths to place the blame for the killing of Jews in Byelorussia on Lithuanian mercenaries (some of whom did serve in Byelorussia). No mention was made of the Byelorussian mercenaries in the northern Ukraine, nor of the police battalions who participated in the *Einsatzgruppen* "actions" against the Jews. The responsibility for the deaths of the civilian population was assigned to Soviet partisans. Selections from Nazi documents, complaining about the lack of support from the natives, were displayed as proof of Byelorussian innocence. No mention was made of the SS and Wehrmacht documents listing the collaborators and their roles in the extermination of the Jews. The BAYO article was a good example of the revisionist party line served up not only to the children of South River but to the equally naïve intelligence community as well.†

_____

*The Belarus usually vacationed together at a hotel owned by a fellow Byelorussian, the Bel-Air Minsk in Glen Spey, New York.
†Ostrowsky followed a similar line in a letter to the editor of the *New York Times* from San Martin, Argentina, that was published on October 13, 1951. He discussed the long history of Byelorussia's fight for independence from Russia and pointed out that such a declaration had been made by the Second National Byelorussian Congress in 1944. "The Byelorussian home guard was fighting against the invasion of the Soviet armies at this

By 1954, it was an open secret among American intelligence agencies that elements of a Nazi puppet Byelorussian regime existed in America. In the middle of that year, Wisner funded an international convention of collaborators in South River that was called the Fourteenth Plenum of the Byelorussian Central Council. A brochure published for the occasion made clear the origins of the organization, for it listed the thirteen previous meetings going back through the exile government in Berlin to the SS-sponsored Minsk congress of 1944. Additional evidence of the collaborationist nature of the wartime Ostrowsky regime was provided by the publication in 1956 of Nicholas Vakar's book *Belorussia: The Making of a Nation.** It caused something of a sensation in the émigré community because it described, quite accurately, the role of the Byelorussian collaborators during the Nazi occupation and mentioned some by name.

The Byelorussians denounced Vakar's book, which, among its other offenses, accurately quoted some of the anti-Semitic, pro-Nazi speeches made at the Minsk collaborators' convention of 1944. Ostrowsky's son, Wiktor, published a pamphlet in London on anti-Semitism in Byelorussia that sought to lay a large measure of the blame on Jewish Communists and Russian repression, while mentioning very little about the actual existence of anti-Semitism among the Byelorussians themselves. The younger Ostrowsky concluded that "the local population took no part in these actions against the Jews."

Ironically, most of the Belarus settlements in America are located near large concentrations of Jews. Occasionally, allegations connecting the Byelorussians to war crimes were forwarded from the Jewish community to the FBI during the 1950s, but all the inquiries were dropped after only a cursory check.[18]

Despite the rumblings, Wisner succeeded in making it easier for the collaborators to become American citizens. Legislation was secured that relaxed the five-year residency requirement for persons sent overseas to work for American institutes of research.

---

time," he added. Ostrowsky signed the letter as "President, Byelorussian Central Council." The *Times* made no mention of the Nazi background of Ostrowsky or his government.
*Vakar drew heavily on material collected by Harvard University's Institute for Russian Research.

The Attorney General designated the institutions that qualified, most of which were subsequently identified as CIA front organizations. An applicant for citizenship was now able to leave the country without breaking his five-year waiting period. Individuals accorded special preference for immigration visas, reentry permits, and citizenship applications had small red cardboard flags stapled to their immigration paperwork. The red flag read simply "American Committee for Liberation from Bolshevism" and gave a New York City address.

Persons whose files were red-flagged received special treatment. Minor discrepancies in their applications were overlooked; background investigations were cut short; paperwork was expedited. Most of the Byelorussian employees at Radio Liberty had red flags in their immigration files.[19] The immigration officials knew that they were performing some kind of anticommunist propaganda or intelligence work and simply assumed that the CIA had already made a thorough background check. That is how Stanislaw Stankievich entered the United States and eventually became an American citizen, in spite of the fact that five previous visa applications had been rejected.* He was naturalized on March 8, 1969, by the U.S. District Court for the Eastern District of New York.[20]

A check of Stankievich's file at Fort Meade, Maryland, reveals that both the Army and the State Department had knowledge of his history of collaboration with the Nazis prior to his entry into this country. These documents state:

. . . Subject attempted to apply for immigration to the United States in 1948 and 1949. It was found in 1948 that subject had made false statements on practically all major points in his personal data form in order to hide his past history. Subject's name appears on the list of persons rejected for immigration to United States under Section 13

*Stankievich gained his citizenship although he spent very little time in the United States. He was admitted in 1959 on a visa obtained by AMCOMLIB. On the day of his arrival, Wisner's staff sent a letter to the Immigration and Naturalization Service requesting that he be issued a reentry permit so he could leave the country for Germany. Over the next ten years Stankievich traveled back and forth between the United States and Germany. He finally took up residence in New York City before being naturalized. Each of his reentry permits bears a red tab with the name and address of AMCOMLIB.

(movement hostile). During World War II, subject collaborated with the Occupation Forces . . . and during the German occupation edited a newspaper, *Ranitsa,* a Nazi propaganda paper. Subject held many positions of trust in the German administration. . . . Also subject participated in the massacre of Polish officers in a forest near Minsk, *and he was guilty of other war crimes.* [Emphasis added.]

For many of the late arrivals who emigrated during the 1950s and 1960s, a red flag in their files was not even necessary. The security staff at Radio Liberty in Munich was told by the OPC that certain persons were needed in the United States, and was instructed to take appropriate action. One staff member recalled in recent interviews that he hand-carried paperwork to the American consulate, where he was well known, in order to expedite visas. Later assigned to the New York headquarters of Radio Liberty, the same bewildered officer said that he was ordered in various cases to expedite everything from green cards to citizenship applications by personally escorting individuals through the immigration bureaucracy, relying mostly on his familiarity with local officials. Ironically, one Byelorussian Nazi—the CIC was convinced he was a Communist spy—was escorted through in just this fashion in order to work for Radio Liberty. As the security officer explained, everyone assumed that the CIA had checked his background.[21]

Yet the Central Registry of the CIA was still denouncing war criminals up to the mid-1950s, apparently unaware that an agency proprietary organization, Radio Liberty, was bringing such people into the United States. Wisner's agents rarely shared their files with anyone else at the CIA, according to one official, and conducted themselves as an agency within the agency.

To this day the CIA maintains that it is unable to locate all the OPC files.[22]

The Truman administration may have negligently allowed the Byelorussian Nazis into the United States, but it was the Eisenhower government that gave them citizenship. Between 1953 and 1958 those persons who had entered under the Displaced Persons Act began completing their five-year waiting period. Once they were granted citizenship by the courts they would be virtually immune from deportation. But to attain citizenship the applicant had to undergo a full investigation by the Immigration and Naturalization Service, including checks with the FBI and CIA. Moreover, the members of the Belarus would have to disclose nearly every organization they had belonged to, every job they had ever held, every address at which they had resided, and swear to the truth of their statements before a federal judge.

At first, the Byelorussians were in a quandary. If they listed their membership in the SS or in the puppet government of Byelorussia, they would be ineligible for citizenship, not only because they had obtained their visas illegally but because such membership was regarded as proof that the applicant lacked the "good moral character" required for American citizenship. If they omitted any mention of their wartime activities, their citizenship applications would be void for fraud. A very sophisticated compromise was reached. They would disclose the organizations to which they belonged but would omit identifying them as Nazi creations. Thus, their applications showed membership in the "Byelorussian Central Council" instead of the puppet government. Participation in the "White Ruthenian Committee in Warsaw" was listed, but it was not identified as a recruiting organization for the *Einsatzgruppen*. They claimed their membership in the postwar "Byelorussian Central Committee" or "Central Representation" but failed to mention that the CIC had considered it an "illegal organization" or that the Displaced Persons Commission had declared them "movements hostile" to the United States. For example, Emanuel Jasiuk, in his petition for naturalization, listed his memberships as the "Byelorussian-White Ruthenian Central Council" and the "Byelorussian-White Ruthenian Congress Committee." Thus, the Byelorussians disclosed memberships in 1955 that would have prevented their emigrating to the United States in 1948.

The Immigration Service noted several such discrepancies—particularly in the naturalization applications of Byelorussian émigrés—and became alarmed when the CIA's Central Registry —still oblivious to OPC's recruitment drive—provided it with a wealth of derogatory information. But Immigration decided that it could not handle the investigations on its own, and turned to the FBI for help. The request created a problem for J. Edgar Hoover. If he disclosed the full extent of FBI knowledge to the Immigration Service, it would make clear the extent to which the bureau had permitted known Nazis to reside in the United States, and would eventually reveal that the FBI had been recruiting these same Nazis to provide information on Wisner's activities. But if Hoover withheld the information entirely, he could be prosecuted for obstructing the Immigration Service.

Hoover contacted the central office of the Immigration Service in Washington and explained the delicate relationship between the Byelorussian Democratic Republic and the American Committee for Liberation. Moreover, he furnished the central office with a copy of the sanitized field investigation reports that he had submitted to the Justice Department several years earlier during the Foreign Agents Registration investigation. The report was a model of bureaucratic fence-walking; it confirmed the AMCOMLIB connection and the anticommunist nature of the Belarus, while archly mentioning unconfirmed snippets of information hinting at World War II collaboration with the Germans.

Copies of the FBI interviews with Kushel and Jasiuk were included with the report, but neither they nor the substance of Hoover's conversation with the INS central office was made known to the Brooklyn immigration office until many years later.[23] This "oversight" was fortunate for Kushel, because his lengthy summary of his collaboration with the Nazis flatly contradicted the sworn statements that appeared on his citizenship application filed in 1955. In the FBI interview, he admitted that he had been a colonel in the police force organized by the Germans and commanded several battalions that accompanied the Wehrmacht on its retreat from Byelorussia in 1944. The FBI never mentioned the discrepancy when it cleared Kushel's citizenship application.

Consequently, the Immigration Service reported to the U.S. District Court in Brooklyn that "Francis" Kushel:

In September, 1939 . . . was taken as a prisoner of war to Staroblesh, USSR, where he remained until May, 1941. He returned to Poland (and resided there) until July, 1943 when he went to Germany where he resided in various cities until 1950. He was employed as a teacher in Poland and also as a farm worker. In Germany he was employed as a farm worker and as a factory worker, until 1945, when he became a camp leader of UNRRA camps at Regensburg and Michelsdorf, Germany. In October, 1948 he became a field worker for the YMCA and was so employed until he departed for the United States. . . .[24]

Thus was Franz Kushel—commander-in-chief of the Belarus Brigade, and Minister of War in a government that had fought against the United States—allowed to become an American citizen.[25]

It was not possible to arrange a mere "oversight" where Jasiuk was concerned. He had already admitted falsifying his visa data to the FBI, and that alone should have barred his application for citizenship. There was only one thing for the FBI to do: The bureau concealed from the local immigration officer the fact that Jasiuk's Nazi collaboration had been confirmed by a number of reliable informants, and urged the Immigration Service to approve his citizenship application, simply because Jasiuk had been determined by the FBI to be "trustworthy."[26] The INS duly reported that:

The Federal Bureau of Investigation was informed of the apparent false claims made by the subject. The subject, when first interviewed by the Federal Bureau of Investigation, claimed residence from 1940 until 1945 in a slave labor camp. During a second interview he admitted furnishing false information concerning his residence. Subsequent investigation revealed that the subject was trustworthy and that he had not collaborated with the Germans. The subject testified before an officer of this Service in July, 1955 that he had not collaborated with the Germans during World War II and that he had never worked for the German Secret Police. . . . The subject was naturalized as a citizen of the United States on November 16, 1956.[27]

Once the FBI had personally certified Jasiuk as "trustworthy," the INS saw no reason to disagree. Moreover, attached to Jasiuk's immigration paperwork was a special letter of character reference from the Stuttgart consulate:

To Whom It May Concern:

The bearer of this letter, Mr. Emanuel Jasiuk, has done excellent work for the undersigned in several confidential cases. He may be depended upon for discretion, intelligence, and reliability.

Mr. Jasiuk is eager to be of assistance to the United States in certain work which he will explain, and it is believed that his service would be of great value.

Cleveland E. Collier
Vice Consul of the United States[28]

Jasiuk's file also contained cryptic references to the fact that he had performed "highly confidential work for an American agency." It should be recalled that the central office of the INS had been informed of the existence of the AMCOMLIB connection two years previously. In spite of all the Counter-Intelligence Corps could do to prevent it, even including personal warnings to Hoover that Jasiuk was a war criminal who had committed atrocities, the man had obtained his citizenship.[29] So thoroughly had the FBI vouched for Jasiuk that the Immigration Service recruited him as its own confidential informant.

The Belarus network, experienced in the art of political maneuvering, went out of its way to ensnare as many American public officials as possible. At first it was local politicians who were asked for endorsements, then the mayor of New York City and the governor of New York State, and members of Congress, with whom they had their pictures taken. Vice-President Richard M. Nixon received one Belarus leader in the White House—probably the only time a major war criminal has been so honored.* Belarus members even testified before a special hearing of the House Committee on Foreign Affairs on July 15, 1953, to outline the struggle of the Byelorussian people for liberation from the Communists. A retired military officer working with AMCOMLIB introduced several prominent Byelorussian collaborators to Congress as "freedom fighters." Among them were SS intelligence officers who had helped recruit advisers for the *Einsatzgruppen*.

In the face of this favorable publicity, the Immigration Service

*The individual is currently under investigation.

did not challenge the decisions of the American intelligence community. The FBI began sending the INS copies of many of its Byelorussian field reports to make it thoroughly aware of the true wartime role of the Byelorussians. From then on Hoover did not need to persuade the Immigration Service to cooperate in the cover-up; he could blackmail them.

Among the documents provided the INS by the FBI was a sixty-three-page report, *Byelorussian Activities in the New York Division.* [30] Before long the INS central office knew virtually every facet of the Byelorussian collaboration with the Nazis, from the time of the creation of Ostrowsky's government by the SS to the collapse of the Hitler regime. Immigration officials in the local field offices quickly caught on to the change in policy at the central office. Between 1955 and 1956 several incriminating FBI files were released to local officials who were examining citizenship applications filed by Byelorussian Nazi leaders. Instead of opening up the pro-Nazi leads, the officials noted that the FBI had determined that these applicants were trustworthy anticommunists, and approved the applications. Among them were two of the key advisers and recruiters for the *Einsatzgruppen*. In view of the bewildering complexity of the Belarus history and the strident anticommunism of the times, it is not difficult to imagine how the Immigration Service bureaucrats rationalized their rule-bending in the interests of national security.

For the first time, the Byelorussians had more than a promise of security in America. If they were ever prosecuted for fraudulently obtaining their citizenship, they would be in a position to threaten to expose high government officials in the FBI, CIA/OPC, and INS who had made their fraud possible. The threat of blackmail was not limited to those few Byelorussians who actually worked with those intelligence agencies, since knowledge of the activities of the secret army was widespread in the émigré community. At most, only a handful of officials in the Immigration Service and the FBI were involved in the cover-up. Apart from a few isolated cases where the Nazi connection was too obvious to be ignored, there is no evidence of any widespread corruption in either agency.

The simple truth appears to be that bureaucratic incompetence and institutional inefficiency accounted for the fact that hundreds of seemingly ineligible applicants were able to obtain citizenship. For instance, the Army, in a request to the CIA for information on Kushel, noted that "he surrendered to the Germans," indicating that Kushel was an anti-Nazi.[31] Perhaps the Army was testing to see how much the CIA knew about the Byelorussians. If the inquiry was sincere, it illustrates the Pentagon's inability to extract information it already possessed from the intelligence archives of the various military services.

It is possible that not even Frank Wisner knew the extent to which the members of the Belarus network conspired to help each other obtain citizenship. Jasiuk once told immigration officials that while he was mayor of Stolpce, he had secretly resisted the Germans and helped save the life of a Jewish doctor named Greenberg. The story sounded so convincing that it was used by another Byelorussian, who did not even bother to change the name of the town or the name of the doctor. The two stories were solemnly sworn to by many of the same South River "character witnesses," yet the Immigration Service apparently never caught on.

Assured of their security, the enclaves of Byelorussian collaborators settled down in their new country. But they refused to give up the dream of returning to Byelorussia in triumph to revenge themselves upon the Soviets. In cellars and suitcases all across America the Belarus network had hidden the records of their wartime regime. They had smuggled their entire archives into the United States: everything from unit rosters of the Belarus Brigade to the minutes of the meetings of the Nazi puppet government. They had even brought some of the captured files that they had located for the SS as the *Einsatzgruppen* swept through Minsk. It may have been reckless to keep so many incriminating documents, but the Byelorussians would not part with these talismans.[32] They were all that was left of the years of power under the Third Reich.

Chapter

9

Under the Eisenhower administration, the CIA's covert activities expanded rapidly. After the end of the Korean War in 1953, the perception of the Soviet threat shifted from the military to the political, and there was a consequent increase in covert operations. Allen Dulles played a major part in defining this role. Dulles's wartime experience in the OSS had been on the operational side of intelligence, and his fascination with undercover work persisted. Rolling back communism became the central theme of CIA operations, and Wisner's shop scored successes: the overthrow of Premier Mohammed Mossadegh in Iran in 1953 and the coup against President Jacobo Arbenz Guzman in Guatemala a year later.

These achievements gave the CIA and the administration a sense of confidence and set the stage for future developments. Ever since the "Anti-Communist Manifesto" of the Doolittle report, the intelligence community had been waiting for a signal to begin making serious trouble for the Soviet Union, especially in the occupied countries of Eastern Europe. Finally, on March 12, 1955, the National Security Council issued a directive to the CIA, entitled NSC 5412/1, which at last authorized Wisner to declare guerrilla war against the Communists:

> In accordance with established policies, and to the extent practicable in areas dominated or threatened by international communism, develop underground resistance and facilitate covert and guerrilla operations. . . .
>
> Specifically, such operations shall include any covert activities related to: propaganda, political action, economic warfare, preventive direct action, including sabotage, antisabotage, demolition, escape and evasion and evacuation measures; subversion against hostile states or groups including assistance to underground resistance movements, guerrillas and refugee liberation groups; support of indigenous

and anti-communist elements in threatened countries of the free world; deception plans and operations and all compatible activities necessary to accomplish the foregoing.[1]

Armed with this mandate, Wisner determined to take "preventive direct action" against a number of Communist-bloc nations that he believed were ripe for revolt. He authorized an operation designed to incite simultaneous revolts against Soviet authority in each of the major cities of Eastern Europe, which were to be followed by a civil war among the ethnic and religious minorities within the Soviet Union. Once the revolt had erupted, underground cells were to seize the government buildings and radio, and call for the people to rise. Within hours, Wisner's "liberation armies" would be dropped in to attack the scattered Soviet garrisons.[2] Roads, bridges, and rail lines would be blown up or blocked to prevent the movement of Russian reinforcements. After the Soviets had been sufficiently weakened, North Atlantic Treaty Organization (NATO) troops would be dispatched as a peace-keeping force, with the declaration that they would remain only long enough to restore order and conduct the democratic elections that Stalin had promised at Yalta in 1945.

Wisner began pouring millions of dollars into training dissident Czechs, Poles, Hungarians, Byelorussians, Latvians, and Romanians to be the spearhead of the operation. Underground resistance networks were to be reestablished, training areas and bases for guerrilla bands opened on the periphery of the Iron Curtain, and arms caches built up. A few years before, as relations with the Russians soured, President Truman had ordered a study prepared for an invasion of the Soviet Union. A review of the study shows that invasion routes had been planned and a timetable set for the early 1950s. Wisner's plan was in a sense more sophisticated than Truman's, which relied heavily on the use of American combat forces to capture strategic targets long enough for the anticipated revolts to gain momentum.

Nevertheless, Wisner's plan was romantic and absurdly impractical. In order for it to have any chance for success two elements were indispensable: complete secrecy in preparation and complete coordination of attack. Not only would Wisner have to train, arm, and equip resistance forces in secret, but he would need to orchestrate each of the internal rebellions so they would culminate at the same time. And secrecy had already been lost, for Gehlen's organization, which was to supply the core of the groups being recruited, had been penetrated by Communist agents who reported to Moscow every facet of the plan.

For example, Gehlen's liaison to NATO headquarters, Heinz Felfe, turned out to be a Soviet mole. A ranking Pentagon official who personally briefed Felfe acknowledged in a recent interview that there was not a secret in the entire NATO archives to which Felfe did not have access, including the plans for Wisner's operation.[3] Felfe was brought to the United States for consultation, but because of his Nazi past he could not be issued a regular visa. This was no obstacle for Wisner. According to Felfe's "blue file" at Fort Meade, a false background was created for him and he was issued false documentation. Felfe's KGB controllers must have been amused at the efforts made by Wisner to circumvent the laws of his own country to smuggle a Soviet mole into the United States.

The blame for the tragic dénouement of the plan should not rest with Wisner alone. During the Eisenhower administration, "no direct action covert operations were initiated without prior White House approval," according to a high-ranking CIA officer.[4] The President himself had difficulty in presenting cover stories to the press and generally preferred not to know about Wisner's cover operations.[5] Instead, a special group, the Operations Coordination Board, which came to be known as the "Twenty Committee," was created to oversee these operations and to serve as a "circuit breaker" so that the President could disavow direct knowledge of such activities. In 1954 Nelson Rockefeller succeeded C. D. Jackson, a former Time, Inc. executive, as "supercoordinator" for clandestine intelligence operations, with the title of Special Assistant to the President for Cold War Strategy. Rockefeller must have known of Wisner's plan, for he received a "family jewels" briefing from Dulles and Wisner apprising him of all covert operations run by the OPC. Moreover, as a confirmed Cold Warrior, he had previously allowed the Rockefeller Fund to serve as a conduit for OPC money.

Rockefeller left the administration at the end of 1955 as a result

of political infighting, and Vice-President Richard M. Nixon replaced him as the President's Cold War strategist. Nixon had a
small boy's delight in the arcane tools of the intelligence craft—
the hidden microphones, the "black" propaganda, the techniques
of interrogation—and Dulles and Wisner were pleased to gratify
his curiosity. Like Rockefeller, he received a deep briefing on OPC
operations, and Wisner personally escorted him to the training
center in Virginia where the "special forces" were being trained.[6]

On June 28, 1956, riots broke out in Poznan, Poland, which
were brutally put down by the Russians. Across America there
were demands that the United States "do something" to help the
embattled Poles in their fight for freedom. Considerable pressure
was brought to bear upon Wisner to order his forces into action,
but he convinced the Twenty Committee that his plan was not yet
ready. Over the next few months he worked at a furious pace to
have the operation ready by the middle of 1958.

But revolt erupted in Hungary in late October 1956. With only
small arms and homemade bombs, youthful rebels drove out the
officials of the Communist government and proclaimed Hungary
a free nation, neutral between East and West. There is no evidence
that OPC provoked the uprising, but Radio Free Europe and
Radio Liberty created the hope of American support. The situation was complicated by an Anglo-French-Israeli invasion of
Egypt to seize control of the Suez Canal, which had been expro-
priated by the Egyptians. The Eisenhower administration opposed
the Suez adventure, and on November 4 Premier Nikita S.
Khrushchev took advantage of the disarray among the Western allies to send 200,000 troops into Hungary to put down the
rebellion.

Fighting for their capital block by block, the Hungarian "freedom fighters" frantically called out to the West for help: "We
appeal to the conscience of the world," Radio Free Rakoczi broadcast on November 6. "Why cannot you hear the call for help of
our murdered women and children? Peoples of the world! Hear
the call for help of a small nation! . . . This is Radio Rakoczi,
Hungary . . . Radio Free Europe, Munich! Radio Free Europe,
Munich! Answer! Have you received our transmission?"

This was followed a few hours later by another broadcast:

". . . Attention, attention, Munich! Munich! Take immediate action. . . . We urgently need medicine, bandages, arms, food, and ammunition. Drop them to us by parachute."[7]

Wisner, who had been on a tour of OPC stations in Europe, was in Vienna as these appeals for help poured in. At the first reports of the uprising he had been in a state of euphoria, expecting the revolt to spread to Poland, Czechoslovakia, and East Germany. He pleaded with Washington for an airlift of arms and reinforcements for the Hungarians—only to be ignored. Rage boiling over, he cursed the British, French, and Israelis, claiming their attack on Egypt had provided the Russians with a cover for intervention in Hungary.*

There was to be no help for the Hungarians. The shock of the Soviet counterattack had stunned the Eisenhower administration. The Joint Chiefs of Staff pointed out that not even an incursion of the special forces would be enough to save Budapest. Only an airlift of weapons could stave off defeat, and that would mean the use of military aircraft and open American intervention. This might lead to war with the Soviet Union—a war, the military pointed out, for which the United States was unprepared.[8] So no relief was sent to the Hungarians. Before the fighting ended in Budapest, upward of 30,000 people may have been killed, and another 200,000 fled the country. "Poor fellows, poor fellows," lamented Eisenhower. "I think about them all the time. I wish there was some way of helping them."[9]

"Liberation" and dreams of "rolling back" the Iron Curtain were exposed for the hollow and misleading generalities they had always been. Short of an all-out war, the United States simply

---

*During a recent interview, a retired intelligence official suggested that Wisner never authorized Radio Liberty to encourage the Hungarian uprising, that the staff did this upon their own authority while Wisner was in Vienna. Although this account differs from the recollection of others, the official did remember that Wisner was never the same after the abortive uprising. In his opinion, the Hungarian episode did not itself shatter Wisner, but it was the straw that broke the camel's back. Years of effort in fighting the Communists had taken their toll. Wisner became a manic depressive—up when OPC was moving against the Communists, down when his networks were eliminated. James Forrestal, one of Wisner's original patrons, is said to have experienced a similar end. According to Charles Higham, who researched this period, nurses found Forrestal lying on the floor of his hospital room, babbling that the Communists and the Jews were trying to kill him. Shortly afterward, he committed suicide.

lacked the means to direct or influence events in the Soviet sphere. General Lucian K. Truscott was assigned by the President to investigate Wisner's operation.[10] He went first to Camp Kilmer, New Jersey, the site of a hastily established reception center for Hungarian refugees, and was disturbed by what he learned. Wisner's agents had led the Hungarians to believe that direct American military intervention would take place once the revolt had started. Truscott also discovered that despite the disaster in Hungary, Wisner was pressing ahead with his plan for Czechoslovakia with the same hope of inciting or assisting a mass uprising. The general succeeded in persuading the President that the outcome would be equally disastrous, and orders were given to close down Wisner's operation and disperse the agents involved.

Upon his return to Washington, Wisner began to act erratically. He told long, pointless stories at conferences and drank more heavily than usual. A worried Polly Wisner told friends that she had seen her husband take out his pistol and talk to it. Not long afterward, Wisner was hospitalized with nervous exhaustion and hepatitis, apparently picked up in Athens from a plate of tainted clams. Over the next few years, Wisner suffered several nervous breakdowns; in 1965 he killed himself with a 20-gauge shotgun on his Maryland farm.[11]

Kim Philby said he was told by a mutual friend that Wisner had committed suicide because of his disappointment over the outcome of the Hungarian uprising.[12] Friends and associates described him as a man who had given his life in the service of his country. "At the very outset of this country's unforeseen and unprepared role as a major power of the world, he was called upon to break new ground of the most dangerous, and for a major power, the most essential ground," they said in a statement issued at the time of his death. "In fact, he had to meet the long prepared challenge of the vast Stalinist intelligence and subversion net. Thereafter, for about a decade, he devoted himself totally to one of the most onerous and difficult tasks any American public servant has ever had to undertake. . . . What never can be broken is the image of Frank Wisner left with those who worked with him. He was brave yet wise, prudent yet strongly determined, and deeply American above all. . . ."[13]

Critics denounced him as a reckless adventurer who had brought the world perilously close to war.

Many years later, one of the men who had succeeded Wisner in DDP* assessed the net results of OPC's programs. Apart from East Germany, he said, OPC did not have even the basic elements of an intelligence system in Eastern Europe and the Soviet Union. There was no network of safe houses, not even a reliable system of couriers. Before he left his post as head of CIA covert operations, Wisner must have realized how thoroughly he had been betrayed by his Nazi protégés. Whether out of embarrassment or anger, he did not brief his successors in DDP on the State Department–Nazi connection.

The CIA, however, continued to use Wisner's old contacts, in utter ignorance of their Nazi backgrounds. In one case, the agency even considered granting a Byelorussian Nazi permanent sanctuary under the Hundred Persons Act, in the belief that he had worked with the Resistance in France, and had been imprisoned by the Gestapo. He was still considered to have been a reliable agent until the CIA was shown a copy of his Gestapo file in the National Archives. All along he had worked for the SS as an intelligence agent until it discovered his extensive Communist background and demoted him. Wisner was not even efficient at smuggling Nazis.

With the disbanding of the few remaining cadres of Wisner's secret army—the "special forces" were taken over by the Army and became the nucleus of the Green Berets†—the Byelorussian collaborators he had helped come to America faced difficult times. The CIA finally realized it had never possessed an organized underground behind the Iron Curtain. Most of the agency's so-called intelligence sources were merely "paper mills," producing scraps of information that had been doctored up to be traded to the gullible Americans in exchange for survival.[14] And by concealing the extent of Soviet penetration within their own ranks, the

---

*Deputy Director of Plans, the head of covert operations for the CIA. Previously, the unit was known as the Directorate of Operations.
†Originally, the Green Berets were made up of foreigners who were trained at the same bases in Germany as Wisner's recruits, and even used the same Special Forces name.

émigrés had helped delude Wisner into believing they could carry on covert operations in secrecy. Now their CIA subsidies were cut off, and there was even talk of scrapping Radio Liberty and Radio Free Europe, which provided jobs for many of them.*

In the years following the collapse of Wisner's operations, the Soviets continued to monitor the activities of the Belarus in America. Soviet officials from the Communist Byelorussian UN delegation even met with Belarus leaders in New York City.[15] Some collaborators contacted the Soviet embassy, asking for transcripts of their school records in Byelorussia. Three or four wrote to Byelorussia and brought over mail-order brides, all of whom professed to unhappiness in America and quickly returned home. The Soviet Union embassy staff collected books and magazines by the Belarus, and criticized them as collaborators in internal Soviet publications. But the Soviets did not repeat the denunciations made before the United Nations in 1947 that numbers of infamous war criminals were sheltered by Americans.

The silence ended in 1961, when Franz Kushel and Emanuel Jasiuk were singled out for special attention. The accusations against them surfaced in a Yiddish-language newspaper, the *Morning Freiheit,* published in New York.[16] Basically, the paper reprinted some accounts of the trials in the Soviet Union of those who had participated in the atrocities at the Koldichevo death camp in Byelorussia. Jasiuk and Kushel were named as key officials in the Nazi administration that had sent thousands of people to their deaths in the camp. Earlier on, when similar accusations had been made, the FBI had consulted Simon Wiesenthal, the noted Nazi hunter, who had warned that the charges might be a Communist Cold War tactic to intimidate the émigré community with false charges of war crimes.[17] Since this was precisely what the FBI wanted to hear, the earlier probes were dropped. But this time the charges had come to the attention of survivors of the Holocaust, and they could not be ignored. There was also a great deal of pressure from Congress, and in 1962 the Immigration and

*The CIA continued to finance Radio Free Europe and Radio Europe at a cost of about $35 million a year until 1971, when a policy of open funding by congressional appropriation was approved (Victor Marchetti and John Marks, *The CIA and the Cult of Intelligence* [Alfred A. Knopf, 1974], pp. 167–70).

Naturalization Service launched an investigation. Once again, the INS turned to the FBI for assistance.

The FBI had known the entire history of the Byelorussian Nazi government since the early 1950s and realized that Kushel and Jasiuk were two of the most important war criminals in the United States. The Bureau also was aware that both men had ties to OPC through the American Committee for Liberation from Bolshevism, which funded their activities. So, citing Wiesenthal's unfortunate comment, the FBI reported to the Immigration Service that the Soviet charges were part of a plot to discredit important anticommunist political figures. When similar denunciations followed, the FBI noted in nearly every case that the accused were staunch anticommunists.

Occasionally, an enterprising newspaper reporter would try to dig into the story. One even managed to interview Kushel, who denied having served with the *Einsatzgruppen* before slamming the door in the reporter's face. Similarly, when one Byelorussian in South River began receiving anonymous letters denouncing him as a war criminal, he wrote to the FBI asking for assistance in identifying his accuser. To understand the self-confidence behind such a gesture, it should be noted that the charges were accurate.[18]

The Immigration Service did not rest on the assurances of the FBI, as it had before. INS officials called the U.S. Army's Investigative Records Repository at Fort Meade, Maryland, and asked if the CIC had any information on Kushel. The CIC, it will be recalled, possessed several classified dossiers dating back to the late 1940s that positively identified him as an SS officer, a member of the Nazi government of Byelorussia, and an informant for SS intelligence. But after a telephone call from CIC in 1963 the Immigration Service noted in its records:

> Mr. Woolwine advised that the CIC records . . . show that Franzishek Kushel was the leader of the Michelsdorf Displaced Persons Camp. No additional information relating to Franzishek Kushel is contained in the CIC Records. In view of this information, Mr. Woolwine was advised that formal report would not be required.

And so, the sanitizing continued. The Pentagon had reason to be grateful that it did not have to submit a formal report on Kushel to the Immigration Service. The agency had previous experience with putting Kushel's false background in writing. In 1956 it had furnished CIA/OSO with a sanitized version of Kushel's history. Undeceived, the CIA had responded with a summary of the hodgepodge of erroneous information concerning Kushel's anticommunist activities, but did note that he was in fact some sort of SS division commander, as the CIC's own records showed. It will be recalled that the FBI had alerted the Immigration Service to Kushel's CIA file when he applied for citizenship in 1955, but through "oversight," the records were never checked.[19] In 1963 the CIA informed the INS that it had "no derogatory information" on Kushel, but included a copy of its 1956 report mentioning the ambiguous reference to the SS division, as well as the fact that the CIC possessed "voluminous information" on Kushel.[20]

The Immigration Service should have realized that the CIA's allegations about Kushel's SS background dovetailed rather neatly with the recent war crimes charges, and it should have gone back to CIC with a demand that the files be produced and the leads followed up. But through incompetence or conspiracy, these leads were never pursued. The Kushel investigation was terminated almost immediately after the CIA reported that it had "no derogatory information" on him.[21]

Recently a CIA official was asked to define "no derogatory information." He responded that it meant there was no evidence of pro-Communist activity. Nazism was regarded as anticommunist, therefore information that a person was a Nazi was not derogatory. This was not simply doublespeak: The intelligence community has a precise language all its own. For example, if the CIA was asked whether it ever employed Nazis as agents, the agency would respond in the negative. Upon further inquiry, if a researcher knew enough to ask, he would discover that an "employee" does not include someone employed by a CIA front organization; and an "agent" does not include persons who worked for Wisner's guerrilla forces, because they were not on the United States government payroll. To a layman it may seem like a distinction without a difference, since they were all paid by the CIA to do work for the CIA.

The FBI employs similar fine distinctions. If the Bureau were asked whether it ever used Nazis as informants, the answer would be no. The FBI distinguishes between confidential sources, casual sources, volunteers who provide information, and people who provide information under investigation. Since the FBI refuses to release the names of its confidential informants even to the assistant attorney general in charge of the Criminal Division, it has normally been impossible to determine whether the Bureau has had a conflict of interest in conducting war crimes investigations.

Moreover, intelligence agencies change their record-keeping procedures with astonishing rapidity. Only the file clerks who suffer through each of these reorganizations can track down the locations of the cold files. The Pentagon could not even find the name of the office within Military Intelligence that coordinated its old Sensitive Document files. As the World War II–era clerks retired from government service during the late 1960s and 1970s, they took with them the institutional memory of Top Secret operations which had been conducted only twenty years previously. With some chagrin, a CIA official has confided that the institutional memory in one section of the agency went back only eighteen months due to the wave of recent retirements. In fact, the CIA has misplaced the entire Gehlen collection and does not know where to find it. It was not able even to begin its search until another agency furnished the exact cryptonym that had originally been used by the CIA twenty years before. As a result, each American intelligence agency carefully maintains acres and acres of cavernous vaults under heavy guard without the remotest idea of their contents.

In the wake of Watergate and other abuses—including alleged CIA involvement in an "anticommunist" coup in Chile that recalled Frank Wisner in his heyday—there were demands for a congressional investigation. President Gerald Ford, who had succeeded Nixon, issued an executive order establishing a presidential commission to investigate the CIA. Nelson Rockefeller, now the Vice-President, was named to head it, and knowledgeable observers compared the appointment to setting the fox to guard the henhouse, because of Rockefeller's links to the intelligence community and his knowledge of its covert activities. A subsequent

Senate investigation concluded that the Rockefeller Commission was only a whitewash effort to divert further investigation from abuses by the intelligence community.

The Rockefeller Commission included Ronald Reagan, who, perhaps unwittingly, had helped years before to raise funds for the Crusade for Freedom, which served as an OPC front, and had publicly urged that the refugee freedom fighters be given a home in America.

The existence of the Rockefeller Commission did not noticeably assuage Congress's urge to investigate, however. On January 27, 1975, the Senate established a Select Committee to Study Governmental Operations with Respect to Intelligence Activities, under the chairmanship of Senator Frank Church of Idaho. The Church Committee's mandate included:

The extent to which the Federal Bureau of Investigation, the Central Intelligence Agency, and any other federal law-enforcement or intelligence agencies coordinate their respective activities, and agreements which govern that coordination, and the extent to which a lack of coordination has contributed to activities which are illegal, improper, inefficient, unethical, or contrary to the intent of Congress. . . . The extent and necessity of overt and covert intelligence activities in the United States.[22]

The committee soon discovered the existence of OPC, the original clandestine service, and was just starting to penetrate the labyrinth of OPC cryptonyms when Richard Welch, the CIA station chief in Athens, was assassinated. The Church Committee was blamed for inadvertently disclosing Welch's identity and thus causing his death. The resulting furor over what was perceived as a reckless investigation contributed to the disbandment of the committee just as it was about to start probing into the Belarus secret and the other Nazi networks that had been smuggled into America at Wisner's direction. In hindsight, it appears that the Church Committee was the victim of false propaganda: subsequent investigations have shown that neither Welch nor his predecessor in Athens had ever concealed their position as CIA station chief. But whether by accident or by design, the investigation was terminated.* Wisner's OPC project files remain buried in the vaults. The Church Committee did (like the Rockefeller Commission) recommend the establishment of a joint congressional oversight committee.[23]

Paradoxically, right across the street from the Senate lay enough information to expose not only the Belarus secret but virtually the entire range of OPC's illegal activities. The Library of Congress had obtained copies of several books published by the Byelorussian Soviet Republic in the late 1960s which described in detail the wartime collaboration of the Belarus, the atrocities its members had committed, and their subsequent involvement with the CIA and the British secret service. One book, *Collaborators in Crime,* displayed photographs of captured Byelorussian paratroopers with their U.S. government–issue equipment.[24] The book also reproduced many of the Nazi documents incriminating the Belarus political leaders, and named their supervisors in Radio Liberty, along with the members of the Eisenhower administration who had hired them and smuggled them to America. Other books recently published in Byelorussia showed the various collaborators, including Franz Kushel, in full Nazi uniform.[25] These volumes had never been translated into English, and none of the accusatory information on the library's open shelves had been discovered by any of the intelligence agencies.

Moreover, the Library of Congress also contained sufficient information to sustain many of the Soviet charges against the Byelorussian collaborators. Books published by the Belarus network in the Byelorussian language contain photographs of the leaders, including Kushel, Jasiuk, Sobolewsky, and many others. Even the sanitized Nazi documents reprinted by the Belarus confirmed the Soviet accounts in nearly every respect. There were admissions that they were being funded by AMCOMLIB, whose name was later changed to Radio Liberty.

The Slavic Reading Room has copies of various other Byelorus-

---

*Recently, it should be pointed out, a staff member stated that the Church Committee had actually decided to stop its investigation *before* the Welch incident, and that most Senators remained eager to investigate abuses in the future.

sian publications, including those in which the various factions accused each other of war crimes and secret collaboration with the Communists. The library's microfilm section contains copies of the *Minsker Zeitung*,[26] the Nazi newspaper published in Minsk during the occupation, which names and discusses the roles of the various collaborators. In the stack sections under "White Russian History" are various eyewitness accounts by the Jewish victims of the Byelorussian holocaust, who describe in detail the atrocities committed by the Byelorussian collaborators and the police battalions during the war.

A few blocks away from the Senate, in the Modern Military Section of the National Archives, repose microfilms of the wartime records of the Nazis for Byelorussia. The weekly SS reports named their key collaborators and reported the total number of Jews killed. The Wehrmacht reports discussed the role of the political collaborators in forming the police battalions to suppress the partisans. There is even an old OPC card index to the Nazi documents (from which the names of its agents had been removed) that could facilitate a search for a particular individual. A general index to each country had already been prepared by one of OPC's research fronts. The index contains such topics for Nazi documents as "Collaborators Civilian," "Atrocities," "Jews," and "Anti-Partisan Operations." There was only one problem: There had never been funds to translate the materials, and so they lay there while various congressional investigating committees searched for proof of illegal activity in the intelligence community.

It was not necessary to search the Library of Congress or the National Archives if one had access to a security agency. In 1977, for example, when the new head of Radio Liberty/Radio Free Europe took over, he was puzzled by the frequent charges in the Soviet press that many of his staff members were war criminals. When he started receiving reports that these same staff members were having difficulties with Jewish employees, he became alarmed. He went to pull their personnel records, only to be informed that the CIA had removed them when custody of Radio Liberty was turned back to the State Department.

A list of suspected employees—among them Stanislaw Stankievich—was submitted to State Department security, which was requested to conduct a thorough background check. Security officers contacted virtually every intelligence agency in NATO and reported the initial raw results. Most of the names were connected to various uncorroborated accusations, but in Stankievich's case, agency after agency had listed him as a former Nazi who had committed dreadful atrocities in Borissow. Stankievich had recently retired, however, and instead of continuing the investigation, Radio Liberty quietly let the matter drop.

But others in Washington were not so content. In 1977, Representative Joshua Eilberg, chairman of the House Judiciary Committee's Subcommittee on Immigration and Naturalization, and Representative Elizabeth Holtzman were convinced that there was something to the persistent rumors about Nazi war criminals residing in the United States.[27] Together they collected a list of some forty-four names which were submitted to various federal agencies. For the first time, the Department of Defense was faced with a specific request for information on war criminals by a member of Congress.

Among the names was that of Emanuel Jasiuk. Although one letter of his name was mistyped,* that should not have hindered the Pentagon's computerized files entry program, which searched out names spelled 75 percent the same. A phone call to the Defense Investigative Service was all that was needed to disclose that the Army CIC possessed a dossier on Jasiuk. In fact, the CIC dossier on Jasiuk in its Top Secret "blue files," or "Special Documents Division," contained a number of documents from different agencies discussing everything from Jasiuk's war crimes to his postwar service as an intelligence informant. It included a discussion of the decision by the consular officials in Stuttgart to condone the fraudulent statements in his visa application. All of this information was on file prior to Jasiuk's obtaining citizenship. There was also another Jasiuk dossier in the Pentagon—an Air Force file that was equally explosive. In it was a copy of the 1950 CIC correspondence with J. Edgar Hoover exposing Jasiuk as a war criminal who had fraudulently entered the United States after working for Air Force intelligence. It would have led Congress straight to the FBI's involvement in the cover-up.

---

*"Emanuel Jastuk" instead of "Emanuel Jasiuk."

Yet, the Department of Defense informed Congress in 1977 that the files of all the service intelligence agencies had been checked and no record for Jasiuk could be found.[28]

Both the Air Force and the CIC use the same computerized record index as the Pentagon. If either the Army, the Air Force, or the Defense Department had checked the computer on a 75 percent search for "Emanuel Jastuk" it would have printed out the following entry:

JASIUK, EMANUEL DB=060819 SS= PB=PL
DOSSIER LOC=AIRR YR=00 NO=X8423082 CTX=SUBJECT

This means that the Army Investigative Records Repository (AIRR) at Fort Meade had a dossier discussing a subject of investigation named Emanuel Jasiuk who was born on August 19, 1906, in Poland. Since both the Army and the Air Force dossiers cross-referenced each other, if either one had run a name trace on its own manual index, or on the Pentagon's computer index, every Jasiuk dossier would have been instantly located. In order not to find any Jasiuk dossiers, two intelligence clerks in two separate military agencies would have had to make the same series of errors simultaneously.

Congressman Eilberg did not give up, and wrote a formal letter of request to the Comptroller General asking that the General Accounting Office begin a full-scale inquiry. So that there would be no doubt as to what Congress was looking for, Eilberg carefully spelled it out:

The Immigration and Naturalization Service, with the cooperation of the Department of State, is presently compiling evidence on alleged Nazi war criminals who entered the United States fraudulently. . . . For the past two years I have been following closely the action being taken by the Service in these cases. Certain allegations have emerged which lead me and some of my colleagues to believe that the existence and backgrounds of these individuals were known to the Service for a long time without any action having been taken.

These people entered the United States and acquired benefits under the Immigration and Nationality Act in contravention of United States law. No adequate explanation has been forthcoming from the

Service as to why they did not proceed against these individuals until Congress brought the matter to their attention.

I would like to enlist the cooperation of the General Accounting Office in conducting a thorough investigation of this situation, especially to determine if Immigration personnel deliberately obstructed active prosecution of these cases or engaged in a conspiracy to withhold or quash any information in its possession.

I intend to explore all avenues to get the true facts behind these cases and the apparent negligent attitude adopted by the Immigration Service. I consider this matter to be of extreme urgency and would consider this investigation on that basis.[29]

As the audit-and-inspection branch of the government, the GAO was accustomed to dealing with bureaucratic feints. It examined a number of Immigration and Naturalization Service files for allegations of war crimes, winnowed the list down to 111 names, including both Kushel and Jasiuk, and prepared to resubmit it to the Defense Department.[30] In order to avoid any confusion over misspellings or insufficient identifying data, the GAO asked INS to list every alternate spelling found in its files, along with the date and place of each person's birth. Each of the GAO's spellings of names for Kushel and Jasiuk was an exact match of a dossier name listed in the CIC and Air Force repositories.[31]

In fact, on October 7, 1977, David Crossland, General Counsel of INS, notified GAO that Immigration had found a CIC dossier for Jasiuk, but that GAO would have to wait until the Department of Defense gave permission to see it under the "third agency rule."* Someone on Crossland's staff then removed all of the CIC material from Jasiuk's immigration file and put an internal route slip on the documents:

RE: Emanuel JASIUK, A7 165 388

Defense material NOT cleared for review by GAO.
DO NOT disclose to GAO until notified to do so.

General Counsel, Washington, D.C.

*In order to avoid inadvertent disclosure of intelligence informants working for Agency A, Agency B may not disclose a given informant's name to Agency C without A's approval. One of the side-effects of the third agency rule is that it frequently hinders, and occasionally blocks, outside investigations.

Crossland's staff at INS then notified DOD that it had come up with a Jasiuk dossier. Apparently, DOD realized that it had previously told Congressman Eilberg that no such file existed. Subsequently, Defense's response was relayed to INS, for the note bears a distinct alteration. Someone had drawn a pencil line through that part about "until notified" so that the final note now read: "Defense material NOT cleared for review by GAO." At the same time, the FBI sanitized its reports in Jasiuk's immigration file by blacking out any mention that Jasiuk had ever worked for State Department or Military Intelligence. The usual procedure is to coordinate with the third agency before attempting such deletions, so again, in 1977, DOD was apparently notified that there was CIC information in Jasiuk's immigration file. Nevertheless, when DOD officials met with the GAO investigators in April, 1978, they stated that it would be unnecessary to recheck Jasiuk's file since they had already done that for Eilberg, and no such file could be found.

When the GAO finally saw Jasiuk's immigration file, all the incriminating information linking him with intelligence operations had been removed. The GAO read the FBI's sanitized discussion of a previous CIC investigation, and concluded that this must have been the report that Crossland had mentioned earlier. There was no indication in the file that any documents had been removed, and, as if to reassure the investigators, they immediately received a letter from DOD:

> We trust our response to your April 7, 1978 letter request for records in support of your report was satisfactory. All available pertinent DOD records were provided your representative for review by April 28.

The GAO did not learn about the note or the missing DOD documents until October, 1980, when I showed them the unexpurgated file. Nor was the Department of Defense the only agency to withhold information. The FBI, the Central Office of the INS, the State Department, and the CIA all had their own dossiers on Jasiuk, containing everything from the CIC's letter to J. Edgar Hoover denouncing Jasiuk as a war criminal working for the Air Force, to the High Commissioner's letter to the State Department reminding State how it had smuggled Jasiuk in. The CIC had copies of letters from Jasiuk recruiting other war criminals for the State Department, including his cousin, Dimitri Kasmowich, whom Jasiuk identified as a former Nazi police chief in Byelorussia. There were CIC reports criticizing State Department officials who intervened to help Kasmowich avoid CIC prosecution. In all, there were about a dozen copies of various Jasiuk dossiers possessed by the intelligence community in 1978. Despite the fact that GAO asked for them from each agency, using the correct spelling of Jasiuk's name, none of the dossiers was disclosed. The only information the GAO saw was an FBI report claiming that there was no information showing Jasiuk to be a Nazi war criminal, and that, in any event, he was determined to be "trustworthy" and a good anticommunist by the FBI after a thorough investigation—hardly reason for suspicion by the GAO.*

Far more incriminating is the response of DOD to the GAO request for dossiers on Kushel. This time there is no doubt that DOD forwarded Kushel's name to CIC.[32] There were no misspellings that could be used to evade a charge of obstruction of Congress.[33] On April 29, 1979, the CIC sent the following letter to the Pentagon to report the results of their search for a Kushel dossier:

In accordance with above reference, an intensive search of the records maintained at the Investigative Records Repository (IRR) USAINSCOM, was conducted. Checks were accomplished with the Defense Central Index (DIS); Name Only Index, IRR; Special Records Division, IRR; and the Microfilm Branch, IRR. . . . The results of this search represent an exhaustive check of the IRR conducted on the basis of the information provided.[34]

The Department of Defense told the GAO it had located a file for Kushel, but that it contained no derogatory information.[35] In fact, the only file mentioned was the sanitized version supplied to the CIA back in 1956, which included just a two-page character

---

*There was not a shred of credible evidence to indicate that the GAO had been negligent in pursuing its investigation of Jasiuk. It would be a different matter if GAO had received Crossland's memo *after* reviewing the file, but I later determined that this was not the case. In any event, that still would not explain why the other agencies failed to respond to GAO's requests for their files.

reference letter, designed to show that the military had no contact with Kushel until the mid-1950s.[36] Yet the CIC had several files on Kushel, under the exact spellings furnished by GAO and exactly where the CIC claimed to have conducted its "exhaustive search."[37] In fact, Kushel was such a prominent Nazi that he was twice indexed as far back as the 1948 *Consolidated Orientation and Guidance Manual* which listed him as the president of the "ZBW," an underground organization of "White Russian War Veterans in Exile." The CIC described Kushel's ZBW as a unit of the "right-wing Kriwiczy party" whose members had collaborated in the "puppet government of White Russia," in which "Oberstleutnant Franz Kushel" was the Minister of Defense. In 1948 the Army files also listed Kushel's entry as:

> Franz (Francizek) Kushel, president (of the ZBW), Michelsdorf, Kriwiczy Chairman, born about 1896 in Novogorod, former Captain in Polish Army, former Lieutenant Colonel in a White Russian battalion created by Germans, last military unit was Russische No. 2, 29th SS Grenadier Division.

Even assuming that no one in the Pentagon or the CIC had consulted this Top Secret reference book in 1978 (which was possible), the CIC had several complete personal background dossiers each filed under alternative spellings of Kushel's name, so there was no possibility of missing any of the files the GAO requested. The individual dossiers in the Investigative Records Repository at Fort Meade included everything from Kushel's affiliation with the SD, the SS intelligence service,[38] to his participation in the Nazi government.[39] Moreover, the cross-references in either of Kushel's personal background dossiers would have led the GAO straight into the thousands of documents which the CIC had compiled on the Belarus network.[40] In fact, the cross-references indicated that there had once been a third personal background dossier on Kushel (not counting the sanitized file) in the Top Secret vault, a dossier that no one now could find.[41] Apparently, Kushel's principal file was destroyed at about the same time that other agencies were destroying theirs according to a "routine purge" in 1962, which coincidentally was the last time Kushel was under investigation for war crimes. However, no one remembered to eliminate the rest of the files for Kushel outside the vault, in the microfilm section, and there they remained, exactly where DOD said it had conducted its exhaustive search.

One of the interesting things about intelligence files is that they are so extensively cross-referenced that it is almost impossible to destroy them completely. Copies always exist in another agency, or even in another file within the same agency. For example, Jasiuk's CIC file had copies of the letter to Hoover, and so did the Air Force, either of which showed that he was a wanted war criminal.[42] Ironically, I discovered the Hoover letter by tracing the CIC documents in Jasiuk's immigration file, which (unknown to the GAO) indicated that CIC had still another Jasiuk dossier containing derogatory information.[43]

In 1979, I requested Kushel's dossiers from the same agencies which told GAO in 1978 that they had furnished all pertinent information. One agency reported to OSI in 1979 that it had no dossiers for Kushel or any of the other Byelorussian Nazis on my list, but when I went back in 1980 with proof that the dossiers existed, I came across an interesting surprise: On top of several of the dossiers there was a memo, summarizing the Nazi background of my suspect, all dated in 1979 and referencing my 1979 request. Like the GAO, I had hit a roadblock.*

With the firm support of OSI in 1980, the roadblocks began to vanish, and the files on Kushel began to appear. One document listed Kushel as a source for OPC, another that he had been working for American intelligence since 1948—a year before he emigrated. Another contained an interview with Kushel that flatly contradicted the information on his citizenship application. Another showed that Kushel was the leader of a group being funded by AMCOMLIB, the OPC front group that later became Radio Liberty. In all, there were nearly a dozen incriminating documents

---

*I asked to see the official who had relayed the message that the files did not exist and was told that he was unavailable. He had been sent away for training and was later transferred to a different job. Most of the people I tried to interview about the withholding of files had just retired or had been transferred out of the country by their respective agencies. Curiously, each of the retirees seemed once to have worked on intelligence operations in Germany around the time Kushel and Jasiuk had emigrated.

on Kushel's Nazi background in five different intelligence agencies. However, the only materials shown to GAO were sanitized file summaries asserting that there was no derogatory information available on Kushel. The GAO only saw files to the effect that Kushel was some sort of Polish freedom-fighter who had once worked in the military wing of the SS against the Communists, which in itself would not even have barred him from citizenship.

There are only two possibilities: either five separate branches of the intelligence community were stricken with simultaneous amnesia in 1978 so that they all inadvertently overlooked nearly two dozen incriminating dossiers indexed exactly as GAO requested, or a small group of individuals who knew how to protect their key informants (and themselves) sanitized, concealed, and manipulated their records so that the Belarus secret would never be made public.

On May 15, 1978, the GAO released its report to Congress entitled "Widespread Conspiracy to Obstruct Probes of Alleged Nazi War Criminals Not Supported by Available Evidence." The report concluded that the GAO had conducted an extensive search of all the intelligence agencies' files and of the twenty-nine background dossiers discovered—including one innocuous file for Kushel—and that none of the documents disclosed derogatory information. Stymied for lack of evidence, the subcommittee terminated its inquiry.

Kushel had died before the inquiry began. But a year or so after the GAO investigation, the Immigration Service was asked to determine whether Emanuel Jasiuk was still alive. The local investigator contacted his most reliable informant in South River.

Mrs. Jasiuk informed him that her husband had died.

Epilogue

March 25 is the traditional National Day of the Byelorussians of South River.

On the Sunday closest to that date—which marks the anniversary of the proclamation of the Byelorussian National Republic in 1918—they gather at the Byelorussian-American Club on Whitehead Avenue to celebrate. Some of the girls and women wear brightly colored national costumes, and there is dancing, drinking, and feasting.

On most days, the club is almost empty except for a few old men drinking in the bar, but there are some interesting customers. One of them had thrown small children into a well and dropped hand grenades on them. A frequent visitor was an executioner at the death camp at Koldichevo. Another patron teased a visitor known to be squeamish about the Holocaust by picking up a cleaver and hacking at some lunch meats. "I wish these were Jews," he declared.

The old men of South River have achieved a certain respectability. In 1978, the New Jersey American Revolution Bicentennial Celebration Commission published an *Ethnic Directory of New Jersey*. Heading the five pages of Byelorussian organizations was the American Friends of Byelorussian Central Council. Its president was listed as Emanuel Jasiuk.

Radislaw Ostrowsky had finally emigrated to America too. There was no controversy concerning his entry, but when he applied for citizenship in 1972, his file shows that the INS was notified of Ostrowsky's complete Nazi background.[1] After considerable consultation among the various intelligence services, the INS noted in his file that he "appears to have been involved in some sort of espionage activity." A reporter for a New Jersey newspaper who learned that Ostrowsky was living in the United States asked the Immigration Service if the rumors were true. The INS noted on the letter that it had no record of any such individual, but filed it in Ostrowsky's folder. When the reporter came back in 1975 with several variants on the spelling of Ostrowsky's name, the INS put that in the folder too, along with the note that the reporter had been advised by telephone that the INS had conducted a full investigation which cleared Ostrowsky completely.[2] And so the highest-ranking Nazi war criminal to enter this country lived on undisturbed until his death in 1979.

The old men of South River might have been more circumspect if they had realized that despite the clean bill of health reluctantly given them by the General Accounting Office, another investigation was closing in on them.

The Eilberg hearings had left the strong suspicion that the INS had not been as thorough as it might have been in investigating the smuggling of Nazis into the United States, and Congress requested the Justice Department to make an inquiry. An Office of Special Investigations was created within the Criminal Division early in 1979, and Walter Rockeler, Jr., who had been a prosecutor at the Nuremberg war crimes trials, was named to head it. I joined OSI a few weeks later and was assigned the cases from Byelorussia.

For two months I read the translations of the books and documents published by the Byelorussians. I learned enough of the Cyrillic alphabet to recognize the names of the leading Byelorussian war criminals and secured access to the stacks of the National Archives, where I discovered more books and documents that had not been translated. Ostrowsky's history of the Minsk convention was among them, and in the index I found numerous references to Stankievich, Jasiuk, and other leading collaborators. I compared this information with captured SS documents stored at the Archives and they corroborated each other. All the evidence clearly suggested that Nazi war criminals had been allowed to emigrate to the United States, and later to become American citizens. There were unanswered questions, however.

Who had helped them, and why?

And who had been responsible for covering up their records all these years and for stonewalling the Eilberg hearings?

As soon as he received my findings, Alan Ryan, my immediate superior, sent a Top Secret report in October 1980 to Attorney

General Benjamin Civiletti stating that this was the single most important matter in which his office was engaged. That report said, "It should be apparent that the matters discussed in this report are extremely sensitive, both because of the number of Byelorussian Nazis who entered this country, and the extent to which U.S. Government agencies apparently assisted that entry, possibly in violation of the law."

OSI was authorized to expand the scope of its investigation. More researchers and translators were hired, and security clearances were raised—my own was three access levels above Top Secret—to permit inspection of the secret records of the various intelligence services. For the first time in thirty years an effort was made to search out and coordinate all the information concerning the Byelorussian Nazis in this country.

A key operative was Marc Masurovsky, a young French-born Jew, who worked under cover among the Byelorussian community for two years. Posing as a historical researcher with a grant from the National Endowment for the Humanities, Masurovsky was accepted into the homes of the Belarus leaders in South River and other communities. He tracked down and authenticated a large number of documents vital to the inquiry, including the records of the puppet government of Byelorussia and the original roster of the militia units that were the nucleus of the Belarus Brigade.

In the vaults at Suitland, Maryland, I discovered a portion of the many dossiers that had been built up on Stankievich. Included among them was the confession that he had made to Military Intelligence in 1948. Another intelligence agency had dossiers on Stankievich in which he admitted in 1954 that he had ordered the massacre of the Jews of Borissow. Upon learning that the Army officer who had taken the 1948 confession was still on active duty, OSI asked to talk with him. The Pentagon's response was that he was working under deep cover on a secret project in Europe. Eventually, however, he was brought back for an interview by OSI.

On his return, the officer was shown a series of reports that he had written more than thirty years before, but at first he failed to remember them. "We had many Nazis working for the Army in

those days," he said. Gradually, however, the names and operations came back as his memory was refreshed by the dossiers, and
he began to recall some of the details of the cases. When told that
the Nazi collaborators mentioned in his reports were now living
in the United States as American citizens, he was shocked. "This
is mutiny," he murmured as he dropped the pages on the
desk.

I asked him how such a thing could have happened.

Someone must have sanitized the records, he replied.

Did he have any idea who had done it?

He recalled that years before there had been a special Army
intelligence unit in Germany that screened sensitive material on
informants before it was turned over to other agencies.

Was it possible that such a unit was still in existence?

He telephoned friends at the U.S. Army Investigative Records
Repository at Fort Meade, where the records had been stored
after being shipped from Germany many years earlier. He found
out that the SOD, a secret unit at Fort Meade, had responsibility
for screening the files before they were given to other agencies.
The following day the two of us went to the post, which is
located only a short drive from Washington. At SOD headquarters, we confronted a civilian employee who readily admitted
that the unit had been routinely ordered by the Department of
Defense to look over all dossiers of intelligence informants and
had deleted sensitive items. He seemed surprised at our questions, saying he was certain that the OSI had been informed of
the arrangement.*

I asked to see material that had been deleted from ten files
which I selected at random. The first dossier contained not only
Army material that had been sent to OSI but also documents

*In fact, a retired Military Intelligence official told me that the SOD was the unit which
at one time served as the principal link between the FBI and military counter-intelligence.
Consequently, the bureau had access to the unsanitized CIC files for each of the Byelorussian Nazis as part of the FBI domestic counter-intelligence program. That may explain why
the FBI files made only cursory reference to the fact that its informants admitted serving
the Germans during the occupation. The FBI had no need to duplicate the voluminous
information provided by the SOD. Perhaps coincidentally, several people associated with
the SOD had been stationed in Germany on intelligence operations after the war. I never
had a chance to interview them, since they retired from the Army or were transferred
overseas immediately after the GAO investigation.

belonging to other agencies as well. I looked at the name on it: Emanuel Jasiuk. In it was a letter to the State Department from the office of John J. McCloy, the new civilian High Commissioner in Germany. Written at the time that Jasiuk had applied for citizenship, the letter reminded the State Department that three of its officials had knowingly allowed Jasiuk to present a fraudulent personal history to the visa-screening officer in the Stuttgart consulate. The file also contained correspondence between the CIC and J. Edgar Hoover in which the FBI director was informed that Jasiuk was a war criminal who had worked for Air Force Intelligence.[3]

None of this material had been supplied to the Eilberg inquiry or to OSI, despite repeated requests. Had it been turned over to the congressional investigators, the cross-references would have uncovered the entire Byelorussian Nazi underground and the subsequent cover-up. Of the ten files I reviewed, three contained clear evidence that U.S. agencies had assisted Nazi collaborators to emigrate to this country. A fourth file included the case history of a Soviet spy who had posed as a Nazi during the war but had later defected to American intelligence and provided eyewitness descriptions of war crimes committed by Byelorussian Nazis, including Jasiuk. After confirming the defector's allegations through its own network of informants, the Army gave him a new identity and helped him to emigrate to a country other than the United States. This information confirmed the reports that some of the Byelorussian émigrés in this country not only were war criminals but that their ranks had been penetrated by Soviet spies.

By backtracking through the labyrinth of the various intelligence agency archives, with the aid of the cross-references provided by these files, the OSI built up a strong case for denaturalization against living Byelorussian collaborators. Unfortunately, the United States has no law to punish the members of the Belarus network for murders committed in their native Byelorussia. Without criminal jurisdiction the only action the Justice Department can take against these ex-Nazi collaborators is to bring suit to revoke their citizenship and try to have them deported, a difficult and lengthy process. These men perpetrated their crimes nearly forty years ago in a foreign country, and most of the surviving witnesses are behind the Iron Curtain. To compound the difficulties, the Soviet government has failed to cooperate—it has withheld evidence against the Byelorussians while providing documentation about other national groups, such as the Ukrainians and Baltic peoples. An educated guess is that this Soviet policy is designed to protect their former—and possibly present—agents who infiltrated the Belarus network.

Stanislaw Stankievich was to have been the first to face proceedings to strip him of his citizenship. There was conclusive proof that he had lied on his visa application, had procured his citizenship by fraud, was an admitted perjurer, a strident anti-Semite, a high-ranking Nazi collaborator, a suspected Soviet agent, and a confessed murderer. But the "Butcher of Borissow" died on November 3, 1980, before hearings could begin in the federal district court in New York City. Oddly enough, the first report we received of Stankievich's death came from the Procurator General of the Soviet Union, whom we had asked to supply witnesses against him.

Yet we had never supplied the Russians with Stankievich's address and, in keeping with Orthodox tradition, an obituary notice did not appear until sixty days after he died.

Late in 1980, the OSI asked John Tipton—the General Accounting Office supervisor who had helped prepare the report downgrading the possibility of a conspiracy to smuggle the Nazi war criminals into the United States—to examine the material we had gathered. We gave him the voluminous files that had been amassed on Jasiuk and Franz Kushel. Tipton was plainly embarrassed as he leafed through the dossiers, saying he had never seen the material before. And when he spotted the most recent entries, which admonished the clerks at the Immigration Service not to reveal the enclosed Army material to the GAO, he shook his head. "My God!" he exclaimed. "How could this have happened?"

The cover-up arose initially out of what were perceived to be the legitimate needs of national security. Imbued with the anticommunist spirit of the Cold War, intelligence officials decided to fight fire with fire—to enlist Eastern European Nazis with anti-Soviet backgrounds in a guerrilla and propaganda war against the Soviet Union. These Americans were not evil or vicious; they believed that moral ends justified immoral means. Allen Dulles put it best. Asked why he made use of someone like Reinhard Gehlen, the Director of Central Intelligence replied: "There are few archbishops in espionage. He's on our side and that's all that matters. Besides, one needn't ask him to one's club."[4]

Over the years, however, the emphasis of the cover-up switched from protecting ongoing operations and agents to protecting the men who had smuggled the Nazis into the United States. Wisner and his associates had violated several laws, including the Trading with the Enemy Act, and some statutes of limitations did not run out until 1961, but there were other reasons for the persistence of the cover-up. The major one was the change in the international climate. The Belarus conspiracy was a product of the Cold War and confrontation between the United States and the Soviet Union. Rightly or wrongly, the American people and American policymakers were convinced that Stalin was determined to dominate the world and tailored their actions to meet the perceived threat. Anything that made trouble for the Russians was permissible—including the enlistment of Nazi collaborators. Critics were isolated as appeasers, enemies of the state, or, in the heyday of McCarthyism, "soft on communism."

In the 1960s there came a change in American attitudes toward foreign policy and covert action. The war in Vietnam, which carried Cold War thinking to its logical end, was deemed too costly in blood and money. Covert action was discredited by the failure of the CIA-sponsored Bay of Pigs expedition, the attempts to assassinate Fidel Castro, and the efforts to undermine the elected government of Salvador Allende in Chile. It was not the time to disclose the embarrassing details about the smuggled Nazi collaborators. Bureaucracies bury their embarrassments in the files.

So the cover-up continued long after there was any legitimate need for it. OPC veterans hoped that the records of the errors of the past would remain undisturbed in the vaults of the various intelligence agencies. As they retired they took with them the cryptonyms needed to unlock these secrets. There were, of course, those for whom the cover-up never ended. During the 1960s Military Intelligence found it necessary to lie to the Immigration Service upon several occasions when asked for information from its files, in order to conceal complicity in the smuggling operation. Within the CIA several old OPC hands still loyal to their Nazi protégés frustrated congressional and Justice Department requests for information. Exculpatory documents were inserted in CIA records, and incriminating SS files were removed from the National Archives. The FBI refused to provide OSI with the complete dossiers on its Byelorussian informants, such as Anton Adamovitch of Radio Liberty. Only heavily censored summaries that did not reflect the full Nazi background of those under investigation were supplied. And at Fort Meade the sanitizing process continued because of bureaucratic inertia. Without knowing why they were doing it—like Japanese soldiers holding out on Pacific islands long after the end of World War II—the SOD clerks continued to delete any information from the files pertaining to intelligence operatives connected with OPC.

Not all the blame for the cover-up belongs to the Cold War intelligence community. The congressmen who were in charge of overseeing intelligence programs at that time must share the responsibility because of their failure to perform the duties assigned them. As long ago as 1956, Senator Leverett Saltonstall of Massachusetts, a member of one of the CIA oversight committees, stated:

It is not a reluctance on the part of CIA officials to speak to us. Instead it is a question of our reluctance, if you will, to seek information and knowledge on subjects which I personally, as a member of Congress and as a citizen, would rather not have, unless I believed it to be my responsibility to have it because it might involve the lives of American citizens.[5]

I asked two former members of OPC and two retired CIA officials if it were true that no one ever told Congress about the Nazi connection or the details of Wisner's secret war. They replied that they learned about the Nazis only from contacts in their individual overseas operations, and none of them had ever known of the Nazis in America. They doubted that Wisner or Dulles informed Congress, but most seemed fairly certain that Congress never asked, because members rarely asked about *any* "operational details." Even Eisenhower's Twenty Committee never pressed for explanations on how the Communists were to be defeated, or just when. If Nixon and Rockefeller were given briefings on the Nazis, it was done privately and not through regular channels. One very senior official interviewed recently did recall that C. D. Jackson of Eisenhower's White House staff was squeezed off the Twenty Committee because he favored psychological warfare rather than the more popular paramilitary and political action programs, which his successors, Nixon and Rockefeller, authorized with enthusiasm.

We talked at length about the traditional methods of security compartmentalization, which keeps all but a handful of officials from knowing the complete picture of an intelligence operation. I asked if it were possible that this same system of compartmentalization had prevented Wisner's rivals from discovering the full extent of his Nazi-recruiting program while he was with the State Department, and even after he left the post of DDP. Yes, they replied, it was possible. Wisner would have needed only a handful of operatives in the visa section of various consulates to bring anyone he wished to America. Once the underground railroad was established, it could continue running even after OPC was merged into the CIA, and neither Congress nor the President would know.

The situation has not improved over the last quarter-century.[6] There is a continuous lack of scrutiny, a heritage of congressional negligence that allows the intelligence community to act on its own authority. Without the assent or knowledge of the present members of Congress, intelligence agencies are believed to be smuggling a modern band of "war criminals" into the United States. The leader of this group, who was installed in power in a Middle Eastern country by the OPC three decades ago and is alleged to have persecuted 200,000 innocent civilians, was recently approved for sanctuary in the United States. Although the leader was reported executed before he could escape to America, it now appears that his followers are entering this country in significant numbers. Because the matter is currently classified, I cannot discuss it further.

Still, Congress and the American people must know this much: The unlocking of the Belarus secret is not the end of the conspiracy. It is only the beginning.

Notes

CHAPTER ONE

1. For background on Wisner see William R. Corson, *The Armies of Ignorance* (Dial Press, 1977), pp. 306–10; Thomas Powers, *The Man Who Kept the Secrets* (Alfred A. Knopf, 1979), pp. 32–33; obituary in the Washington *Post,* October 30, 1965.

2. Gehlen's operations are described in E. H. Cookridge, *Gehlen: Spy of the Century* (Random House, 1972).

3. *Ibid.,* pp. 203–04.

4. The best account of the history of Byelorussia is Nicholas P. Vakar, *Belorussia: The Making of a Nation* (Harvard University Press, 1956).

5. For post-World War I activities in Byelorussia and émigré politics, I have relied upon V. Kalush, *In the Service of the People for a Free Belorussia: Biographical Notes on Professor Radislav Ostrowski,* which was published in Byelorussian in London in 1964. A reliable source indicates that this work is actually an autobiography written by Ostrowsky under a pen name. It will be cited below as Ostrowsky's biography.

6. Polish oppression in Byelorussia is discussed in Stephan Horak, *Poland and Her National Minorities, 1919–1939* (Vantage Press, 1961), pp. 170–80.

7. According to "Parliament Rzeczypospolitej Polskiej" (Parliament of the Republic of Poland) 1919–1927, edited by Professors Henryk Miscicki and Woldzimierz Dzwonkowski, published by Lucjan Zlotnicki for the Polish Government in Warsaw in 1928, "Sobolevsky was deputy to the Polish Parliament in 1926, representing the Byelorussian Socialist Party and this was a Communist Party." Ironically, allegations about Sobolewsky's Communist background were previously known to the FBI. See letter of December 21, 1950, from J. Edgar Hoover to Chief, Security Division, U.S. Department of State.

8. According to Ostrowsky's biography, pp. 28–29, he was accused of receiving funds from Bolshevik sources to finance subversive activities of the Gramada.

9. The Vilna trials are described in Henryk Frankle's *Poland: The Struggle for Power, 1772–1939* (Lindsey Drummond Ltd., 1946), pp. 155–56.

10. The Gramada leaders who fled to the Soviet Union were executed on Solovky Island as Polish spies. Union Calendar No. 929, 83rd Congress, Second Session, "Communist Takeover and Occupation of Belorussia," Washington, 1955, p. 14.

11. For Russian émigré politics in the pre–World War II period see Geoffrey Bailey, *The Conspirators* (Harper & Bros., 1960).

12. For an overview of the SS structure, see Heinz Hohne, *The Order of the Death's Head* (Coward-McCann, 1970).

13. According to the Nazi historical work *Weissrutheniein Volk und Land* by Eugen Freiherr von Engelhardt (Volk und Reich Verlag, 1943), the leading representatives of the "Byelorussian Union of University Students" before World War II were: Abramchyk, M. (Paris, France); Cherepukan, I. (Chicago, U.S.); Kasmovich, D. (Belgrade, Yugoslavia); Rusak, V. (Prague, Czechoslovakia); Tsikota (Rome, Italy); Vasileuski, K. (Ghent, Belgium); Waronka, J. (Chicago, U.S.); Zakharka, V. (Prague, Czechoslovakia). Over half of the persons on this list became Nazi collaborators during the war.

14. The Self-Help Committee was described by Stanislaw Hrynkievich as an agency that "provided help, mostly financial, for needy White Ruthenian subjects, after they had been investigated and found 'worthy' by Nazi standards." Interrogation Report, No. 2, Third Army, May 12, 1945.

15. For an overview of Byelorussia from the SS perspective, see "Tätigkeiten & Lageberichte No. 2651," pp. 29–34, microfilm frames nos. 226392–397.

16. In his biography, pp. 34–35, Ostrowsky admits that in the summer of 1940 he was already in contact with the Byelorussian committees at Warsaw, Poznan, and Berlin. His biography names the leaders of those various committees, many of them former students of Ostrowsky. In a confidential interview with a Western intelligence agency, Ostrowsky admitted that the work of the committees was secretly funded by the Gestapo.

17. Extensive documentation concerning the role of the *SS Einsatzgruppen* in conducting mass executions is set forth in Raoul Hilberg, *The Destruction of the European Jews* (Octagon, 1978).

18. Background on Dr. Six is in Cookridge, *op. cit.,* p. 242.

19. A list of the Byelorussian guides and the particular cities to which they were assigned by the SS is contained in interview M-34 (GBV).

CHAPTER TWO

1. For an overview of Operation Barbarossa see Alexander Werth, *Russia at War, 1941–1945* (Dutton, 1964), pp. 131–58. The major work on the German occupation of the Soviet Union is Alexander Dallin, *German Rule in Russia 1941–1945* (St. Martin's Press, 1957).

2. Ostrowsky's biography mentions that the Byelorussian National Committee in Warsaw furnished forty members who were assigned to administrative jobs under the Germans. It was Ostrowsky who devised the system of putting them in pairs.

3. The recruitment of pro-German administrators from among the Byelorussian collaborators is described in "Tätigkeiten & Lageberichte No. 1," National Archives Nuremberg Collection Document No. 2651.

4. According to captured German documents in the National Archives, the local collaborators were required to register the Jews with provisional visas. The "purpose of the visa: possibility of elimination of all undesirables." Document of 20 July 1941, Military Administration Group, Army Group Center, National Archives Microfilm Section T120, Roll 2533, frames 292820–821.

5. Captured Nazi documents clearly establish that the Jews in the ghettos were under the control of the civilian police. Report No. 70, National Archives Microfilm Section T175, Roll 233, frames 2722148–152.

6. The connection of the collaborators to the civil administration under the Germans is described in SS document Ereignesmeldungen No. 97 (1941), National Archives Microfilm Section T175, Roll 233, frames 2722679–688.

7. The effect of the Nazi instructions to the collaborators can be seen by comparing Report No. 27 (19 July 1941), "Greater Cooperation Is Expected Considering the Catching of . . . Intelligence, Jews, etc." with the next week's report (24 July 1941), "In Minsk, the whole Jewish Intelligentsia Has Been Liquidated." National Archives Microfilm Section T175, Roll 233, frames 2721633–637.

8. According to captured SS records, White Ruthenian collaborators were appointed to positions in the civil administration in all cities touched by the *Einsatzgruppen* (the mobile killing units). Ereignesmeldungen No. 43, National Archives Microfilm Section T177, Roll 233, frames 2721772–782.

9. Although many of the Byelorussians claimed that they were elected to their offices, captured German documents clearly established

that it was they who installed the collaborators as mayors. National Archives Microfilm Section T120, Roll 2533, frames 292820–830.

10. The connection between the *Einsatzgruppen* and the provisional administration established in Byelorussia is discussed repeatedly in several captured SS documents contained in the National Archives. See, for example, National Archives Microfilm Group T175, Roll 233, Report No. 27, frame 2721570; Report No. 21, frames 2721490–91; Report No. 21, frame 2721496; Report No. 36, frames 2721692–93; Report No. 90, frames 2722485–87; Report No. 97, frame 2722688. It should be emphasized that these are the actual weekly reports from the mobile killing units themselves.

11. Stankievich is discussed in Volume 5 of the Nuremburg documents series (Red Set).

12. Stankievich's role as mayor of Borissow is described in the following German documents and SS reports: Microfilm Group T194, Roll 235, frames 429–433; Microfilm Group T454, Roll 26, frame 71; Microfilm Group T315, Roll 1586, frame 359; and Nuremberg document PS-3047.

13. Soennecken's report is in the *Congressional Record Appendix,* August 7, 1948. Nuremberg Document No. 3047-PS.

14. Evidently, Ehoff was pardoned by the Communists after the war. According to the Soviet propaganda booklet "How They Served the People," p. 34, "David Ehof, a Russianized German from the Volga Region and one of the active participants of the bloody events at Borisov in 1941, now lives in A Free Settlement in the Soviet Union. . . ."

15. The role of the White Russian police in the systematic slaughter of the Byelorussian ghettos is described in the English section of the 550-page Yiddish-language book "Sefer Steibtz-Swerzene" [Memorial Book of Stolpce] (Israel, 1964). According to Jewish eyewitnesses, the method of extermination was quite systematized:

For two days they dug a pit that was 150 meters long and 2½ meters deep. The Jews were loaded on lorries. Those who refused to climb up were beaten savagely or killed on the spot.

The shrieks of the poor people split the heavens. The lorries were driven by local White Russian drivers. Beside the pit stood Germans, Letts and White Russian police with machine-guns. The Jews were ordered to take their clothes off. Men, women and children stood naked. Their belongings, their rings, their money and everything else was taken away from them. These were placed in a row on the edge of the pit and the machine-guns began chattering and killing. Living people also fell into the pits which were then covered with a layer of sand.

16. The *Encyclopedia Judaica* lists hundreds, perhaps thousands, of small Byelorussian and Ukrainian villages that were subjected to the same treatment.

17. On November 1, 1941, General Wilhelm Kube wrote a letter to the Reichs Kommissar for the Eastern Territories, Gauleiter Heinrich Lohse, at Riga, protesting the Slutsk massacre:

Peace and order cannot be maintained in White Ruthenia with methods of that sort. To bury seriously wounded people alive who work their way out of their graves again, is such a base and filthy act that this incident as such should be reported to the Fuehrer and Reichs Marshal. The civil administration of White Ruthenia makes very strenuous efforts to win the population over to Germany in accordance with the instructions of the Fuehrer. These efforts cannot be brought in harmony with the methods described herein. . . .

18. Paromchyk Galina, *The Tragedy of Koldychevo,* from the library of the newspaper "Voice of the Motherland" (Minsk, 1962), discusses the 1962 war crimes trial in Baranovitche, Byelorussia, of four accused murderers. The book also contains detailed allegations against Ostrowsky, Franz Kushel, Boris Ragulia, Sergei Gutyrchik, and Victor Zhdan, all of whom were alleged to be living in the United States.

19. Solomon Schiadow, Memoirs, FBI files.

20. Vakar, *op. cit.,* Chapter 12, contains an objective account of the Nazi occupation of Byelorussia.

21. Many of the collaborators had religious backgrounds. The Orthodox theological schools had lower fees than grammar schools in Byelorussia, although their graduates were restricted to academic careers at the theological seminaries. Up to 1906, theological scholars were barred from the universities (Ostrowsky, biography, pp. 10–11).

22. On partisan warfare, see Vakar, *op. cit.;* Werth, *op. cit.,* pp. 710–26; and V. K. Kiselev, *Partizanskaya Razvedka* (Partisan Intelligence Work) (Minsk, 1980).

23. Ostrowsky admitted that he had no idea whether the Communists in his administration were secretly planted by the NKVD. However, both the SS and the German administration agreed that the shortage of trained collaborators made the hiring of Communist officials necessary (Ostrowsky's biography, pp. 44–45).

24. Vakar, *op. cit.,* chap. 12.

25. For Gehlen's memorandum, see Dallin, *op. cit.,* pp. 545–46.

26. Ostrowsky's biography, pp. 49–50, notes that on December 20, 1943, Sobolewsky sent him a telegram from Minsk, as chairman of the Byelorussian Relief Organization (Self-Help) inviting him to a conference the next day with SS General von Gottberg. Sobolewsky's version of the meeting is contained in "The Truth About ABN" by Niko Nakashidze (Munich, 1960), p. 54.

CHAPTER THREE

1. Ostrowsky's biography.

2. Decree No. 2 of the President of the Byelorussian Central Council, City of Minsk, January 15, 1944, appointed Kushel, Sobolewsky, and Hrynkievich among the first fourteen members of the Byelorussian Central Council. Copy of document in Byelorussian propaganda book *For the National Independence of Byelorussia* (London, 1960; copy in Library of Congress).

3. The *Minsker Zeitung* is a useful source for identifying the names and ranks of the various collaborators. For example, a man named Russak was identified as the city mayor for Baranovitche and Stankievich was reported as the representative of the Byelorussian Central Council for the region of Baranovitche at the time Ostrowsky visited the city to conduct an anti-partisan propaganda campaign. According to the Nazi press accounts, first Russak spoke of the role of the Central Council in undertaking the war against the "Jewish Bolsheviks." Stankievich spoke next on the need for building better trust with the German civil administration. Ostrowsky then spoke of the terrible atrocities being perpetrated by the NKVD.

4. Minutes No. 1A of the Byelorussian Central Government meeting of Regional Deputies, and the Byelorussian Regional Defense Chiefs, Minsk City, March 28, 29, and 30, 1944, contains a transcript of the discussion on organizing the draft mobilization for the Nazis. During the meeting, Stankievich complained that their forces were more poorly equipped than the other collaborator military units. One of the other collaborators replied that when we were talking about the "uniforms the question was not to look handsome but to have strength." Stankievich in return claimed that he had organized a force of some 64 officers, 382 sub-officers, and 6,000 riflemen. (Copy in Byelorussian propaganda book *For the National Independence of Byelorussia,* Library of Congress.)

5. Ostrowsky cooperated wholeheartedly with General von Gottberg's request for assistance in combating the partisans. See, for example,

letter of June 8, 1944, from Ostrowsky to the commander of the Slutzk Byelorussian Regional Defense Force (BRD):

> Attached please find a copy of my letter to General Commissar of Byelorussia from 5-25-44 and a copy of his answer from 6-6-1944. I am ordering you to send to the most endangered part of the villages special units of BRD battalions under the command of the most qualified officers.

Copy of letter in Byelorussian propaganda book *For the National Independence of Byelorussia* (London, 1960; copy in Library of Congress).

6. Sven Steenberg, *Vlasov* (Alfred A. Knopf, 1970), pp. 71–73.

7. The planning for the congress in Minsk took place just as the news of the British and American landings in Normandy were reaching Byelorussia. During one of the planning conferences, Ostrowsky's vice-president, Shkelonak, realized that the invasion meant the end of the German Reich, and suggested that it might not even be wise to hold the congress. When Ostrowsky heard of the blunder, he called the SS official directly and explained that Shkelonak's German was not that good, and that he really meant the time was right for the congress to begin (Ostrowsky's biography, pp. 56–59).

8. *Ibid.*, pp. 59–60.

9. Ostrowsky's close relationships with the SS and the Wehrmacht gave him special standing among the collaborators in exile in Berlin: "Here I should stress that the BCC at that time had such standing that the leaders of the other non-Russian nations looked to it in matters of policy. This is probably the reason why Himmler put the BCC most under pressure. Due credit should be given in this connection to the late Professor Dr. Von Mende, who is opposed to Himmler's policy and who is a great friend to all the non-Russian peoples enslaved by the Bolsheviks." (Ostrowsky's biography, p. 62).

10. Franz Kushel insisted that the Byelorussian army should be organized and used only in the struggle against Bolshevism. Apparently, he too was concerned that his troops might be used on the western front. Copy of document in Byelorussian propaganda book *For the National Independence of Byelorussia* (London, 1960; copy in the Library of Congress).

11. Minutes of the meeting of the Presidium of the Byelorussian Central Council of September 26, 1944 (Berlin) indicated that permission had been received to reorganize the Byelorussian legion. "From the conversation, it can be seen that the German military authorities in principle agree to the organization of Byelorussian military forces, the

word army is even used . . . initially two divisions are to be created, a combat one and reserve one . . . the outlook for the organization of Byelorussian forces is quite good." Copy of document in Byelorussian propaganda book *For the National Independence of Byelorussia* (London, 1954; Library of Congress).

12. The SS unit designation is described in National Archives document microfilm roll T45426/85–86. According to the Army letter of November 30, 1956, from the ACSI-CDO0, "Under the auspices of the German Wehrmacht Kushel was placed in command of Belo-Russian Brigade which subsequently was expanded into a division. Kushel was made division commander (2-star general) and fought until the end of the war. He surrendered to the Germans in what became the French zone of Germany." The last sentence erroneously suggested that Kushel fought against the Germans, not for them.

13. Minutes of the meeting of the Presidium of the Byelorussian Central Council in Berlin, December 12, 1944. The minutes note that Dr. Stankievich, the editor of the newspaper *Ranitsa,* was invited to the meeting along with Colonel Kushel and several others. Ostrowsky discussed the position of the BCC with regard to General Vlasov's army. Ostrowsky spoke of the continued need to prevent the Byelorussian forces from being absorbed into Vlasov's divisions. Copy in Byelorussian propaganda book *For the National Independence of Byelorussia* (London, 1954; Library of Congress).

14. According to one version, as the Allies were approaching, General Kushel went to see General Maltsov of General Vlasov's army. Maltsov and Kushel decided to defect to the U.S. Army. Between them and the U.S. troops was a German SS division stationed in Eisenstein-stadt. According to a knowledgeable source, Maltsov and Kushel sent emissaries to the American commander and at his direction fought through the German SS division until they reached Zwissel, where they joined the U.S. troops and were interned as prisoners of war.

CHAPTER FOUR

1. On Bradley's telephone call to Patton, see Omar N. Bradley, *A Soldier's Story* (Henry Holt, 1951).

2. Patton's comments on the Soviets are quoted in Cookridge, *op. cit.,* p. 127.

3. The most detailed account of Operation Keelhaul is in Nicholas Bethell, *The Last Secret* (Basic Books, 1974).

4. The flight from Berlin to the western regions of Germany is described in Ostrowsky's biography, p. 63.

5. General Anders was trying to keep the members of his "Polish Army" intact in the camps until a more permanent home could be found. *New York Times,* May 20, 1946.

6. From an OSI informant.

7. Among Stankievich's many employers was the Language Institute of the World Church Service at Ulm/Danube where he was employed from March 10, 1949 to May 1, 1950. It should also be noted that the World Church Service was frequently listed as sponsor of Byelorussian Nazis into the United States under the Displaced Persons Act.

8. According to Ostrowsky's biography, p. 70, the members of the BCC remained in hiding in the British, American, and French zones of western Germany "because the majority of them were afraid that they might be called to account before the Allies for collaboration with the Germans during the War." Ostrowsky recognized that it was necessary to suspend the activities of the BCC and create another front group for the U.S. zone, the Byelorussian National Committee, formed at the Regensburg DP camp (where most of the Belarus SS legion was then located).

9. The history of the various postwar conventions, the attempts to escape repatriation as war criminals, and the subsequent reorganization in the United States is more fully described in FBI File NY97-1251. According to the FBI, Ostrowsky's BCR organization in the DP camps had about 4,000 members, about half of whom later emigrated to America. This, of course, does not include those members of the Belarus who sided with Abramtchik's faction, such as Kushel and Stankievich. As of 1954, according to the FBI, this faction had more than a thousand members living in the United States.

10. Abramtchik's Gestapo background in Paris is also noted in a document contained in the Stankievich "blue file," USAIRR, Ft. Meade, Maryland.

11. Paragraph 189 of the 1948 CIC *Consolidated Guidance Manual* noted that the Abramtchik faction apparently had connections to the NTS and also received funds from the Vatican.

12. The most complete account available of Gehlen's activities is in Cookridge. Gehlen's own memoirs are less candid.

13. For background on the OSS, see Kermit Roosevelt, *The War Report of the OSS* (Walker, 1976).

14. The dismembering of OSS was accomplished in a letter from President Truman to Secretary of State Byrnes, September 20, 1945. *Public Papers of the President of the United States, Harry S. Truman, April 12 to December 31, 1945* (Government Printing Office, 1961), p. 331.

15. For the breakup of the OSS see *Final Report, U.S. Senate Select Committee to Study Intelligence Operations* (Government Printing Office, 1976), Book IV, pp. 5–6.

CHAPTER FIVE

1. Quoted in Andrew Tully, *CIA, The Inside Story* (William Morrow, 1962) p. 16.

2. The organization of the CIG is outlined in *Select Committee Report, op. cit.,* pp. 6–12.

3. Immediately after the war there was a great deal of controversy about the possibility of Nazis residing in the DP camps. See *New York Times,* March 2, 1946, p. 1 ("U.S. Must Turn Over Members of Axis Army"); March 10, 1946, p. 5 ("Weeding Out Nazis in POW Camps"); May 12, 1946, p. 18 ("Army Screening to Seek Imposters"); March 24, 1946, p. 16 ("Nazis Living in Camps"); March 30, 1949, p. 17 ("Nazi Camp Guard Posing as Displaced Person"); April 1, 1949 ("Former Camp Guard Held at Ellis Island").

4. The existence of the Belarus SS and other collaborationist units did not go entirely unnoticed in the DP camps. See *New York Times,* March 24, 1946, p. 16.

5. Kushel's transformation of the White Russian "Boy Scouts" into the military formation of the BVA is discussed in paragraph 204 of Chapter V, p. 50, 1948 CIC *Consolidated Guidance* report.

6. Friedrich Buchardt's unpublished manuscript is entitled "Die Behandlung Des Russischen Problems Wahrend Der Zeit Des Nationalsozialistischen Regimes in Deutschland." (The Treatment of the Russian Problem During the Period of the Nazi Regime in Germany). Top Secret, ACSI—Sensitive Document File, Suitland, Maryland.

7. For a discussion of how the ex-Nazis assisted Soviet intelligence agents in the Byelorussian DP camps after the war, see Stankievich's "blue file," USAIRR, Ft. Meade, Maryland.

8. Text of the Byelorussian charges is in UN Record of Debates, October 31, 1947.

9. The first request for the apprehension of Bandera was by letter from General Sidlov, Chief Soviet MVD, Brandenberg, Germany, dated June 29, 1946, to the Assistant Chief of Staff, United States Forces, European Theatre. A reply was sent by the Army in July 1946 entitled "Bandera, Stephen Andrew, war criminal." Apparently unsatisfied with the reply, Sidlov wrote another letter to General Sibert in August 1946. Sibert, of course, was Gehlen's supervisor, and Gehlen was Bandera's

employer. Copies of the Army's subsequent false denial of any knowledge of Bandera's whereabouts can be found in the Stankievich "blue file." The Soviet Union continued its denunciations of the United States for failure to cooperate with the return of their nationals from European refugee camps. See *New York Times,* January 5, 1953, p. 3.

10. After his confession, the military forwarded the following secret report up the CIC chain of command referencing the UN charges:

> Stanislaw Stankevich is probably identical with Stanislas Stankevich who resides in Osterhoffen, D.P. Camp. Allegedly he was the former commander of the White Ruthenian S.S. in Minsk. Later he published a White Ruthenian language paper in Germany during the Nazi regime. Currently he is the leader in the US zone of the BNC White Ruthenian National Center, an illegal organization which apparently serves as a steering committee for the rightist elements of the White Ruthenian immigration. . . . Many of its members were officials of the Nazi puppet government in Minsk during 1941–43 and continued as a government-in-exile in Berlin in 1944.

The document goes on to indicate that the Army had knowledge of the whereabouts of many other Byelorussian and Ukrainian Nazis who were at that time denounced in the United Nations as war criminals. (Copy in Stankievich's "blue file," Ft. Meade, Maryland.)

In 1951 a letter was sent by the Army in response to the January 1948 UN General Assembly charges that the U.S. was harboring persons listed as war criminals. Included on the list was Stankievich, "allegedly in charge of massacres in the Borrissov region and later editor of the fascist newspaper *Ranitsa.*" The Army, of course, already possessed extensive information on Stankievich, but told Washington that:

> A check of files on informants of CIC revealed one Stankiewicz, first name unknown, Deputy President of White Russian Committee, and an anti-communist group existing in the US and French zones of Germany, location unknown.
>
> 2. The G2 record section further contains information quoting to one Stankiewycz, Dr. Stanislav as follows:
>
> Member of the organization "Byelorussian National Center," a speaker at an Edinburgh Conference of the International Conference of Refugees held under the auspices of the Scottish League for European Freedom," an anticommunist organization.
>
> 3. All other indicated files checked on 21 November 1951 disclosed no derogatory information.

Prior to submission of the sanitized report, the Army had received corroborating information from other intelligence agencies that the "Stankiewycz" who attended the Edinburgh Conference was the same person who was charged with having committed atrocities in Borissow during the German occupation, and later became editor of *Ranitsa.*

11. For organization of the CIA see *Select Committee Report, op. cit.,* pp. 12–20.

12. Leonard Mosley, *Dulles* (Dial Press, 1978), p. 114.

13. The CIA and the Italian election is discussed in Powers, *op. cit.,* pp. 29–30.

14. The Clay "war scare" cable is discussed in *Select Committee Report, op. cit.,* p. 29.

15. Founding of OPC is discussed in *ibid.,* pp. 29–36.

16. Corson, *op. cit.,* p. 307.

17. Top Secret State Department Decimal Files, 1948–49. National Archives.

18. Powers, *op. cit.,* pp. 55, 73. But until his death Wisner's name rarely appeared in print. For example, *The Nation* devoted its whole issue of June 24, 1961, to Fred J. Cook's 44-page article on the CIA and its operations without mentioning Wisner or the OPC.

19. Stewart Alsop, *The Center* (Harper & Row, 1968), pp. 215–16.

20. William Colby, *Honorable Men* (Simon & Schuster, 1978), p. 73.

21. Quoted in Mosley, *op. cit.,* p. 243.

22. General Clay was apparently aware of the connection between the Byelorussians and the Nazi government. FBI File NY97-1251 has a copy of a letter from the Byelorussians to Clay in 1948 which describes the political institutions established in Byelorussia "although under the difficult circumstances of the German occupation."

23. Paragraph 175, Chapter 5, p. 45 of the 1948 CIC names several other Byelorussians who had been denounced as war criminals and whose extradition was sought by the Soviets.

CHAPTER SIX

1. The 1948 CIC *Consolidated Guidance* report, paragraph 167, reported that on the previous December 10, leading White Russian personalities including "Radislau Ostrowsky (former president of the Nazi puppet state), and several other senators who had remained in comparative obscurity after the war, met in a small village near Aalan to rebuild an organization dedicated to the unity of all White Russian people in exile."

2. The military had a very difficult time sorting out the accusations flying back and forth between the factions, as a document in Stankievich's "blue file," USAIRR, Ft. Meade, Maryland, shows:

The denunciations are not all logical and consistent. It is noted that some of the leaders are denounced for being Soviet agents and for having collaborated with the Nazis, and Stankievich, mentioned above, was denounced for being a Soviet agent, a Nazi collaborator and as a collaborator with U.S. Occupation Forces.

Apparently, it did not occur to the military that all of the denunciations might have had some basis in fact.

3. Cookridge, *op. cit.*, pp. 245–52.

4. The United States Army not only recruited the labor service companies but gave them arms as well. *New York Times,* February 4, 1946, p. 1.

The *Times,* March 13, 1947, p. 7, said that about 10,000 non-Germans were used for guard duty in the U.S. and British zones of Germany.

5. According to the 1948 CIC *Consolidated Guidance* report, a group known as the "White Russian National Counterintelligence" revealed in February 1948 that it was organizing a group of young White Russians in guerrilla warfare and intelligence and was planning to dispatch them on missions to White Russia. The group indicated that it would be in contact with U.S. authorities as soon as this organization was ready for action. The leaders of the training group were also noted by the CIC as persons whom the Soviets had desired extradited because of their participation in atrocities in Byelorussia.

6. The extent of the Soviet attempts to gain information on Wisner's plans can be readily understood from a review of what Stankievich was requested to obtain by Nina Litwinczyk. Summaries of the Soviet espionage requests are contained in Stankievich's "blue file," USAIRR, Ft. Meade, Maryland.

7. The incident of the partisan mole living in the United States is described in FBI File No. NK105-1478.

8. In the July 12, 1955, issue of *Novoye Russkoye Slovo,* Abramtchik was interviewed concerning the charge that he had been a Communist in his youth. Instead of denying the allegation, Abramtchik said that "I don't consider it necessary to react with slander. And finally, even if I had been a Bolshevik once, there is nothing criminal in that." The newspaper went on to report that Abramtchik had lost several votes in

the Paris émigré organization because the delegates could not elect a man "who had gone to the Soviet Union several times."

9. Kim Philby, *My Silent War* (Grove Press, 1968), p. 193.

10. Donald Maclean's penetration of the atomic bomb program is discussed in *The Secret History of the Atomic Bomb* (Brown and MacDonald, eds. Dial Press, 1977).

11. Operation Paperclip file, OSI.

12. Top Secret State Department Decimal File, 1948–49, National Archives.

CHAPTER SEVEN

1. The text of Congressman Klein's discussion is printed in the *Congressional Record* for August 7, 1948, at page A5155.

2. 8 U.S.C. 1427a(3) requires that every applicant for American citizenship have "good moral character." Ironically, during the late 1950s the Immigration Service considered people who were unfaithful to their wives as lacking good moral character, while prior membership in the SS was not a bar.

3. This legislation was requested by the intelligence community because all too often agents brought in under the 100 Persons Act would simply refuse to work after they had been granted a visa for permanent immigration. The Parole Powers Provisions allow the intelligence community to bring in an unlimited number of illegal entrants for a "temporary" stay. Once the agents are here, their visas can be voided if they refuse to cooperate.

4. The Hrynkievich file is contained in Blue File No. D95605, USAIRR, Ft. Meade, Maryland.

5. Ostrowsky's list of delegates at the Minsk convention of 1944 contains the following entry for "Lapitski, Mikalaj": "Protopresbyter, graduate of the Vilna Theological Seminary, graduate of the Theological Department of the Orthodox Theology at the Warsaw University, member and president of the Theology Student Circle, Superior of various parishes in the region of Hlybokaje and in the City of Minsk, member of the Metropolitan Bureau of the Byelorussian Orthodox Church Administration of the Byelorussian Autocephalic Church, member of the Preparatory Commission to the Byelorussian Autocephalic Sobor of the Byelorussian Orthodox Church in Minsk 1942, member delegate from the clergy to the Second All-Byelorussian Congress."

6. Copy in Kushel's Immigration file.

7. According to a letter from the CIC Central Registry to the Ameri-

can consulate general in Stuttgart (copy located in Stankievich's "blue file," USAIRR, Ft. Meade, Maryland), Stankievich also attempted to immigrate to the United States during the mid-1950s under the Refugee Relief Act. In this document the Army informed the State Department that Stankievich admitted holding the following positions under the Nazis:

July, 1941–February, 1944	Town Mayor, Borissow, USSR, German Military Administration, Borissow, USSR (Left) to take up another job
February, 1944–June, 1944	Delegate of the White Ruthenian Central Committee, Baronovichy, Poland (Reason for leaving) fled
June 1944–August 1944	Unemployed, enroute to Berlin, Germany
August 1944–March 1945	Editor, White Ruthenian Newspaper *Raniza* (Morning) German Ministry for the East Address unknown, Berlin, Germany

8. State Department files, Foreign Affairs Information Management Center, 1953 Agreement with the CIA.

9. Conversations with former staff members of the U.S. consulate in Stuttgart.

10. According to the CIC screening officer who handled Jasiuk's application for a DP visa, Jasiuk "has been doing work of a highly confidential nature for an American agency as was proved specifically at interview of subject by the persons in the agency for whom he was working." Wagenaar was one of those who testified. At that time Jasiuk submitted a false background history concealing his Nazi collaboration. None of the State Department officials present made any objection, even though they must have known that the information was false.

11. CIC file on Arendt Wagenaar.

12. *Ibid.*

13. The Kasmowich incident is described in a confidential memo from the American consulate general in Munich, Germany (January 19, 1955). Following his arrest, Kasmowich was not only released but was later returned to the U.S. zone and given a job with the U.S. Army as an accountant. As of 1966, he was still living in Germany.

14. Letter from Weckerling to Hoover. Copy in the AFOSI file for Emanuel Jasiuk, Bolling AFB, Washington, D.C.

15. INS files, OUN/SB.

CHAPTER EIGHT

1. Smith's term as DCI is discussed in *Select Committee Report, op. cit.,* pp. 36–38; also Corson, *op. cit.,* pp. 323–26.

2. On Dulles and Wisner, see Mosley, *op. cit.,* pp. 272–73.

3. In 1967 Stanislaw Stankievich wrote a monograph entitled "Byelorussian Literature Under the Soviets." Stankievich's immigration file stated that he served as chairman of the "Institute for the Study of the USSR" in Munich, Germany, from July 1954 to June 1962.

4. AMCOMLIB's activities were hardly a major secret. See *New York Times,* August 12, 1951, p. 17 ("Five Major Refugee Organizations Map Plans to Set Up Subversive Activities Center in Munich Financed by the American Liberation of Peoples of Russia Committee").

5. The American Committee for Liberation was founded in 1950 and its first broadcast went on the air March 1, 1953. According to their brochure, Radio Liberation was a completely independent venture from the older Free Europe Committee which sponsored Radio Free Europe. According to the letterhead of the American Committee for Liberation, 6 East 45th Street, New York 17, N.Y. (supporting the Institute for the Study of the U.S.S.R.), the Board of Trustees included Mrs. Oscar Ahlgran, John R. Burton, William Henry Chamberlain, Charles Edison, J. Peter Grace, Jr., Allan Grover, H. J. Heinz II, Isaac Don Levine, Eugene Lyons, Howland H. Sargent, Leslie C. Stevens, Dr. John W. Studebaker, Reginald T. Townsend, William L. White, and Philip H. Willkie.

6. Appended to the "Conference on the 450th Anniversary of the Statute of the Grand Duchy of Lithuania, sponsored by the Belorussian Institutes of Arts and Sciences and in Cooperation with the Ethnic Heritage Studies, Cleveland State University, August 31, 1980," is a complete list of all the conventions held by the Byelorussians in the United States. It is worthy of note that several of the speakers were persons who were accused by the Soviet Union of having committed war crimes and atrocities, including Stanislaw Stankievich.

In discussing the recent wave of immigrants from Byelorussia who came to the Cleveland area in 1949–51, one commentator noted that "the progress of the more recent immigrants was quite impressive." The children attended college, and the immigrants themselves had a very high percentage of professional members. Unlike most refugees, the new

Byelorussian immigrants were mostly registered as Republican. Michael S. Papp, monograph, *The Ethnic Communities of Cleveland* (1973).

7. FBI File NY97-1251 (1952) describes some of the front groups formed by members of the Byelorussian Central Council "which governed Byelorussia under German occupation from 1944 to 1945." The FBI report also notes that "all of its officers are now in the U.S."

8. At that time, the Argentine headquarters of the Belarus network was called the "Zhurtavnie Belorusau U-Argentinie" and was located at Calle Itapariu 2681 V. Alcina, Buenos Aires.

9. Jasiuk's participation in the Ukrainian American Congress is described in FBI File NY97-1251. In the same file appears the notation that "another governmental intelligence agency, in report of September 19, 1950, advised that Jasiuk in 1942, when White Russia was occupied by the Germans, allegedly worked in one of the departments of the Security Police at Baronovichy, Poland, and allegedly submitted a list of Polish residents to the German Secret Service which resulted in some of the people listed being shot." The FBI subsequently reported to the Immigration Service that Jasiuk was "trustworthy" and a good anticommunist.

10. *Byelorussian Independence Day,* BAA (New York, 1958), contains photographs of ex-Nazis with prominent politicians.

11. Philby, *op. cit.,* p. 202.

12. The extent of Soviet infiltration of the various ex-Nazi émigré organizations is described in Cookridge, *op. cit.,* pp. 254–55.

13. Sobolewsky's letter to the Assistant Attorney General is contained in Department of Justice File 149-06-2-12, Section 4, May 19, 1952.

14. By memorandum of July 17, 1952, James M. McInerney, Assistant Attorney General, Criminal Division, U.S. Department of Justice, Washington, D.C., advised the FBI that the facts submitted on the Byelorussian Central Administration (also known as the Byelorussian Central Representation) did not constitute them as an agent of a foreign principal as defined by Section 20(a) of the Internal Security Act of 1950. The FBI was advised that the Justice Department had decided to conduct a further investigation of the Byelorussians under the Foreign Registration Act of 1938 (FBI File NY97-1251). By memorandum of September 9, 1952, Charles B. Murray of the Criminal Division, United States Department of Justice, subsequently advised the FBI that he had received a letter from Jury Sobolewsky submitting additional information on the organization. On the basis of Sobolewsky's statement, the Justice Department concluded that the Byelorussians were not agents of

a foreign principal within the meaning of the Foreign Agents Registration Act of 1938.

15. Victor Marchetti and John D. Marks, *The CIA and the Cult of Intelligence* (Alfred A. Knopf, 1974).

16. The Doolittle Committee's "Anti-Communist Manifesto" is in *Select Committee Report, op. cit.,* pp. 52–53 *n.*

17. The Harvard Russian Research Center's program for interviewing exiles is discussed in an interview with Dr. Robert A. Bauer in the *New York Times* of September 5, 1951, p. 11.

18. FBI files (citation deleted).

19. Interview with Security Office, Radio Liberty, 1980.

20. Stankievich was issued Certificate of Naturalization No. 9198868.

21. Interview with former Security Officer, Radio Liberty, 1980.

22. Interviews with DDP officers, Langley, Virginia, 1980–81.

23. A copy of FBI File NY97-1251 containing the June 5, 1954, interview with Kushel was never placed in his immigration folder. Rather, a copy was sent to the central office of the Immigration Service under the title "Byelorussian Democratic Republic, Central Council, USA." The reason for the omission was significant. Within a year after his FBI interview, Kushel gave contradictory information on his application for citizenship. For example, in his FBI interview he admitted that he had become a colonel in the Byelorussian Land Defense for Police organized by the Germans. Kushel also admitted that by the time the Byelorussians fled to Germany in 1944, he was in command of several battalions of Byelorussians and he retreated with the German army.

24. INS Memo for record, February 8, 1963 (Kushel).

25. Immigration and Naturalization Service, File No. C7514221 (Kushel).

26. FBI files on Emanuel Jasiuk, quoted by INS.

27. Immigration files on Emanuel Jasiuk.

28. *Ibid.*

29. On May 12, 1949, Emanuel Jasiuk was issued Immigration Visa No. 5828/54 by the American vice consul at Stuttgart, Germany. On November 16, 1956, Jasiuk was issued Certificate of Naturalization No. 7481379 by the Bergen County Court of Bergen County of Hackensack, New Jersey.

30. FBI File No. 105-40098 is a 63-page book entitled *Byelorussian Activities in the New York Division.* The report is a summary of many previous FBI reports on Byelorussian activities dating back to 1951. According to this report, the FBI knew that "the Byelorussian Central

Council (BCR) based its claim to leadership upon the fact that it was established at the Second Byelorussian Congress held at Minsk in 1944 under the German occupation" (p. 23). "In July, 1945, when the Soviets were threatening the Minsk area, the Germans evacuated Ostrovsky, Sobolevsky, and many other functionaries to Germany" (p. 24). "Sobolevsky stated that a German S.S. general, Gottenberg, [sic] who was the nominal head of the German forces of occupation, allowed the Byelorussian Central Administration to set up its own government" (pp. 25–26). "Under the German occupation of Western Poland, [Sobolevsky] was appointed Mayor of Baronovichy, and later was responsible for acts of brutality against the people of that city. In 1943, a German S.S. general, Gottsberg, [sic] named Sobolevsky chief of the 'Zentral Rada' of Byelorussia" (p. 57). "Sobolevsky in 1942–1943 was chief of the White Ruthenian Self-Aid Committee in the Minsk area" (p. 60). "Sobolesky said that it was true that the organization and he himself cooperated with the German forces in World War II" (p. 62). "The BAA (Byelorussian American Associates) as of May, 1955 had about 1,000 members including the families of members. It had 12 branches throughout the U.S. with the majority of membership residing in New York, New Jersey and Connecticut. Ninety per cent of the membership were new immigrants" (p. 35). "In September, 1945, Eshersbacken, Germany, there was a meeting of the members of Byelorussian Central Council and a new organization called the Byelorussian National Center was formed with Ostrowsky as its leader. The new organization was so-named so the members could avoid being called war criminals during the time of crisis in Germany" (p. 28). A copy of this book was also found in the classified file section of the Central Office of the Immigration and Naturalization Service, Washington, D.C.

31. Letter of November 30, 1956, from Charles G. Dunn, Colonel, GS Chief Collection Division, ACSI/CDO0. In their request for CIA information, the Army reported that:

Under the auspices of the German Wehrmacht, Kushel was placed in command of Belo-russian brigade which subsequently was expanded into a division. Kushel was made division commander (two-star general) and fought until the end of the war. He surrendered to the Germans in what became the French zone of Germany. From there, he immigrated to the United States and is presently residing in the New York area.

32. Interviews with Marc Masurovsky, 1980–81.

CHAPTER NINE

1. The text of NSC 5412/1 is in *Select Committee Report,* Book 1, p. 51.

2. OPC had previously floated several trial balloons in the American press. See for example the article of June 4, 1953, in the *New York Times:*

A group of refugee East European politicians have proposed to their western colleagues the recruitment of a volunteer "liberation army" of half a million Russian refugees to form part of a unified American-West European force, according to an Austrian editor who acted during the war as a German army expert on Russia.

The editor, Dr. H. A. Kraus, has outlined the plan in [the] Salzburg organ of the Austrian Institute for Economic and Political Research. After pointing out that the United States is faced by the dilemma whether to try to defend Western Europe or let it go and trust air attacks to defeat Russia in the long run, Dr. Kraus observes that in the present stage of public opinion it would be impossible for Washington to send enough troops to Europe to match the Soviet army. But with the aid of refugees from Communism, who must be supported in any case as displaced persons, this could be accomplished, it is argued.

"The chief task of this 'national liberation army,'" Dr. Kraus writes, "would be to strike the Soviet Union at its weakest point—that is, to mobilize resistance to Soviet domination of the Russian hinterland, to transform the eventual war from an imperialistic war to a fight for freedom. . . ."

3. Confidential source, Pentagon interview, 1981.

4. Harry Rositzke, *The CIA's Secret Operations* (Reader's Digest Press, 1977), p. 190.

5. Peter Collier and David Horowitz, *The Rockefellers: An American Dynasty* (Holt, Rinehart & Winston, 1976), p. 273 *n.*

6. Corson, *op. cit.,* pp. 36–37.

7. Quoted in Wise and Ross, *op. cit.,* p. 327.

8. Mosley, *op. cit.,* pp. 419–21; Powers, *op. cit.,* p. 75.

9. Quoted in Charles C. Alexander, *Holding the Line: The Eisenhower Era, 1952–1961* (Indiana University Press, 1975), p. 180.

10. Truscott's role in terminating OPC's covert action programs is detailed in *ibid.,* pp. 368–72.

11. Mosley, *op. cit.,* p. 421; Powers, *op. cit.,* pp. 75–77; *Washington Post,* October 30, 1965.

12. Mosley, *op. cit.,* pp. 491–92.

23. The final conclusions of the Church Committee are in *Select Committee Report, op. cit.,* pp. 424–26.

24. Romanouski, Vasily Pilipavich, *Saudzel'niki u Zlachynstvakh* (Collaborators in Crime) (Minsk: "Belarus" Publishing House, 1964). This is possibly the best unclassified Soviet account of Byelorussian war criminals and their subsequent escape to the U.S.

25. A photograph of Kushel in Nazi uniform is contained on p. 81 of *Collaborators in Crime,* White Ruthenian History Section, Library of Congress.

26. See *Minsker Zeitung,* February 23, 1944, for an article in German, "With Deutschland for a Free White Ruthenia."

27. An article in the *Morning Freiheit,* "More Names of Jew Murderers Who Live Undisturbed in the Free World," provides the following account of Jasiuk's activities:

> When the Germans entered Baronovichy, they appointed Jasiuk as head of the town administration of Kletzk. I was working for him for some time. The Germans and Jasiuk ordered me to prepare a deep ditch outside the town, and to bring over 300 arrestees to do the work. Soon thereafter the Jews in Kletzk were rounded up and summarily shot. Jasiuk personally directed the operation (action) and gave all orders to the police squads. Later on he regularly dispatched consignments of victims to the Koldychev Concentration Camp.

The article also briefly denounced Kushel and gave his address as Alabama Avenue, East New York, Brooklyn.

28. Interview with GAO investigator John Tipton, November 1980.

29. Letter of January 13, 1977, from Joshua Eilberg, Chairman of the House Subcommittee on Immigration, Citizenship and International Law (Committee on the Judiciary), to Elmer B. Staats, Comptroller of the General Accounting Office.

30. Letter of April 7, 1978, from the GAO to Secretary of Defense Harold Brown, with enclosed lists of names. Kushel was number 45 on the list.

31. Jasiuk's "blue file" "XE8423082" was readily located in April 1980 at the USAIRR in Ft. Meade, Maryland. The entire dossier (blue file) is still stored in the vault at Ft. Meade.

32. Letter of April 17, 1978, from Department of the Army, Military Intelligence—Counter-Intelligence Section (DAMI/CIS) to USAIRR, Fort Meade, Maryland, requested the Army to check their files for persons listed on the GAO request. Both agencies had access to the Defense Investigative Service's computerized index.

13. Washington *Post,* October 30, 1965.

14. Lyman Kirkpatrick, *The Real CIA* (Macmillan, 1968), p
states:

> By this time (1952) we knew that there was not only a false network invo
> although there were some sources that occasionally did produce some i
> mation of value, but we knew further that a large number of their so-c
> intelligence sources were nothing but "paper mills." These "paper mills"
> organizations of refugees or émigrés producing alleged intelligence re
> from interrogating other refugees and emigres or from the "cocktail circ
> These reports were worthless and unreliable and most frequently dedi
> to selling a point of view.

15. Various meetings in America between Communist official:
the BSSR delegation to the UN and the leaders of the Belarus org
tions are described in FBI File No. NY105-35905. During one of
meetings, one of the Soviet delegates requested and received coj
some of the books published by the Belarus.

16. Allegations of war criminals residing in the United States a
several times in the *Morning Freiheit.* For example, April 13, 1962
10, 1962; July 6, 1962; March 22, 1964.

17. FBI files: Notes of an Interview with Simon Wiesenthal.

18. FBI file citation has been deleted because the subject is a po
target of investigation.

19. Dossier AC645873, USAIRR, Ft. Meade, Maryland. It
be noted that the Central Registry of the CIA was not privy to th
comprehensive data on Kushel available to the OPC. Consequently
background information on Kushel was sketchy, to say the leas

20. Over the years, some of the intelligence agencies noted tl
29th was not an SS division. Upon further research it was discover
the source of this interesting bit of disinformation was General l
himself.

21. INS reopened the Kushel investigation in 1973 in respo
allegations of war crimes received from Dorothy Rabinowitz, a re
and from the World Jewish Congress. Again the investigation
terminated.

22. Senate Resolution 21 adopted by the Senate on January 27
established the Select Committee to Study Governmental Ope
with Respect to Intelligence Activities (the Church Committee) to
mine whether "illegal, improper, or unethical activities were eng
by *any* agency of the Federal Government" (emphasis added).

33. Title 18, Section 1505 of the United States Code makes it a crime to obstruct a congressional inquiry:

> Whoever corruptly . . . influences, obstructs or impedes or endeavors to influence, obstruct or impede the due and proper administration of the law under which such proceeding is being had before such department or agency of the United States, or the due and proper exercise of the power of inquiry under which such inquiry or investigation is being had by either House, or any joint Committee of the Congress . . .
>
> . . . shall be fined not more than $5,000 or imprisoned not more than five years or both.

Similarly, Title 18, Section 371 makes it a felony to conspire to defraud the United States, and Title 18, Section 4 (misprision of felony) punishes those who knowingly keep silent on crimes that have been committed against the federal government.

34. Copies of the pertinent correspondence are located both in the GAO investigation records and in the files of the Army Special Actions Officer, USAIRR, Ft. Meade, Maryland.

35. The sanitized Kushel file is listed as File No. AC645873, USAIRR, Ft. Meade, Maryland.

36. One comment in the sanitized report for Kushel is that "President Abramtchik of the Belo-Russian Rada, who is also president of the Paris Bloc, is now staying with General Kushel." One of the interesting but unanswered questions raised by this document is how Abramtchik managed to get a visa to visit the United States in the first place. Abramtchik has an immigration file, but there is no visa in it. There is, however, a letter from an intelligence officer to the Canadian border guards.

37. File No. XE198433-I18I045, classified FOUO (For Official Use Only) for "Kusiel, Franciszek," was readily retrieved by the staff at Ft. Meade, even though that particular spelling of the name was not requested during a subsequent OSI investigation.

38. The CIC file for "Kusiel, Franciszek," File XE198433-I18I045, contains index cards showing that Kushel controlled the White Ruthenians veterans league and was a leading figure in the German SD. Another index card indicates that he was an SS officer in "Siegling's Division" (subsequently identified as the 30th Waffen-SS Division).

39. The file for Kushel, Francisek, No. 152 628 (USAIRR, Ft. Meade, Maryland), contains a photocopy of Kushel's 1947 CIC index card indicating that he was a member of the Byelorussian Central Council and that further references can be found on secret list 700-4. The index card naming Kushel as the leader of the Michelsdorf DP camp is

in this file, along with various Top Secret document replacement sheets indicating that even more sensitive documents had once belonged to the file but now could no longer be located. The Army has no idea what happened to the missing documents.

40. Among the general subject matter files relating to the Byelorussians at Ft. Meade are the following: "White Russian National Center," "White Ruthenian BNC," "Association of White Russian Veterans," "White Ruthenian Student Organization," "Sakavir Monthly Papers" (March), "Bakauscyna Newspaper" (Fatherland), "White Ruthenian DP Group," "White Ruthenian Propaganda," "BNR White Ruthenian National Public," "White Ruthenian Committee," "White Ruthenian National Committee."

41. An interesting thing about the sanitized Kushel file was that it was kept in the Top Secret vault at Ft. Meade, although all Top Secret information in it had been removed from it, and all his other dossiers. There were no sign-out sheets indicating who had taken the Top Secret information. Moreover, there was no record of the dossier ever being signed out of the vault. Even the punch-card index for Kushel's file was missing. Apparently, whoever went to the trouble to create the sanitized file for Kushel went to extreme steps to insure that it could not be readily located.

42. Jasiuk's CIC dossier No. X847230A2 also contains copies of the CIC report of Jasiuk's connection with Air Force Counterintelligence. These documents were among those forwarded to J. Edgar Hoover by General Weckerling, along with allegations that CIC informants had conclusively established that Jasiuk was a war criminal who was

well known for his cruelty and persecution of the Polish populace in the area and was responsible for sending many persons to forced labor in Germany. In 1942, during the liquidation of the Polish intelligentsia, subject submitted a list of certain residents of Nieswicz and other cities to the Sicherheits Dienst (German secret service) in Baranowicz, and as a result a number of these persons were shot.

43. According to a note on the reverse of the Immigration and Naturalization Service's background investigation form, in 1975 the CIC reported that it had at least two dossiers for Jasiuk, one of which was missing, but the available dossier represented "possible derogatory information learned about subject after he had departed to the US." The information was not shown to the GAO.

EPILOGUE

1. Ostrowsky's immigration file number is A12866178, C9098434. He received his American citizenship in Michigan in 1972.

2. The FBI was aware of illegal immigration in some cases even before it occurred. See, for example, FBI File NY97-1251. "The president of this organization, informant said, is R. Ostrowsky who lives in Argentina and expects to come to the United States in the near future." This file, and others, are replete with information that Ostrowsky was the president of the Nazi government in Byelorussia during the German occupation.

3. Top Secret files, Emanuel Jasiuk, USAIRR, Ft. Meade, Md.

4. Mosley, *op. cit.*, p. 275.

5. Senator Saltonstall's statement has been described as the so-called "want to know" principle. Corson, *op. cit.*, p. 306, citing U.S. Congress Senate Select Committee to Study Governmental Operations with Respect to Intelligence Activities, First Report (1976), p. 149.

6. The Soviet Union continues to charge in its propaganda broadcasts that American intelligence is still secretly maintaining its financial support for the ex-Nazi émigré organizations. BBC "Summary of World Broadcasts," December 20, 1979. My earlier assertions that the OPC used these same private organizations to launder funds comes neither from Soviet sources nor from classified files. All that is necessary to identify the CIA conduits is to check publicly available lists for those organizations which contributed money to Radio Liberty from 1951 to 1971. Radio Liberty has since admitted that during this period 99.8 percent of its income came from the CIA. Monograph, "Radio Liberty —Basic Facts," Library of Congress, P-134 SC (72) 53.

In spite of all that has happened, I remain convinced that an *efficient* intelligence service is essential to the defense of democracy. Somehow, Congress must strike a better balance between secrecy and supervision.

Index

Abramtchik, Mikolai, 48, 106, 108–12, 119, 171, 185; British recruit, 77, 80, 81; in Byelorussian Central Council, 37; collapse of faction led by, 109–10; communist background of, 17–18, 175; factional battles with Ostrowsky, 52–3, 77, 99, 115; Free Polish army and, 44; French secret service and, 49; and Wisner, 110–12

Abwehr, 16

Acheson, Dean G., 70

Adamovitch, Anton, 119, 159

AEG Company, 93

Air Force, U.S., 100–1, 144–7, 150, 156; Human Resources Research Institute of, 118

Akula, Konstantine, 22 n.

Allende, Salvador, 158

Allgemeine-SS (General SS), 16

Alliance of Russian National Solidarists (NTS), 16, 42, 80, 81, 171

Alsop, Joseph, 72

Alsop, Stewart, 72

American Committee for Liberation from Bolshevism (AMCOMLIB), 107, 112–13, 115, 122, 125, 127, 138, 142, 150, 178

Amt/Ausland Abwehr, 16

Anders, Wladyslaw, 44, 49, 98, 99, 171

"Anti-Communist Manifesto" (Doolittle), 117, 130

Arbenz Guzman, Jacobo, 130

Army, U.S., 95, 97 n., 106, 129, 136, 145, 156, 173; G-2 intelligence system of, 55; Investigative Records Repository of (USAIRR), 90, 138, 145, 148, 149, 155; Third Army, 46,

47; see also Counter-Intelligence Corps (CIC)

Army Group Center, 19, 21

Bandera, Stephan, 15, 66, 101–2, 172

Barkley, Alben, 108

Barnes, Tracy, 72

Bartishevic, Jury, 51, 62

Bay of Pigs invasion, 158

Berlin blockade, 8, 11

Bissell, Richard, 72

BKA (home defense corps), 35, 36, 39

"Black Cats," 42, 43, 100 n.

Blood Purge (1934), 16

Bohlen, Charles, 72

Bolsheviks, 13, 163

Borissow massacre, 20, 25–9, 65–6, 119

Bradley, Omar N., 46

British Secret Service, 47, 80, 142

Buchardt, Friedrich, 10, 41, 63, 85

Bundesnachtrichtendienst, 56

Burgess, Guy, 110 n.

Byelorussian Activities in the New York Division (FBI report), 128

Byelorussian-American Youth Organization (BAYO), 120

Byelorussian Central Council (BCC), 35, 37, 46, 47, 51, 52, 64–6, 94, 108, 109, 112, 124, 168–70, 179; American Friends of, 152; Fourteenth Plenum of, 121

Byelorussian Central Representation (BCR), 52, 109, 112, 124

Byelorussian Democratic Republic, 125

Byelorussian Liberation Movement, 113, 115
Byelorussian National Republic (BNR), 13, 15, 52–3, 152
Byelorussian Peasants and Workers Party, *see* Gramada
Byelorussian Union of University Students, 164

Canaris, Wilhelm, 16
Carnegie Fund, 107
Carter, Ledyard & Milburn, 8
Castro, Fidel, 158
Central Intelligence Agency (CIA), 72–3, 77 *n.*, 78–80, 85, 105–7, 115, 128–9, 136–7, 139–40, 143, 160; congressional investigation of, 141–2, 159; creation of, 58, 67, 84; Doolittle committee and, 116; under Eisenhower administration, 130, 132; "Hundred Persons Act" and, 89; immigration checks by, 92, 96, 122–4; in Italian elections (1948), 68–9; Jasiuk dossiers of, 147; military intelligence and, 67–8; Nuremberg trials and, 75; OPC, formation of, 69–70; OPC funding by, 103, 104; Philby and, 110 *n.*; Rockefeller Commission investigation of, 140–1; visas issued by, 94
Central Intelligence Group (CIG), 58, 59, 66–7
Cheka, 13, 14
Chicago *Tribune,* 56
Christian Democrats, Italian, 69
Church, Frank, 141
Church Committee, 141–2 and *n.*
Churchill, Winston S., 47, 49
Civiletti, Benjamin, 154
Clark, Tom C., 89
Clay, Lucius D., 66, 69, 71, 73–5, 77, 78, 84, 90, 92, 93, 107, 174
Clifford, Clark, 82 *n.*
Colby, William, 72

Cold War, 49, 65, 68 *n.*, 69, 76, 77 *n.*, 137, 158, 159
Collaborators in Crime, 142
Collier, Cleveland E., 127
Committee for the Liberation of the Peoples of Russia, 41
Communist Party, 17, 114
Congress, U.S., 73, 104, 127, 137, 153, 159–61; CIA investigated by, 141–2; immigration laws and, 86, 88, 89, 92; war crimes investigation by, obstructed, 144–7, 151
Congressional Record Appendix, 86
Consolidated Orientation and Guidance Manual (CIC), 74, 92, 105, 149
Corson, William R., 71
Counter-Intelligence Corps (CIC), 103, 117 *n.*, 123, 124, 155 *n.*; arrest of war criminals by, 47; Gehlen and, 59–60, 62; in immigration screening process, 88–97, 99–101, 105; investigation of Nazis by, 73–5, 79, 82–4; Jasiuk and, 99–101, 111, 127, 144–8, 150, 156; Kushel and, 92–3, 138–9, 149–50; Stankievich and, 66, 80, 93–4
Crossland, David, 146, 147, 148 *n.*
Crusade for Freedom, 107, 118, 141

Danikevich, Joseph, 79
Dashkevich, Yosif, 66
Defense, Department of (DOD), 144–8, 150, 155
Dewey, Thomas E., 68, 72, 73
Displaced Persons Act (1948), 86, 88, 94–5, 104, 123, 171
Displaced Persons Commission, U.S., 88, 93–5, 96 *n.*, 101, 124
Donovan, William J., 55–6, 59
Doolittle, James, 116, 117, 130
Dulles, Allen, 68, 130, 158, 160; in OSS, 54, 67; Wisner and, 71, 73, 106, 115–16, 132–3
Dulles, John Foster, 68, 71, 73
Dunn, Charles G., 181

Ehoff, David, 26–7, 166
Eichmann, Adolf, 24–5
Eilberg, Joshua, 144–7, 153, 156
Einsatzgruppe B, 19–21, 25, 63
Einsatzgruppen, 31, 46, 51, 76, 92, 124, 127–9, 138; Jasiuk in, 97–8; Nuremberg trials of commanders of, 63, 64, 78; Ostrowsky in, 34; slaughter of Jews by, 18–19, 25, 29–30, 38, 85, 120
Einsatzkommandos, 19
Eisenhower, Dwight D., 107, 109, 123, 142, 160; CIA covert activities and, 130, 132; Hungarian uprising and, 133–4; OPC investigation ordered by, 116; in World War II, 46, 50, 105
Ermachenko, Ivan, 33 and n., 91
Ethnic Directory of New Jersey, 152
European Command Intelligence School (EUCOM G-2), 62, 78
Expected Elements of Information (EEI's), 74

Federal Bureau of Investigation (FBI), 55–6, 58, 80–1, 92, 119, 121, 140, 141, 155 n., 159, 179, 187; background checks on immigrants by, 96, 124–8; Jasiuk and, 101, 111, 126–7, 137, 138, 144, 147, 148, 156; Kushel and, 125–6, 137–9; OSS denounced by, 67; Sobolewsky and, 111–13
Felfe, Heinz, 132
FitzGerald, Desmond, 72
Ford, Gerald R., 140
Ford Foundation, Russian Research Committee of, 107
Foreign Agents Registration Act, 112, 113
Forrestal, James A., 68, 71, 134 n.
Free Polish Intelligence, 64
Fremde Heere Ost (FHO), 10, 54, 57
Fuchs, Klaus, 83

Gehlen, Reinhard, 10–11, 49, 140, 158, 172; American military intelligence and, 53–6; CIA and, 67, 158; DP camps and, 60–2; Ostrowsky and, 36, 58; postwar German operation of, 56–7, 59–60; Soviet infiltration of operation of, 80, 132; Wisner and, 75–80; during World War II, 32–3, 36, 42
General Accounting Office (GAO), 145–51, 153, 155 n., 157
Gestapo (Geheime Staatspolizei), 16, 34, 57, 97, 103, 136; Abramtchik and, 52; BCC and, 35, 37, 46; Soviet infiltration of, 32, 80
Goebbels, Joseph, 31
Golubovich, Geny, 65
Gottberg, General Kurt von, 33–7, 51, 168
Gramada, 14, 15, 34, 113, 163, 164
Green Berets, 136
G-2 Military Intelligence Service, 55, 59, 67
Guderian, Heinz, 54 n.

Hadley, Morris, 116
Harvard Institute for Russian Research, 117–18, 121 n.
Hilger, Gustav, 10, 41–2, 70, 75, 84, 85, 107 n.
Hillenkoetter, Roscoe H., 67–9, 72, 105
Himmler, Heinrich, 16, 40–2, 87
Hitler, Adolf, 10, 15–17, 21, 33, 35–7, 39, 44, 48, 54 n., 74, 128
Hitler-Stalin Pact, 17, 70
Holocaust, 84, 86–7, 137, 143, 152; see also Jews: slaughter of
Holtzmann, Elizabeth, 144
Hoover, J. Edgar, 55–6, 101, 111–13, 125, 128, 144, 147, 150, 156
House of Representatives, U.S.: Committee on Foreign Affairs, 127; Judiciary Committee Subcommittee on

House of Representatives, U.S. (*cont.*) Immigration and Naturalization, 144

Hoxha, Enver, 110

Hrynkievich, Stanislaw, 46–8, 71, 91, 164

Hull, Cordell, 68 *n.*

Hundred Persons Act (1949), 89, 136, 176

Hungarian uprising (1956), 133–5

Immigration and Naturalization Service (INS), 92, 96, 102, 103, 122 *n.*, 124–9, 137–9, 145–7, 151–3, 159

Institute of Russian Research (Munich), 107, 119

Internal Security Act (1950), 113

International Refugee Organization (IRO), 60, 61, 86–8, 91, 92, 95, 101

Iron Guard, 9

Jackson, C. D., 132, 160

Jasinki, Max, *see* Jasiuk, Emanuel

Jasiuk, Emanuel, 20, 51, 108–9, 113, 142, 177, 179, 186; emigration to U.S. of, 99–100, 105, 124, 180; FBI and, 101, 111, 126–7, 137, 138, 144, 156; GAO investigation of, 144–8; grave of, 6; INS investigation of, 125–7, 129; as mayor of Kletsk, 97–8; OSI investigation of, 150–3, 157; recruited by Americans, 99–101

Jews: *Einsatzgruppen* and, 18–19; fascist attitude toward, 15; in Pale of Settlement, 12; resettlement of, 24–5, 29; slaughter of, 22 *n.*, 23–30, 63, 86, 98, 108, 120, 121, 143, 154, 166, 167

Joint Intelligence Objectives Agency, 90 *n.*

Joyce, Robert S., 68, 70, 71 *n.*, 77, 84

Judenrat, 23, 24, 26

Justice Department, U.S., 3, 7, 83, 92, 112, 113, 125, 153, 154, 156, 159,

179; *see also* Office of Special Investigations (OSI)

Kasmowich, Dimitri, 36–7, 50, 100 and *n.*, 113, 115, 148, 177

Kennan, George A., 68–70, 72, 77, 84–5, 107

KGB, 114, 132

Khrushchev, Nikita S., 133

Kirkpatrick, Lyman, 183

Kissinger, Henry A., 117

Klein, Arthur G., 86, 87

Koldichevo camp, 30

Kolubovich, Evgeni, 65

Korean War, 105, 130

Kraatz, General, 21–2

Kraus, H. A., 182

Kriminalpolizei (Criminal Police), 16

Krock, Arthur, 72

KTsAB, 77

Kube, Wilhelm, 32–5, 91, 117, 167

Kushel, Arsenieva, 65

Kushel, Franz, 48 *n.*, 50 *n.*, 51, 61, 76, 77, 129, 142, 146, 157, 169, 170, 180, 183, 185, 186; Anders and, 44, 45; as DP camp coordinator, 61, 65, 76, 88, 120; emigration to U.S. of, 92–3, 105; GAO investigation of, 146, 148–51; INS investigation of, 125–6, 137–9; as leader of American Abramtchik faction, 106, 108, 119; pro-Nazi police under, 22, 25, 29, 36, 39; recruitment of, 63–4

Lapitski, Mikalaj, 92, 176

Lenin, V. I., 13

Levy, Larry, 68

Library of Congress, Slavic Reading Room of, 142–3

Litwinczyk, Nina, 32, 37, 80, 175

Maclean, Donald, 82, 110 *n.*

Maltsov, General, 170

Masurovsky, Marc, 154

McCarthy, Joseph, 116

McCarthyism, 158
McCloy, John J., 78, 156
McInerney, Joseph M., 113, 179
McNarney, Joseph T., 47
Melnik, Andrei, 101
Mende, Gerhardt von, 10
Meyer, Cord, Jr., 72
Military Intelligence Service (MIS), 88–90, 97 n., 101, 140, 147, 154
Minsker Zeitung (newspaper), 143
Montevideo, Treaty of, 89
Morning Freiheit (newspaper), 137, 184
Mossadegh, Mohammed, 130
Murray, Charles B., 113, 179
Mussolini, Benito, 42
MVD, 60, 65, 80

National Archives, Modern Military Section of, 143
National Committee for a Free Albania, 85
National Committee for a Free Europe (NCFE), 84 n., 107
National Endowment for the Humanities, 154
National Security Council, 68, 69, 90 n., 130; Directive 10/2, 9, 69
New Jersey American Revolution Bicentennial Celebration Committee, 152
New York Times, 72, 120 n.
Nixon, Richard M., 127, 133, 140, 160
NKVD, 32, 42–3, 51
North Atlantic Treaty Organization (NATO), 131, 132, 143
NTS, 16, 42, 80, 81, 171
Nuremberg War Crimes Tribunal, 28, 49, 57, 63, 64, 75, 78, 86–9, 104, 153

Office of Policy Coordination (OPC), 8, 70–3, 77 n., 84–5, 97, 104, 136, 142–3, 158–60; AMCOMLIB and, 107, 112, 138, 150; autonomy of, within CIA, 104, 105–6; charter of, 9, 69; Church Committee and, 141–2; Doolittle committee and, 116–17; during Eisenhower administration, 132–3; Gehlen and, 10 n., 76, 78; Hungarian uprising and, 133–4; illegal immigration arranged by, 89 and n., 95, 96, 103 n., 123, 124, 128; Jasiuk in, 99–101; Ostrowsky faction and, 112–15; Philby and, 81; propaganda agencies of, 118–19; research programs of, 117–18; Stankievich and, 93; State Department control of, 69–70
Office of Special Investigations (OSI), 150, 153–9
Office of Special Operations (OSO), 59, 69, 85, 96 n., 106, 115, 139
Office of Strategic Services (OSS), 47, 67–8, 70, 77, 85, 86; dismantling of, 55–6, 58, 59; Dulles in, 54, 68, 116, 130; Wagenaar in, 97; Wisner in, 8–9, 84, 116
OGPU, 14
ONI, 55
OPC, see Office of Policy Coordination
Operation Barbarossa, 21, 78
Operation Keelhaul, 48
Operation Paperclip, 82–4, 90
Operation Pow-wow, 117
Operations Coordination Board, 132
Operations Research Office (ORO), 117
Operation Tobacco, 59, 60, 71
Organisation Gehlen (ORG), 11
Organization of Ukrainian Nationalists (OUN), 80, 102–4
Ostrowsky, Radislaw, 20, 49, 51, 63, 66, 81, 94, 117, 120, 171, 174; Abramtchik faction and, 52–3, 77, 80, 99, 115; in Argentina, 105, 108; British and, 48, 52, 53; emigration to U.S. of, 152–3, 187; FBI and, 110–12; Gehlen and, 57, 58; Gestapo and, 164; in Gramada, 14, 163;

Ostrowsky, Radislaw (*cont.*)
  grave of, 6, 92; OPC and, 112–15;
  Patton and, 46; during Russian civil
  war, 13; during World War II, 22,
  24, 33–45, 98, 128, 167–70
Ostrowsky, Wiktor, 44, 121
Pale of Settlement, 12, 19, 25
Panzer units, 19
"Parole Powers Provision," 176
Patton, George S., 41, 45–7, 49–50, 52,
  71
"People's Police" (VOPO), 11
Philby, Harold A. R. (Kim), 49, 80,
  81, 109–10, 135
Polish Central Commission, 99
Polish Military Mission, 50, 64
Polish riots (1956), 133
Polish Secret Service, 14, 45 *n.*, 85
Potsdam meeting, 49
Pravda, 89
"Prometheus" program, 49

Rabinowitz, Dorothy, 183
Radio Corporation of America, 107
Radio Free Europe, 118, 133, 137, 143,
  178
Radio Free Rakoczi, 133
Radio Liberty, 76 *n.*, 118–19, 122,
  123, 133, 134 *n.*, 137, 142–4, 150,
  159, 178
Ranitsa (newspaper), 17, 25, 65, 66,
  94, 123
Reagan, Ronald, 107, 141
Red Army, 13, 17, 21, 32, 38, 39, 41,
  48, 74, 98
Reich Central Security Office, 16
Reston, James, 72
Riga, Treaty of (1921), 13
Rockefeller, Nelson A., 68 and *n.*,
  132–3, 140–2, 160
Rockefeller Fund, 107, 132
Rockeler, Walter, Jr., 153
Roosevelt, Franklin D., 8 *n.*, 47, 49,
  55–6

Roosevelt, Kermit, 72
Russian Army of Liberation, 47
Russian Revolution, 12, 34, 52
Ryan, Alan, 153

SA (Sturmabteilung), 16, 18
Saltonstall, Leverett, 159
Schiadow, Solomon, 4, 30–1
SD (Sicherheitsdienst), 16, 17, 35, 76,
  93, 149
Secret Intelligence Service, 49
Senate, U.S., 140–1; Church Commit-
  tee, 141–2 and *n.*, 183; Foreign Re-
  lations Committee, 59
Sibert, Edwin L., 54, 71, 172
Sicherheitspolizei (security police), 19
Sidlov, General, 172
Sikorski Institute (London), 45 *n.*
Six, Franz, 19–22, 25, 33, 63, 78, 97
Skorzeny, Otto, 42, 43, 50
Slavic Reading Room, 142–3
Smith, Walter Bedell, 105–6, 110
Sobolewsky, Jury, 14, 20, 51, 105, 108,
  111–13, 117, 142, 163, 168, 179
Soennecken, Sgt., 26–8, 86
Souers, Sidney W., 58
Special Operations Detachment, 155,
  159
SS (Schutzstaffel), 10, 16–20, 22, 31,
  32 *n.*, 33, 42, 48, 51, 57, 87, 89, 92,
  120, 124, 127, 136; Abramtchik and,
  52; captured files of, 129, 143, 153,
  159; Jasiuk and, 97–100, 111;
  Kushel and, 139, 149, 151; Ostrowsky and, 34–5, 37, 38, 41, 128;
  OUN and, 103–4; recruitment of
  former members of, 71, 76; and
  slaughter of Jews, 24–6, 28, 33, 143;
  see also Waffen-SS
Stalin, Josef, 11, 17, 21, 26, 47–9, 114,
  131
Stankievich, Stanislaw, 63, 64, 77, 80,
  143–4, 153–4, 157, 168, 170–8
  passim; Borissow massacre and, 20,
  25–8, 65–6, 119; in DP camp, 50, 61;

emigration to U.S. of, 79, 86–8, 93–4, 122; OPC and, 93, 107, 119
Stankievich, Ziniaide, 93
State Department, U.S., 55, 56, 58, 66, 75, 82, 84–5, 96 *n.*, 103 *n.*, 119, 136, 145, 160; AMCOMLIB and, 107; Bureau of Latin American Research of, 68 *n.*; immigration process and, 88–90; Jasiuk and, 99–101, 147–8, 156; OPC controlled by, 69–71; Policy and Planning Staff of, 68–70, 71 *n.*, 77; Stankievich and, 143–4; Wagenaar hired by, 97
State-Navy-War Coordinating Committee, 90 *n.*
Strategic Services Unit, 56
Suez crisis (1956), 133
Sûreté, 100

Theismann, Joe, 5
Time, Inc., 132
Tipton, John, 157
Trading with the Enemy Act, 158
Truitt, Marc, 71 *n.*
Truman, Harry S, 8, 49, 70, 72, 109, 123, 131; CIA and, 58, 68, 105; immigration of ex-Nazis banned by, 82; OPC and, 73; OSS disbanded by, 56
Truscott, Lucian K., 135
Tucci, Niccolò, 68 *n.*
Tumash, Vitold, 22 *n.*
Twenty Committee, 132–3, 160

Ukrainian American Congress, 179
Ukrainian collaborators and Nazis, 80, 85, 101–4; *see also* Bandera, Stephan
ULTRA, 48
United Nations, 64–5, 101, 104, 137, 173
United Nations Relief and Rehabilitation Agency (UNRRA), 50, 126

Vakar, Nicholas, 121
Vandenberg, Arthur H., 59

Vandenberg, Hoyt S., 58–9, 67
Vedeler (State Department official), 96 *n.*
Vietnam War, 158
Vitushka, Michael, 42, 43, 100 *n.*
Vlasov, Andrei A., 41, 48, 170
von Braun, Wernher, 83
Vorkommando, 19–21

Waffen-SS (Armed SS), 16, 18, 39–40, 47, 76, 78
Wagenaar, Arendt, 96–7, 99–101
Waldmann, Erich, 10 *n.*, 117 *n.*
Wallace, Mike, 22 *n.*
War Department, U.S., 56
Warsaw uprising, 40
Watergate scandal, 140
Weckerling, John, 101
Wehrmacht, 16, 18, 21, 26, 33, 35, 36, 78, 120, 125, 143
Welch, Richard, 141
White Ruthenian Committee in Warsaw, 124
White Ruthenian Institute of Arts and Sciences, 106
White Ruthenian Veterans League, 93
Wiesenthal, Simon, 137, 138
Wisner, Frank G., 8–11, 70–3, 94, 110, 123, 129, 130, 136, 139–42, 158–60, 175; Doolittle committee and, 116–17; emigré institutes established by, 106–7; ex-Nazis brought to U.S. by, 81–4, 86, 89–90, 92, 96, 121; failure of operations of, 115–16; Gehlen and, 75–80; Hungarian uprising and, 133–5; Jasiuk and, 99; OPC appointment, 70–1; Ostrowsky and, 110, 113–15; Philby and, 80, 81, 110; plan for direct action against Soviets by, 131–3; propaganda agencies of, 118; research programs of, 117–18; Smith and, 105–6; suicide of, 135; Ukrainian Nazis and, 101–4

Wisner, Polly, 72, 135
World Church Service, 96; Language
   Institute of, 171
World Jewish Congress, 183
World War II, 8, 10, 16–46, 99, 105,

112, 116, 120, 125, 126; *see also*
Holocaust

Yad Vashem, 45 *n.*
Yalta conference, 47, 131

A NOTE ABOUT THE AUTHOR

JOHN LOFTUS is a former trial attorney for the Justice Department's Office of Special Investigations, in which capacity he investigated the war crimes and subsequent activities of Byelorussian Nazis. He is 32 years old, from an Irish Catholic family, and a graduate of Boston Latin School and Boston College. After serving as an army officer, Mr. Loftus completed his studies for, and received simultaneously, his Master's degree in Public Administration and his Doctor of Laws degree. He has served as editor of the *Suffolk Review*, and has worked in several political campaigns. He is now in private practice with the law firm of Bingham, Dana and Gould in Boston.

NATHAN MILLER is the author of several books, including *The U.S. Navy: An Illustrated History,* and the forthcoming *FDR: An Intimate History.* He has worked as a Washington correspondent for the Baltimore *Sun,* and as a member of the staff of the U.S. Senate Appropriations Committee. Mr. Miller lives in Chevy Chase, Maryland.

A NOTE ON THE TYPE

The text of this book was set via computer-driven cathode ray tube in a face called Times Roman, designed by Stanley Morison for *The Times* (London) and first introduced by that newspaper in 1932.

Among typographers and designers of the twentieth century, Stanley Morison has been a strong influence, as typographical adviser to the English Monotype Corporation, as a director of two distinguished English publishing houses, and as a writer of sensibility, erudition, and keen practical sense.

Composed, printed and bound by
The Haddon Craftsmen, Inc., Scranton, Pennsylvania

DESIGNED BY ALBERT CHIANG